Mastering Excel Through Projects

A Learn-by-Doing Approach from Payroll to Crypto to Data Analysis

Hong Zhou

Apress®

Mastering Excel Through Projects: A Learn-by-Doing Approach from Payroll to Crypto to Data Analysis

Hong Zhou
University of Saint Joseph
West Hartford, CT, USA

ISBN-13 (pbk): 978-1-4842-7841-3   ISBN-13 (electronic): 978-1-4842-7842-0
https://doi.org/10.1007/978-1-4842-7842-0

Managing Director, Apress Media LLC: Welmoed Spahr
Acquisitions Editor: Joan Murray
Development Editor: Laura Berendson
Coordinating Editor: Jill Balzano

Cover image designed by Freepik (www.freepik.com)

Distributed to the book trade worldwide by Springer Science+Business Media LLC, 1 New York Plaza, Suite 4600, New York, NY 10004. Phone 1-800-SPRINGER, fax (201) 348-4505, e-mail orders-ny@springer-sbm.com, or visit www.springeronline.com. Apress Media, LLC is a California LLC and the sole member (owner) is Springer Science + Business Media Finance Inc (SSBM Finance Inc). SSBM Finance Inc is a **Delaware** corporation.

For information on translations, please e-mail booktranslations@springernature.com; for reprint, paperback, or audio rights, please e-mail bookpermissions@springernature.com.

Apress titles may be purchased in bulk for academic, corporate, or promotional use. eBook versions and licenses are also available for most titles. For more information, reference our Print and eBook Bulk Sales web page at http://www.apress.com/bulk-sales.

Any source code or other supplementary material referenced by the author in this book is available to readers on GitHub via the book's product page, located at www.apress.com/9781484278413. For more detailed information, please visit http://www.apress.com/source-code.

Printed on acid-free paper

To all those who once helped me

Table of Contents

About the Author

Hong Zhou is professor of computer science and mathematics at the University of Saint Joseph in Connecticut. Before returning to school for his doctoral degree, Dr. Zhou worked as a Java developer at Silicon Valley. Since 2004, Dr. Zhou has been teaching various courses in computer science, data science, mathematics, statistics, and informatics. His major research interests include data mining, bioinformatics, software agents, and blockchain. Dr. Zhou became interested in Excel through teaching computer skills and using it for research purposes, for example, applying Excel in teaching data mining, encryption, and health informatics. He also enjoys applying his Excel skills to help colleagues on their research projects.

About the Technical Reviewer

Kolyu Minevski is an Excel enthusiast who has worked with spreadsheet programs for about 25 years. His main experience is in the financial and IT industry where he has utilized Excel for creating various regular and ad hoc reports, analyses, budgets, and financial models. He loves Excel because it is a flexible, powerful, and easy-to-learn-and-use tool that is capable of solving a wide range of analytical tasks in almost every organization. He is always keen to learn and apply new ways of Excel, even pushing it beyond what is accepted to be its limits. For the last three years, he has shared his knowledge and experience on his blog `https://excel-do.com` with the main purpose to help other users work more efficiently with Excel and save precious time for more important tasks.

Acknowledgments

First of all, this book would not be possible without the assistance from the Apress editing team including Joan Murray and Jill Balzano. Many thanks go to them. Great thanks go to the technical reviewer Kolyu Minevski who thoroughly examined the book for accuracy and provided many valuable suggestions. Kolyu's suggestions significantly improved the quality of this book. I would also like to thank my son David Zhou who reviewed the book before it was submitted to Apress. In addition, I would like to thank my colleagues Dr. Katie Martin and Dr. Joseph Manthey who motivated me to learn more about Excel.

Introduction

Different people master Excel skills through different approaches, but example-based is probably the most common. However, simple examples cannot help you develop deeper problem-solving skills, that is, they do not offer you the challenge and practices to connect dots. This book introduces a unique project-based approach that can lead you into creative usage of various Excel skills in addition to formulas/functions. There are eight projects, each covering a different topic, including word game, food nutrition ranking, payroll (tax withholding) calculation, encryption, two-way table, Kaplan-Meier analysis, data analysis via PivotTable, and the data mining method K-means clustering. Through these projects, you will experience how Excel skills are organized together to accomplish missions that seem impossible.

A project is different from a simple example dedicated to a specific single skill. To complete a project, you must assemble all your Excel knowledge and skills to find an optimal solution. You must analyze the given information, arrange the data in an easy-to-access setup, find optimal Excel functions, and fabricate formulas. In most cases, you have to refine your solution. This step is equally important because it requires retro-thinking and creativity. In one sentence, a project is much more than an example.

The book starts with a simple but interesting project, the word game, which asks users to find English words that have exactly 100 points given the 26 alphabets having points 1, 2, 3, ..., 26, respectively. Not only does the book show you step by step how to disassemble a word into letters and then sum up their points, it takes you one step further by considering how to make the product, the completed Excel worksheet, more user-friendly and completely automatic. In this sense, the book is talking about developing a software product in the form of Excel worksheets.

Take the project Payroll calculation as another example. The focus of this project is tax withholding calculation. We know that there are a number of software tools which can automate tax withholding, and large accounting offices do not use Excel for this purpose. However, Excel is still a critical and popularly used tool for small business owners. Education-wise, Excel is not replaceable in accounting. Once you have finished this project, you will find out that you have a worksheet product that can automatically calculate tax withholding amount for your employees (assume you have employees).

One unique value of this textbook is that it emphasizes the idea of automation. Fundamentally, why we need Excel is to automate our procedures. Thus, all the projects endeavor to show how you can maximize the automation. To maximize automation, not only do you need to refine our formulas, but you also need to set up tables creatively and apply other built-in features in Excel. This book can guide you step by step on such skills.

No matter if you are a beginner or an experienced user of Excel, this book can definitely serve you well to further elevate your Excel knowledge and skills. For a beginner, the small examples in each chapter will warm you up before you dive into the projects. For experienced users, the projects, especially those with table setup considerations, can help you become more creative in your future endeavors.

I have been teaching and using Excel for more than a decade. My experience tells me that students can quickly forget what they have learned if the examples do not impress them deeply. Projects, however, can always burn a deeper impression than simple examples. For instance, in a Math class, I taught RSA encryption (public and private key) through an Excel project, and this does arouse students' interest in Excel.

CHAPTER 1

Master Excel Through Projects

There are quite some books that teach us how to master Excel worksheets, and many of them are excellent. Some books go into every detail and are so valuable that they can be referenced as an encyclopedia for Excel. Nevertheless, this book takes a unique route to practice and master Excel.

Why Learn Through Projects

Different people learn/master Excel skills through different approaches, but example-based is probably the most common. Unfortunately, simple examples cannot help us develop deep problem-solving skills, that is, they do not offer us the practices to connect dots. This book introduces a unique project-based approach that can lead us into creative usage of various Excel skills in addition to formulas/functions. There are eight projects, each covering a distinct topic, including word game, food nutrition ranking, payroll (tax withholding) calculation, encryption, two-way table, Kaplan-Meier analysis, data analysis via PivotTable, and the data mining method k-means clustering. Through these projects, we will experience how Excel skills are organized together to accomplish missions that seem very far away.

A project is different from a simple example dedicated to a single and specific skill. To complete a project, we must assemble all our Excel knowledge and skills to come up with an optimal solution. We often have to learn new skills for a new project. In addition, we must analyze the given data and arrange the data in an easy-to-access setup before we fabricate optimal formulas. This indeed offers a valuable and unique experience.

© Hong Zhou 2022
H. Zhou, *Mastering Excel Through Projects*, https://doi.org/10.1007/978-1-4842-7842-0_1

I have been teaching and using Excel for nearly two decades. My experience tells me that students can quickly forget what they learned if the examples do not impress them deeply. Projects, however, can always burn a deeper impression than simple examples. For instance, in a Discrete Mathematics class, I taught RSA encryption (public and private keys) through an Excel project, and this did arouse students' interest in Excel.

When we study simple examples, we finish the learning and immediately move on. However, learning through projects is different because frequently we want the end result of a project to be a product, a functional Excel workbook/worksheet that can be delivered as an application. This requires us to spend additional effort to maximize the automation of our worksheet(s). Fundamentally, the reason why we make use of Excel is to automate our data processing procedures, isn't it?

In one sentence, Excel is for storing, managing, and analyzing data. In two words, managing data. Certainly, we do not want to manage or process data manually; we want to use Excel to help us automate the process to speed up. That is why we are going to study Excel from the perspective of automation, that is, whenever we work on a project, we should keep asking ourselves: how can we make it more automatic?

There are four elements in Excel that can help automate data processing (excluding VBA and macros). They are cell reference, autofill, built-in features, and formulas. The first two elements are fairly simple but critical. The built-in features are easy to understand, too. The biggest challenge lies with formulas which require familiarity with and creative uses of Excel functions. Don't worry, we will go through all the four elements by simple examples and projects, though we won't be able to cover every Excel function. However, once we have gone through all the projects in this book, we should have a fair learning ability to self-learn Excel functions not covered here.

The book starts with a simple but interesting project: the word game, which asks users to find English words that score exactly 100 points given that the 26 alphabets have points 1, 2, 3, ..., 26, respectively. Not only does the book show us step by step how to disassemble a word into letters and then sum up their points, but also it leads us one step further by considering how to make the product, the completed Excel worksheet, more user-friendly and automatic. In this sense, the book is also talking about developing a software product in the form of Excel worksheet(s).

The confidence in self-learning is critical in our life. This type of confidence is built up through and can be reinforced by accomplishing tasks we feel unfamiliar with. This book will offer such a type of experience through the projects.

One advantage of this book is that the content is very much version-independent, that is, most skills introduced in this book are independent of the version of Excel we are using. So, some new features including some new functions only available to Office 365 or Excel 2019, for instance, MAXIFS, TEXTJOIN, and XLOOKUP, won't be explained in this book.

Cell Reference and Formula

Open a blank Excel worksheet, and what jumps into our eyes is a huge table. Yes, Excel is just a huge table with columns and rows. As we can notice, the columns are labeled A, B, C, …, and the rows are numbered 1, 2, 3, etc. Each cell can be identified by a reference, that is, each cell has a unique name. The cell reference represents the cell. For example, the top left cell is referenced as A1, that is, column A and row 1. Observe that a cell reference must have two parts: the column index (A in A1) and the row index (1 in A1).

Excel is case insensitive. Cell reference A1 is treated the same as a1. This case insensitivity applies to almost everything in Excel. Keep this in mind, please.

The first usage of Excel cells is to store data. There are four common data types we will see in cells: text, number, date, and formula. We can type in cell A1 any value we want. For example, we can type in cell A1 the text "Hello World" (without the quotation marks), or a number 3.1415926, or a date "3/14/1970" (without the quotation marks), or a formula which is our next topic.

Formula

What is a formula? A formula is simply an expression that can perform operations on data. To write a formula, we always start our expression with the symbol =, and there should be no space(s) in front of =. When the content in a cell starts with the symbol =, for example, =1 + 2, the content becomes special because it is in fact a formula. Generally, expressions not starting with = are not treated as a formula but rather as a plain text string in Excel. The only exceptions are those starting with either + (plus) or – (minus) sign. Excel recognizes such expressions as a formula and automatically adds the symbol = at their beginning.

3

A formula is like a mathematical expression that conducts a calculation and then presents the result inside the cell. For example, if we type =1+2 in cell A1 and hit the Enter key, the expression 1+2 is calculated. Since the calculation result is 3, 3 is returned. In other words, 3 is displayed in cell A1 by default.

Mathematical expressions are the most commonly used formulas. Be aware that * is the multiplication operator, / is the division operator, and ^ is the exponent operator in Excel. Let's conduct one experiment.

Suppose one can live up to 110 years, and each year has exactly 365 days. How can you use Excel to calculate the number of seconds equivalent to 110 years?

Open an Excel worksheet. In cell A1, type the following expression, and then hit the Enter key:

=110 * 365 * 24 * 60 * 60

This is a formula since it starts with =. Recall that * is the multiplication operator. Be aware if what we typed is 110 * 365 * 24 * 60 * 60 in cell A1, then it is not a formula but a text string only.

Cell Reference in Formulas

Assume we type the integer 67890 inside A1. At this point, the cell reference A1 represents the integer 67890. For example, if we type in cell B1 the formula =A1, 67890 will be displayed in B1 because the formula =A1 is translated to =67890.

Now, let's assume a friend is looking for a job and this integer 67890 is the proposed salary of one job offer. Our friend wants to know, given this salary, if paid monthly, biweekly, or weekly, what is the amount of every pay? Let's do the following experiment.

Experiment

Enter 67890 in cell A1 (we can also enter it like $67890). Enter the formula =67890/12 in cell B1. This calculates monthly payment. Again, there should be no space before =.

Enter =67890/26 and =67890/52 in cells C1 and D1, respectively, as shown in Figure 1-1. C1 is for biweekly payment, and D1 is for weekly payment.

Take a close look at cells B1, C1, and D1 shown in Figure 1-1. We should notice again that there is no space before the operator =.

	A	B	C	D
1	67890	=67890/12	=67890/26	=67890/52
2				

Figure 1-1. *Use the value inside cell A1 directly*

After entering the formulas in cells B1, C1, and D1, our worksheet should look like Figure 1-2. Be aware that the decimal digits in our cells may look different from those in Figure 1-2.

	A	B	C	D
1	67890	5657.50	2611.15	1305.58
2				

Figure 1-2. *The calculated results are presented*

Assume that after some negotiation, the salary of the job offer becomes $70896, and, therefore, our friend wants us to recalculate the monthly, biweekly, and weekly pay for her/him. What shall we do?

We have to retype the number 70896 in all the cells A1, B1, C1, and D1. This is truly inconvenient. What if the number in A1 needs to be changed again?

This is where cell reference comes into the play. As mentioned before, the reference A1 represents whatever is inside cell A1. Note that if the cell has a formula, then the cell reference represents the calculated result instead of the formula itself. Thus, when we enter the formulas inside B1, C1, and D1, we should not type the number 67890. Instead, we should replace 67890 with the reference A1. This is shown in Figure 1-3.

	A	B	C	D
1	67890	=A1/12	=A1/26	=A1/52
2				

Figure 1-3. *Use cell reference in formulas*

Since we have replaced 67890 with the cell reference A1 in cells B1, C1, and D1, whenever we change the number in A1, the results in cells B1, C1, and D1 will be updated automatically. This is because the formulas in cells B1, C1, and D1 automatically recalculate.

So, the first lesson in this book is that we should always use the cell reference to represent the value inside a cell instead of using the cell value itself literally.

Excel Options and Show Formulas

In the recent experiment, we have learned that we need to use cell references as much as possible in our formulas so that any changes can be immediately reflected by automatic formula recalculation. In fact, Excel automatically encourages users to use cell references by setting the Workbook Calculation option to be "Automatic." Let's take a look at the following data.

Please click File ➤ Options as shown in Figure 1-4. The Excel Options window comes up.

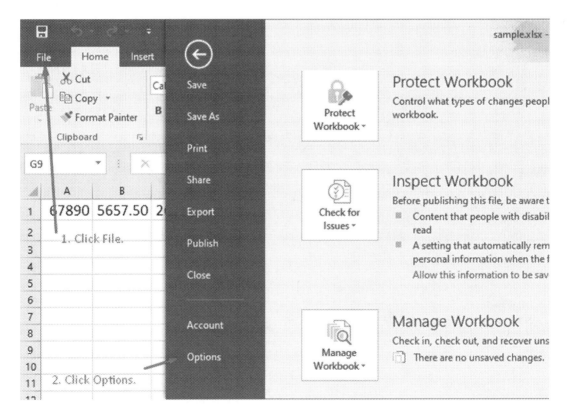

Figure 1-4. *Access Excel options*

On the Excel Options window, please select Formula as illustrated in Figure 1-5. Figure 1-5 reveals that we can disable the Automatic option for Workbook Calculation, but I won't suggest so. Once we disable the Automatic option for Workbook Calculation, cells B1, C1, and D1 won't automatically update their results when A1 is changed. So, let's keep the Workbook Calculation as Automatic for this book. Figure 1-5 also displays other Excel options that are related to how formulas work. Keep the default settings unless I instruct you to change them.

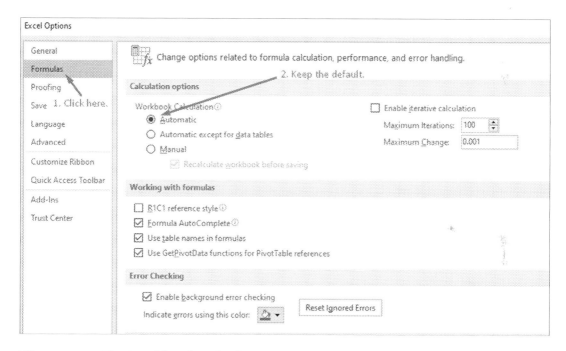

Figure 1-5. *The Workbook Calculation options*

Have you ever wondered how we can display formulas like Figure 1-1? Figure 1-1 and Figure 1-2 display the same worksheet in two different views. Figure 1-2 displays the regular outlook of a worksheet in which cells display the calculated results instead of the formulas inside.

If we want a worksheet to display the formulas so that we can examine the formulas visually, we can click the Formulas tab ➤ Show Formulas as illustrated in Figure 1-6.

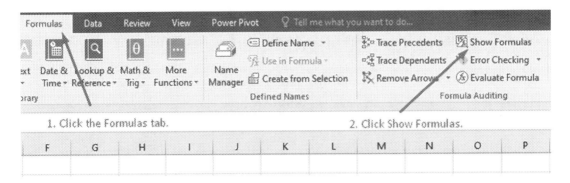

Figure 1-6. *Show Formulas*

To go back to the regular view, click Show Formulas again.

Autofill or Copy

Autofill is a critical feature of Excel because it makes Excel capable of working with a relatively large dataset automatically. Autofill is also called "copy" by some people. Because autofill is so critical, we are going to learn this skill through multiple experiments.

Experiment 1

Let's conduct the following experiment:

1. Enter 1 in cell A1.

2. Enter 2 in cell A2.

3. Select both cells A1 and A2 by clicking cell A1 and dragging the cursor down to cell A2.

4. Release the left mouse button. It is very important to release the left mouse button at this step.

5. Move the mouse cursor to the bottom-right corner of cell A2 until the cursor becomes a black cross (shown in Figure 1-7).

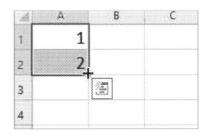

Figure 1-7. *The mouse cursor becomes a black cross*

6. Press the left mouse button, and drag down to cell A6.

The cells A1:A6 are automatically filled with numbers 1, 2, 3, 4, 5, and 6. This process is called autofill, somewhat different from copy. Note that A1:A6 reads "A1 to A6," meaning from cell A1 to cell A6.

So, how does Excel achieve this type of autofill?

Well, Excel is kind of smart. When our first two cells have numbers 1 and 2, Excel automatically computes the increment (or decrement) step value to be 1 (2 - 1 = 1). Thus, Excel automatically increments the values by 1 when we autofill the cells downward.

When we enter 0 and 0.5 in cells B1 and B2, respectively, and repeat the previous autofill process to cell B6, we will obtain values 0, 0.5, 1, 1.5, 2, and 2.5. This time, the step value is 0.5.

Experiment 2

Let's do this experiment in column C:

1. Enter 100 and 98 in cells C1 and C2.

2. Select both cells C1 and C2.

3. Release the left mouse button.

4. Move the cursor to the bottom-right corner of cell C2 until the cursor becomes a black cross (shown in Figure 1-8).

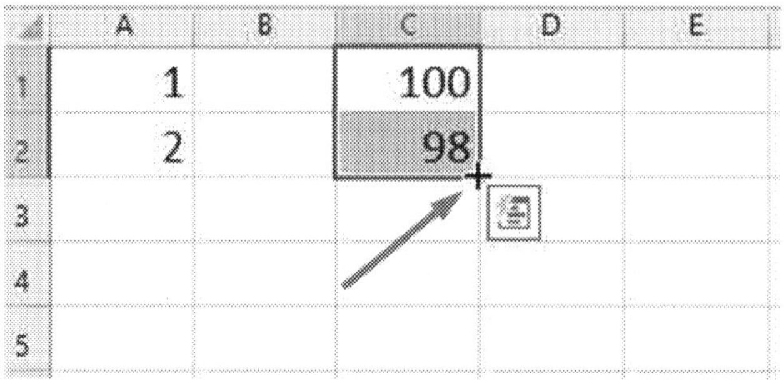

Figure 1-8. *The mouse cursor changes to a black cross*

5.   Press the left mouse button and drag down to cell C6.

What do we see? We should get 100, 98, 96, 94, 92, and 90 in cells C1:C6. This time, the step value is -2.

How to manipulate the mouse cursor is important in working with any computer software, especially with Excel. Try to autofill to cell C100, and then to C1000, and then to C10000 for exercises.

Experiment 3

Autofill can go horizontally, too. Let's do the following experiment:

1.   In cell A1, type Monday.

2.   Select cell A1, and release the left mouse button.

3.   Move the mouse cursor to the bottom-right corner of cell A1 until the mouse cursor becomes a black cross.

4.   Press the left mouse button, and drag to the right until cell G1 is reached.

We should notice that Excel automatically fills the seven weekdays in cells A1:G1.

Functions to Learn

Before we start to learn any Excel functions, we need to understand an important Excel notation. Something like A1:A5 or B2:D6 are commonly seen. We know A1 and A5 are two distinct cells, so it is natural for us to guess that A1:A5 means "A1 to A5," that is, the one-dimensional array containing cells A1, A2, A3, A4, and A5.

B2:D6 stands for "B2 to D6." This is a two-dimensional array including cells B2:B6, C2:C6, and D2:D6. B2 is the top-left cell, while D6 is the bottom-right cell.

We must represent the array "B2 to D6" as B2:D6 (must be in ascending order). We cannot write it reversely as D6:B2. If we happen to write an array as D6:B2, Excel automatically corrects it to be B2:D6.

Since this is the first chapter, we need to learn quite a few functions. In later chapters, we will only learn functions that haven't been explained but must be used. A few functions explained in this chapter won't be used in this chapter's project such as AVERAGE and COUNT. As they are so popular and they will be used later, I am explaining them here, too.

SUM, AVERAGE, MAX, MIN, and COUNT

My experience tells me that SUM and AVERAGE are the most used functions in Excel. These five functions, SUM, AVERAGE, MAX, MIN, and COUNT, have the same syntax:

```
function_name(value1, [value2], ...)
```

For example, the SUM function's syntax is SUM(number1, [number2], ...). This function can take one or more arguments, and each argument can be a literal number, a cell reference, or an array. It then sums up all the arguments. For instance, the formula =SUM(A1, C2, E1:E10) adds up cells A1 and C2 and those cells from E1 to E10.

Let's start a blank Excel worksheet and enter the contents as shown in Figure 1-9.

◢	A	B	C	D	E	F	G	H	I	J
1	4	3	0	9	10	SUM	AVERAGE	MAX	MIN	COUNT
2	1	1	4	4	1					
3	9	3	6	2	3					
4	3	-1		1	4					
5	x2	hello		B	3.14Pi					

Figure 1-9. *Learn the five commonly used functions*

In Figure 1-9, there are two blank cells (C4 and C5). Enter formulas =SUM(A1:E4) and =SUM(A1:E5) in cells F2 and F3, respectively. Notice that both F2 and F3 have the same result: 67. In Excel, blank cells such as C4 and C5 are ignored by the SUM function. The same applies to other non-numerical cells.

Test Yourself: type the formula =SUM(A5:E5) in cell F4. What should we expect?[1]

The AVERAGE function calculates the average of its arguments. Enter the formula =AVERAGE(A1:E4) in cell G2. This formula calculates the average of cells A1 to E4.

Enter the formula =AVERAGE(A1:E5) in cell G3. We shall discover that G2 and G3 have the same answer 3.5263 or something close. However, we should notice that A1:E4 has 20 cells and the sum of A1:E4 = 67, but 67/20 = 3.35, which is different from 3.5263. What happened?

Like the SUM function, the AVERAGE function automatically skips blank cells and other non-numerical cells. To the AVERAGE function, both A1:E4 and A1:E5 have only 19 cells. If we place 0 inside both C4 and C5, then both G2 and G3 display 3.35.

As the names suggest, the MAX function finds the maximum in a number of values, the MIN function finds the minimum in a number of values, and the COUNT function counts how many cells are hosting a numerical value.

Let's enter the formulas =MAX(A1:E4) and =MAX(A1:E5) in cells H2 and H3, respectively. These two formulas find the maximum value in A1:E4 and A1:E5, respectively.

Enter the formulas =MIN(A1:E4) and =MIN(A1:E5) in cells I2 and I3, respectively. These two formulas find the minimum value in A1:E4 and A1:E5, respectively.

Enter the formulas =COUNT(A1:E4) and =COUNT(A1:E5) in cells J2 and J3, respectively. These two formulas count how many cells contain numbers in A1:E4 and A1:E5, respectively.

Our worksheet should look like Figure 1-10. We shall notice that all the five functions skip blank cells and other non-numerical cells.

	A	B	C	D	E	F	G	H	I	J
1	4	3	0	9	10	SUM	AVERAGE	MAX	MIN	COUNT
2	1	1	4	4	1	67	3.526316	10	-1	19
3	9	3	6	2	3	67	3.526316	10	-1	19
4	3	-1		1	4					
5	x2	hello		B	3.14Pi					

Figure 1-10. *The five common functions skip blank and other non-numerical cells*

---

[1] We should expect 0.

CHAR and CODE

Computers store everything in the form of integers. The famous ASCII table defines the integer values for characters on our keyboard. For example, uppercase letters A–Z are stored as integers 65–90, respectively. The CHAR function can convert a number to its equivalent character. For instance, =CHAR(65) gives the uppercase letter A and =CHAR(97) returns the lowercase letter a.

Function CODE reverses CHAR. The CODE function converts a character back to its equivalent integer. For example, the formula =CODE("A") generates 65. We are not going to use the CODE function in our project.

MID

MID is a text function that fetches one or more characters from the middle of a text string, given the starting position and the number of characters to fetch. Its syntax is MID(text, start_num, num_chars), where the argument text is the string from which characters are taken, start_num is the starting position, and num_chars specifies how many characters to fetch.

For example, =MID("The United States", 2, 5) returns "he Un" (without the quotation marks). Be aware that the space between "The" and "United" is counted.

Test Yourself: given A1 stores the text string "COMPUTER," what will be returned by the formula =MID(A1, 6, 1)?[2]

Two other functions are worth mentioning here: LEFT and RIGHT. These two functions fetch characters from the left terminal or the right terminal of a text string. For example, =LEFT("The United States", 5) returns "The U," while =RIGHT("The United States", 5) returns "tates."

RANDBETWEEN

This function generates a random integer inside a given range. Its syntax is RANDBETWEEN(bottom, top). For example, if we want to generate a random integer between 1 and 10 inclusively (both 1 and 10 are included), our formula should then

---

[2] T

be =RANDBETWEEN(1, 10). Be aware that RANDBETWEEN recalculates every time we make a change in our worksheet. So, the numbers generated by this function can keep changing.

Test Yourself: to generate random integers between 0 and 1, what is the formula?[3]

LOOKUP

LOOKUP is one of my favorite functions. It looks up a value in a one-dimensional array, either a row or a column. Its default syntax is LOOKUP(lookup-value, lookup-vector, [result-vector]). To explain this function well, we need to try several small experiments.

Let's open a blank worksheet and enter some data exactly like Figure 1-11.

	A	B	C	D	E	F	G	H
1	0	F	1	A	C	F	G	Z
2	60	D	2					
3	70	C	3					
4	80	B	4	0	60	70	80	90
5	90	A	5	F	D	C	B	A

Figure 1-11. *Sample data for LOOKUP function experiments*

Let's assume a test grading scenario. Suppose A1:A5 stores the score brackets and B1:B5 stores the corresponding grades. The score brackets are 0 ➔ 60, 60 ➔ 70, 70 ➔ 80, 80 ➔ 90, and 90 or above. The symbol ➔ in the expression "0 ➔ 60" indicates "from 0 up to but not including 60."

Bracket is a common concept in test grading and income tax filing. In this test grading example, we do not assign letter grades for every score number from 0 to 100. Instead, we divide the scores into discrete brackets, each with a lower boundary and an upper boundary. LOOKUP function can be used to find the **lower** boundary of a bracket to which an integer belongs.

---

[3] =RANDBETWEEN(0, 1)

For example, if the score is 55, the corresponding bracket is 0–60, and so the lower boundary is then 0. If the score is 70, the lower boundary of its bracket is 70. If the score is 100, the lower boundary of its bracket is then 90. The grades are assigned based on the lower boundary.

Experiment 1

LOOKUP function can be used to find the lower boundary of a destination bracket. However, this function has a prerequisite: the lookup-vector must be sorted in ascending order. Assume we have entered data as shown in Figure 1-11; to obtain the lower boundary of the bracket of integer 75, we can enter the formula =LOOKUP(75, A1:A5) in cell D3.

Observe that D1:H1 is also sorted in ascending order. Let's enter in cell E3 the formula =LOOKUP("H", D1:H1). What will E3 display?

Now, let's enter in cell F3 the formula =LOOKUP("E", B1:B5). We shall notice that A is displayed in cell F3, but A is not the correct result. This is because B1:B5 is not sorted in ascending order.

Our worksheet should look like Figure 1-12.

◢	A	B	C	D	E	F	G	H
1	0	F	1	A	C	F	G	Z
2	60	D	2					
3	70	C	3	70	G	A		
4	80	B	4	0	60	70	80	90
5	90	A	5	F	D	C	B	A

Figure 1-12. *Experiment 1 of the LOOKUP function*

Experiment 2

In this experiment, we want to convert a score into a letter grade.

In cell G3, enter the formula =LOOKUP(88, A1:A5, B1:B5). Here, B1:B5 is the result-vector. When the result-vector is given, LOOKUP works this way:

1. Finds the bracket 80 → 90 for the lookup-value 88.

2. The lower boundary is 80 which is at position 4 in A1:A5.

3. The position 4 of B1:B5 is B4; thus, "B" is displayed in cell G3.

The beauty of LOOKUP function is as long as the lookup-vector is sorted in ascending order and it matches the result-vector in length, the two vectors can be stored far away, and one can be a row, while the other is a column. Enter the formula =LOOKUP(54, A1:A5, D5:H5) in cell H3. H3 should correctly display F.

We can also convert from letters to integers. Enter the formula =LOOKUP("D", D1:H1, C1:C5) in cell H3; what do we expect to be displayed in cell H3?

By now, our worksheet should look like Figure 1-13.

	A	B	C	D	E	F	G	H
1	0	F	1	A	C	F	G	Z
2	60	D	2					
3	70	C	3	70	G	A	B	2
4	80	B	4	0	60	70	80	90
5	90	A	5	F	D	C	B	A

Figure 1-13. *Experiment 2 of LOOKUP function*

Experiment 3

Another beauty of LOOKUP function is when the two vectors are nearby each other, either two columns like A1:A5 and B1:B5 or two rows like D4:H4 and D5:H5, as long as the lookup-vector is sorted in ascending order and is before the result-vector (either on the left or above), the use of LOOKUP can be simplified.

Let's follow the following instructions to complete Experiment 3:

1. Enter 75 in cell A7.

2. Enter =LOOKUP(A7, A1:B5) in cell B7.

3. Enter =LOOKUP(A7, D4:H5) in cell C7.

We should observe that both B7 and C7 display the grade C, as shown in Figure 1-14.

	A	B	C	D	E	F	G	H
1	0	F	1	A	C	F	G	Z
2	60	D	2					
3	70	C	3	70 G	A	B		2
4	80	B	4	0	60	70	80	90
5	90	A	5 F	D	C	B	A	
6								
7	75 C		C					

Figure 1-14. *Experiment 3 of LOOKUP function*

IF

The IF function is also a very popular function whose syntax is IF(logical-test, value-if-true, value-if-false). Let's follow the following instructions to experience this function.

1. Inside a worksheet, make sure that cell A1 is blank. If there is anything inside, clear it.

2. Enter the formula =IF(A1="", "empty", "not empty") in cell B1. What should we expect to see in B1?

Because A1 has nothing inside, the logical test A1="" is true. Thus, "empty" is returned and displayed in B1.

Now, if we enter "Hello" or a number like 59 in A1, the logical test A1="" returns false; therefore, "not empty" is returned and displayed in B1.

IFERROR

This function is a combination of the two functions IF and ISERROR (we will talk about ISERROR later). To write robust formulas, we need to ask ourselves what if a formula or expression goes wrong. For example, given the example shown in Figure 1-11, ask yourself what the formula =LOOKUP(-1, A1:B5) will get.

Well, because there is no bracket for the number -1 in A1:A5, =LOOKUP(-1, A1:B5) fails and, therefore, returns a Value Not Available Error expressed as #N/A. Normally, such an error won't happen, but what if it does? That is why we are studying the IFERROR function.

The IFERROR function takes in two parameters in order: value and value-if-error. The first parameter is usually an expression such as =LOOKUP(-1, A1:B5); the second parameter is the designated value when an error happens.

For instance, if we want 0 to be returned when =LOOKUP(-1, A1:B5) fails, we can have the formula =IFERROR(LOOKUP(-1, A1:B5), 0). When the expression LOOKUP(-1, A1:B5) works, whatever it returns will be returned by the formula =IFERROR(LOOKUP(-1, A1:B5), 0). Zero is returned only when the expression LOOKUP(-1, A1:B5) fails.

Often, we want an empty string to be returned when an error occurs. In this case, our formula should be =IFERROR(LOOKUP(-1, A1:B5), "").

Test Yourself: what will be returned by the formula =IFERROR(LOOKUP(88, A1:B5), "") if our worksheet looks like Figure 1-11?[4]

Autofill Formulas

The greatest power of Excel comes from the combination of autofill and formulas. This combination realizes automation in Excel.

Relative Cell Reference

Correctly and creatively constructing formulas is a must if we want to be an expert in Excel. A formula can be very complicated, but we need to start from simple examples. For this chapter's exercises, please download the sample Excel files from https://github.com/hhohho/master-Excel-through-projects.

Please open the file chapter-1-1a.xlsx. We shall see a worksheet as shown in Figure 1-15.

---

[4] The answer is letter grade B, because LOOKUP(88, A1:B5) works, and, therefore, its result B is returned.

	A	B	C	D	E
1	EmployeeID	Name	Salary	Bi-weekly-pay	
2	553987	Jake	109724		
3	177187	Sam	116838		
4	346568	Rose	79146		
5	627344	Ally	107002		
6	933713	Scarlet	91473		
7	900647	Michael	90163		

Figure 1-15. *Example payroll-1*

As you can imagine, we are going to compute the biweekly pay for each employee based on their salaries, assuming there are 26 biweekly pays in a fiscal year. Let's follow the following instructions:

1. Enter the formula =C2/26 inside cell D2. This calculates the biweekly pay for Jake.

2. Select cell D2. Lift up the left mouse button.

3. Move the mouse cursor to the bottom-right corner of cell D2 until the cursor becomes a black cross, and then double click.

   Because the columns left to column D already have values and we are trying a downward autofill, we don't need to drag down the mouse cursor. A double-click can do the job much nicer.

We should observe that Excel automatically fills in the desired formulas in the cells D3:D21 for us. We might have attempted to enter =C3/26 inside cell D3, =C4/26 inside cell D4, and so on and so forth. No, we don't want to do that. We always want to enter the formula once and let autofill do the rest for us. That is the greatest beauty of Excel.

Now the question becomes: How does Excel achieve what we desire? Well, to explain this clearly, let's display all the formulas. By default, Excel displays the calculated results of formulas inside a worksheet. But we can force Excel to display the formulas instead of the calculated results. Please click the Formulas tab ➤ Show Formulas. Recall that we have learned this skill as shown in Figure 1-6.

Our worksheet looks like Figure 1-16. As we can discover, the formulas inside cells D3 and D4 are automatically revised to be =C3/26 and =C4/26, respectively. We can notice that the row index in the original formula =C2/26 is incremented from 2 to 3, then

4, and then furthermore. In autofill, if it is a downward autofill, every row index in a formula will increment by one across down. As we can imagine, if the autofill is upward, then the row indices will decrement by 1 all the way up (note that a row index cannot go smaller than 1).

	A	B	C	D
1	EmployeeID	Name	Salary	Bi-weekly-pay
2	553987	Jake	109724	=C2/26
3	177187	Sam	116838	=C3/26
4	346568	Rose	79146	=C4/26
5	627344	Ally	107002	=C5/26
6	933713	Scarlet	91473	=C6/26
7	900647	Michael	90163	=C7/26
8	681211	Tim	111445	=C8/26
9	639117	Nancy	59313	=C9/26

Figure 1-16. *Autofill formula (relative reference)*

Bear in mind that when we autofill horizontally from left to right, Excel automatically increments the column indexes of all the cell references in a formula (from A to B, B to C, etc.).

Excel has two types of cell references: relative reference and absolute reference. By default, all cell references, either row index or column index, are relative references. For example, the cell reference "C2" inside the formula =C2/26 is a relative cell reference. A relative cell reference automatically increments or decrements its row index or column index during an autofill or copy action. What we are experiencing in the previous example is the automatic update of a relative cell reference's row index in an autofill operation. We will experience this very often, and I will explain more later.

To hide the formulas (which is common), click the Formulas tab ➤ select Show Formulas again.

Absolute Cell Reference

Assume that we are going to give every employee a salary raise. Our job is to compute the raised salary for each employee. This time, let's start everything from scratch. Follow the following instructions to complete the experiment:

1. Open a blank Excel worksheet. Enter texts "ID," "Salary," "Raise," "Updated Salary," and "Percentage" in cells A1, B1, C1, D1, and E1, respectively. Enter "5%" inside cell E2 (without quotation marks). The 5% may be displayed as 0.05. If we want to force Excel to display 5%, please click cell E2 to select it ➤ click the Home tab ➤ click the symbol % inside the Number group. This is shown in Figure 1-17.

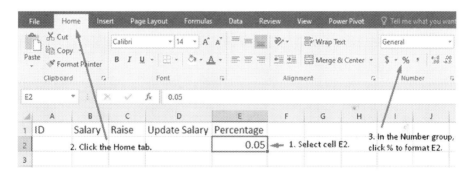

Figure 1-17. *Percentage format*

2. In cell A2, enter the formula =RANDBETWEEN(100000, 999999). This formula randomly generates an integer between 100000 and 999999 inclusively as an ID (a 6-digit integer).

3. Autofill from A2 to A12.

4. In cell B2, enter the formula =RANDBETWEEN(50000, 150000). This formula generates an integer between 50000 and 150000 inclusively as the salary for the first employee.

5. Select cell B2 ➤ move the mouse cursor to the bottom-right corner of cell B2 until the cursor becomes a black cross ➤ double-click.

This double-click action automatically fills in formulas from B2 to B12.

Again, autofill by double-click works only because column A already has values and the operation is a downward autofill.

6. In cell C2, enter the formula =B2 * E2. This formula calculates the 5% raise for the first employee. Everything looks perfect at this point.

7. Autofill from C2 to C12 by the double-click action. Our worksheet now looks like Figure 1-18. If we click cell C3, we shall see a formula =B3 * E3.

	A	B	C	D	E
1	ID	Salary	Raise	Update Salary	Percentage
2	984536	78327	3916		0.05
3	556701	136400	0		
4	731461	84325	0		
5	881164	122896	0		
6	161093	132558	0		
7	564796	148386	0		
8	908445	145646	0		
9	590411	63225	0		

Figure 1-18. *Autofill failed on salary Raise*

As we have learned, in a downward autofill action, the row indexes of cell references automatically increment by 1. That is exactly what is happening. From cell C2 to C3, the original formula =B2 * E2 is automatically updated to be =B3 * E3.

But this is not what we want. We want the formula in cell C3 to be =B3 * E2, that is, cell E2 should not be changed. More specifically, the row index of the cell reference E2 should remain unchanged.

Given the original formula =B2 * E2 in cell C2, how can we ask Excel to automatically update B2 to B3 while keeping E2 unchanged? To make E2 stay the same during a vertical autofill, we should revise the formula in cell C2 to be =B2 * E$2. By placing the $ before the row index 2 (like paying a tip to Excel ☺), the row index 2 will stay the same during this autofill action. Note that a pure vertical autofill never changes the column index of a cell reference.

Placing $ before the row index and/or column index of a cell reference makes the cell reference an absolute cell reference. An absolute cell reference stays unchanged during an autofill or copy action.

We can certainly write the formula in cell C2 as =B2 * $E$2. By placing an extra $ before the column index E, E won't change even when we perform a horizontal autofill. However, because in this case it is a vertical autofill, the $ is not needed next to the column index as it remains constant anyways. In the future, we will run into cases where we must make use of $ to keep either the row index or the column index but not both unchanged for a cell reference in an autofill action.

So, when we autofill formula(s), we must be very clear which cell reference should automatically change and which cell reference (or part of a cell reference) should stay unchanged. We will run into many such occasions. Developing a clear understanding of absolute reference is critical in Excel formula construction.

Now, autofill from C2 to C12. We should get the right result.

8. In cell D2, enter the formula =B2 + C2.

9. Autofill from D2 to D12. Part of our worksheet should look like Figure 1-19.

	A	B	C	D	E
1	ID	Salary	Raise	Update Salary	Percentage
2	389038	139970	6999	146968.5	0.05
3	949266	105912	5296	111207.6	
4	391112	123303	6165	129468.15	
5	557117	118612	5931	124542.6	
6	104743	124227	6211	130438.35	

Figure 1-19. *The example of absolute reference completed*

In the beginning, it could be very confusing regarding when we should use absolute reference and when we should not. This does take practice to become comfortable. One way to get us a good start is to write down the formulas in both the starting cell and the stopping cell without including any $, and then compare them to find out what reference(s) should remain unchanged. The following experiment explains this technique:

1. Assume the starting cell is D5 and its formula is =A2*C2 + D1/B2. Enter this original formula in cell D5.

2. Assume we need to autofill from D5 to E20. The will-be formula in cell E20 must be =B17*D17 + E16/C17.

3. Write down the should-be formula in E20. Assume it is =B17*C17 + D1/C2.

4. Compare the should-be formula and the original formula, then revise the original formula inside the starting cell as illustrated in Figure 1-20.

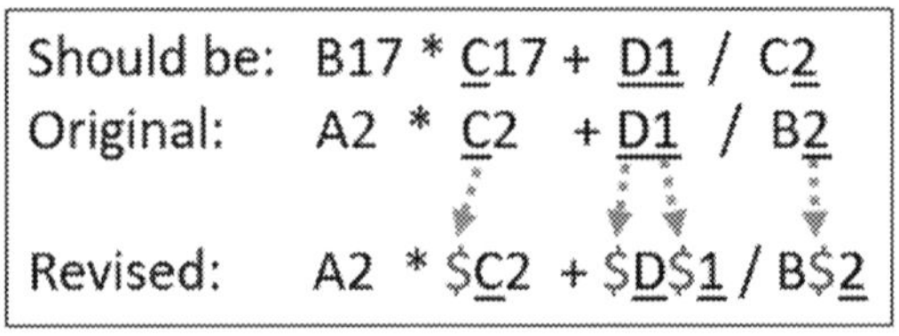

```
Should be:  B17 * C17 +  D1 /  C2
Original:   A2  *  C2  +  D1 /  B2

Revised:    A2  * $C2 + $D$1 / B$2
```

Figure 1-20. *Explains where to place $ for absolute reference*

In Figure 1-20, between the original formula and the should-be formula, the unchanged cell references, either row index or column index, are marked in red and underlined, indicating that they should remain unchanged during the autofill operation. Matching back to the original formula, we then revise the original formula by placing $ right before those row indexes and column indexes that are underlined.

Work on the Project

As mentioned before, this book is project-based such that every chapter has a project to go through. This chapter's project is a relatively simple but fun one. It is an English word game.

Assume that the alphabets A, B, C, ..., Z have integer values 1, 2, 3, ..., 26, respectively. We are going to develop an Excel worksheet to help find what words can score exactly 100. For example, the word Excel scores 5 + 24 + 3 + 5 + 12 = 49. Note that this is case insensitive.

Another example would be Hello = 8 + 5 + 12 + 12 + 15 = 52.

From the previous two examples, we can figure out what we need to accomplish:

- Matching a letter to a specific number, for which we can use the LOOKUP function. To use the LOOKUP function, it's better to leave the 26 letters and their matched numbers together. The question is where to leave them.

- Dissecting a word into individual letters, which can be achieved by means of the text function MID. This also raises a setup question: where to store those individual letters dissected from a word.

- Summing individual numbers, for which we can use the SUM function.

There is no best way to set up the worksheet for this project. An important rule is that the setup should facilitate the automation of the project.

Let's open a new Excel workbook. Follow the following instructions to complete this project:

1. Type numbers 1 and 2 in cells B1 and B2, respectively. Select both cells to autofill to cell B26 such that the number sequence 1, 2, 3, ..., 26 is inside B1:B26.

2. Certainly, we can type the 26 alphabets in cells A1:A26. But we may want to try a slightly easier way.

    In cell A1, type the formula =CHAR(64 + B1). Because B1=1, this formula generates the uppercase letter A. Autofill from cell A1 to A26.

3. In cells C1 and D1, type "Word" and "Score" (without the quotation marks), respectively. These are used to indicate where to enter a word (C2) and where to store the score (D2).

4. Assume that no word has more than 26 letters. So, enter 1 and 2 in cells E1 and E2, respectively, and autofill together to cell E26. Column E is used to tell which character to fetch from the word stored in cell C2. At this point, part of our worksheet looks like Figure 1-21.

⬙	A	B	C	D	E	F
1	A	1	Word	Score	1	
2	B	2			2	
3	C	3			3	
4	D	4			4	
5	E	5			5	
6	F	6			6	
7	G	7			7	
8	H	8			8	
9	I	9			9	
10	J	10			10	
11	K	11			11	

Figure 1-21. *Game setup*

5. Enter in cell C2 the word "Excel" as our example.

6. Enter the formula =MID(C$2, E1, 1) in cell F1. Since E1 = 1, this formula fetches the first character from "Excel," which is letter E.

Pay attention to why the cell reference C2 is written as C$2. Since we are going to autofill from F1 to F26 and every character is taken from the same word stored in cell C2, we need C2 to be absolute reference partially. Test Yourself: will $C$2 work for the same purpose?[5]

Autofill from F1 to F26 (we can use the double-click skill to autofill here).

7. Now that the individual letters are stored in column F, we need to convert them into numbers by using the LOOKUP function.

Please type formula =IFERROR(LOOKUP(F1, $A$1:$B$26), "") in cell G1. In this formula, the array A1:B26 is written in absolute reference as $A$1:$B$26. Why? This is because the array's cell references should not be changed during autofill.

Like we experienced before, the LOOKUP function will fail if its lookup value does not exist. As most English words won't have enough letters to fill cells F1:F26, errors can happen. In this specific case, the LOOKUP function fails in cells G6:G26. For example, in cell G6, the expression LOOKUP(F6, $A$1:$B$26) fails because F6 is a blank cell. The function IFERROR is used to make sure that if a cell in column F is empty, an empty string is returned. Recall that an empty string does not affect the SUM function which we will use in the next step.

The IFERROR function can safeguard another unexpected occasion. People may not enter a single word in cell C2. What if a short phrase such as "Hello World" is entered? Our formula can handle such an unexpected case correctly.

Autofill from G1 to G26.

---

[5] Yes.

8. In cell D2, enter the formula =IF(SUM(G:G)=0, "", SUM(G:G)).

SUM(G:G) sums up all numbers inside the whole column G. We do not have any unnecessary numbers in column G; SUM(G:G) is a perfect use as it sums up every number in column G.

When the game is not played, there is no word inside cell C2. The formula SUM(G:G) will generate 0 inside cell D2. However, it would be nice to make sure when no word is present or SUM(G:G)=0; cell D2 does not display 0 but remains empty. This is why the IF function is used here.

At this point, part of our worksheet should look like Figure 1-22 (showing formulas only).

	A	B	C	D	E	F	G
1	=CHAR(64+B1)	1	Word	Score	1	=MID(C$2, E1, 1)	=IFERROR(LOOKUP(F1,$A$1:$B$26), "")
2	=CHAR(64+B2)	2	Excel	=IF(SUM(G:G)=0, "", SUM(G:G))	2	=MID(C$2, E2, 1)	=IFERROR(LOOKUP(F2,$A$1:$B$26), "")
3	=CHAR(64+B3)	3			3	=MID(C$2, E3, 1)	=IFERROR(LOOKUP(F3,$A$1:$B$26), "")
4	=CHAR(64+B4)	4			4	=MID(C$2, E4, 1)	=IFERROR(LOOKUP(F4,$A$1:$B$26), "")
5	=CHAR(64+B5)	5			5	=MID(C$2, E5, 1)	=IFERROR(LOOKUP(F5,$A$1:$B$26), "")
6	=CHAR(64+B6)	6			6	=MID(C$2, E6, 1)	=IFERROR(LOOKUP(F6,$A$1:$B$26), "")
7	=CHAR(64+B7)	7			7	=MID(C$2, E7, 1)	=IFERROR(LOOKUP(F7,$A$1:$B$26), "")
8	=CHAR(64+B8)	8			8	=MID(C$2, E8, 1)	=IFERROR(LOOKUP(F8,$A$1:$B$26), "")
9	=CHAR(64+B9)	9			9	=MID(C$2, E9, 1)	=IFERROR(LOOKUP(F9,$A$1:$B$26), "")
10	=CHAR(64+B10)	10			10	=MID(C$2, E10, 1)	=IFERROR(LOOKUP(F10,$A$1:$B$26), "")
11	=CHAR(64+B11)	11			11	=MID(C$2, E11, 1)	=IFERROR(LOOKUP(F11,$A$1:$B$26), "")
12	=CHAR(64+B12)	12			12	=MID(C$2, E12, 1)	=IFERROR(LOOKUP(F12,$A$1:$B$26), "")

Figure 1-22. *The complete formulas*

Enter the word ATTITUDE inside cell C2. We should get a perfect score of 100. This tells us that attitude is the key! It is our attitude that makes a perfect score. See Figure 1-23. We can also enter "Hello World" in cell C2, and our worksheet works fine, too.

◢	A	B	C	D	E	F	G
1	A	1	Word	Score	1	A	1
2	B	2	ATTITUDE	100	2	T	20
3	C	3			3	T	20
4	D	4			4	I	9
5	E	5			5	T	20
6	F	6			6	U	21
7	G	7			7	D	4
8	H	8			8	E	5
9	I	9			9		
10	J	10			10		

Figure 1-23. *Attitude is the key*

9. Should we stop here? I won't. Suppose we want to give this Word Game worksheet to our friend Jack who has no Excel skill at all. Jack might mess up something in the worksheet and find out later that it does not work anymore. To avoid something like this to happen, we should protect our worksheet so that Jack can do nothing to this worksheet except for entering English words in cell C2.

To achieve this, we need to have our worksheet password-protected. Be aware that password protection applies to locked cells only and by default all cells inside a worksheet are locked. As we need Jack to enter words in cell C2, we then need to unlock cell C2 before we apply password protection to our worksheet. Let's try the following.

Select cell C2, and then click the Home tab ➤ Click the arrow inside the Font group ➤ on the upcoming window, select Protection ➤ uncheck Locked ➤ click OK. This process is illustrated in Figure 1-24.

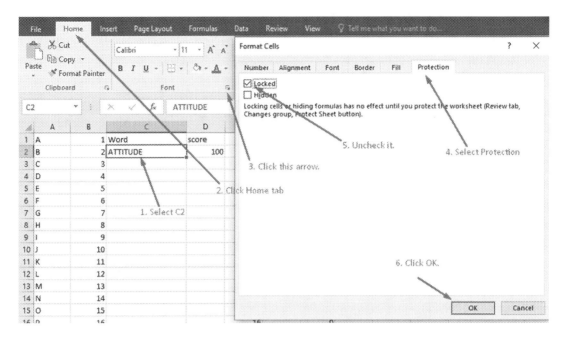

Figure 1-24. *Unlock cell C2*

10. Now, we need to protect all locked cells except C2. Follow the instructions in Figure 1-25 to enter a password to protect our worksheet.

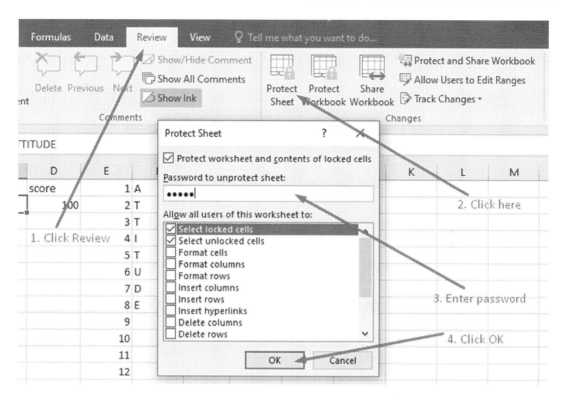

Figure 1-25. *Protect worksheet*

11. We will be asked to re-enter our password. Once it is finished, Jack can edit cell C2 provided he does not have the correct password to stop the protection.

The file chapter-1-2b.xlsx presents the final product as a password-protected worksheet. The password is Excel.

Challenge: Our current worksheet product can examine a maximum of 26 characters. What if we want to allow a maximum of 35 characters? What should we revise? The file chapter-1-2c.xlsx presents a worksheet that can allow a maximum of 35 characters. It is password protected, and the password is Excel.

Chapter Tip

Since this is the first chapter, we are going to experience two tips instead of one.

Open a new Excel file. In cell A1, enter the date 12/1/2021. Then, autofill from A1 to G1. We should see something like Figure 1-26. Be assured that there is nothing wrong. When cells do not have enough spaces for their contents inside, they may display a string of #. To force the cells to show their contents, double-click the vertical bar between two letters as shown in Figure 1-26. We can also simply drag the column to expand its space.

	A	B	C	D	E	F	G
1	12/1/2021	########	########	########	########	########	########
2							
3		Double click here to					
4		expand cell B1.					

Figure 1-26. *Cells without enough spaces display ########*

Should your autofill action fail to generate something like Figure 1-26, please open the Excel file chapter-1-3a.xlsx to practice this skill inside the worksheet named Sheet1.

The second tip is to access data on a different worksheet. Open the file chapter-1-3a.xlsx. This file has three worksheets named Sheet1, Sheet2, and Sheet3. The cells B2 and C2 in Sheet2 have a text message "I am in Sheet2" and the number 59, respectively. Now, let's click Sheet3; we want to display the content of cell B2 of Sheet2 in the cell A1 of Sheet3.

A worksheet can be accessed by name, but the name must be followed by the exclamation mark "!". The exclamation mark denotes that the name is a sheet reference. Thus, we should enter the formula =Sheet2!B2 inside the cell A1 of Sheet3.

Assume we want to multiply the value in cell C2 of Sheet2 by 10 and leave the result in cell B1 of Sheet3. What would be the correct formula?

The two formulas are presented in Figure 1-27.

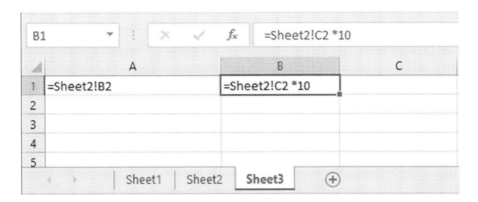

Figure 1-27. *Access another worksheet by name*

Review Points

1. Cell reference and Excel formulas.

2. Excel options and displaying formulas inside a worksheet.

3. Excel autofill skill including autofill by double-clicking.

4. Relative cell reference and absolute cell reference.

5. Excel functions SUM, AVERAGE, MAX, MIN, COUNT, CHAR, CODE, MID, LEFT, RIGHT, RANDBETWEEN, LOOKUP, IF, and IFERROR.

6. Password protection of a worksheet.

7. Accessing data on another worksheet.

CHAPTER 2

Food Nutrition Ranking

Please download the sample Excel files from `https://github.com/hhohho/master-Excel-through-projects` for this chapter's exercises. This chapter's project is about food nutrition ranking. This Excel project derives from a request from a dear colleague, Dr. Katie Martin (thanks to both Dr. Katie Martin and Dr. Joseph Manthey).

In some food banks and food pantries in the United States, foods are classified into different nutrition ranks, each representing a different nutritional level. The ranks can be visually represented by different colors. For example, foods can be marked as Green, Yellow and Red, each indicating a different nutritional level. Such a ranking process can be based on the content levels (amount per serving) of saturated fat, trans fat, cholesterol, sodium, and sugar in each food item. In this chapter's project, we only consider saturated fat, sodium, and sugar. In addition, Green stands for "healthy," Yellow for "neutral," and Red for "unhealthy."

Be aware that different categories of foods have different standards. Let's take a look at Figure 2-1 which presents a sample list of food categories and their standard amount per serving levels regarding saturated fat, sodium, and sugar. As we can see, the sodium criteria for green Fruit is less than or equal to 32 mg, but for green Grains, it must be no larger than 230 mg.

© Hong Zhou 2022
H. Zhou, *Mastering Excel Through Projects*, https://doi.org/10.1007/978-1-4842-7842-0_2

	A	B	C	D	E
1	Food category	Rank by Color	Saturated Fat	Sodium	Sugar
2		Green	< 1 g	< 32 mg	< 12 g
3	Fruit	Yellow	≤ 1 g	33 - 50 mg	13 - 25 g
4		Red	≥ 1.5 g	≥ 51 mg	≥ 26 g
5		Green	< 1 g	< 140 mg	< 4 g
6	Vegetables	Yellow	≤ 1 g	141-230 mg	5 - 7 g
7		Red	≥ 1.5 g	≥ 231 mg	≥ 8 g
8		Green	< 2 g	< 230 mg	< 6 g
9	Grains	Yellow	≤ 2 g	231 - 400 mg	7 - 12 g
10		Red	≥ 2.5 g	≥ 401 mg	≥ 13 g
11		Green	< 2 g	< 200 mg	< 5 g
12	Protein: Plant-based	Yellow	2.5 - 5 g	201 - 480 mg	6 - 9 g
13		Red	≥ 5.5 g	≥ 481 mg	≥ 10 g

Figure 2-1. *A sample nutrition ranking system*

The goal of our project is to develop an Excel worksheet which can offer the following functional features:

- Let users add or remove food categories and specify their ranking standards.

- Allow users to add a specific food item and assign this food item into a category selected from a given list.

- Let users enter the saturated fat level, sodium level, and sugar level for the newly added food item.

- After all the required data has been entered, our worksheet should automatically rank this specific food item into a different color, either Green, Yellow, or Red.

The idea can be better explained by Figure 2-2 and Figure 2-3. In Figure 2-2, we just added a food item named "USA cookie." All the required information has been entered except for the sugar. Thus, no ranking shows up for this food item. In Figure 2-3, the sugar level is completed, and this food item is automatically ranked Yellow.

	A	B	C	D	E	F
1	Food name	Category	Saturated Fat(g)	Sodium(mg)	Sugar(g)	Color Ranking
2	Toto apple	Fruit	0	1	10	Green
3	cola A	Beverages	0	200	30	Red
4	USA cookie	Snacks/Desserts	1	250		
5						
6						

Figure 2-2. *Information is not complete; no ranking is shown*

	A	B	C	D	E	F
1	Food name	Category	Saturated Fat(g)	Sodium(mg)	Sugar(g)	Color Ranking
2	Toto apple	Fruit	0	1	10	Green
3	cola A	Beverages	0	200	30	Red
4	USA cookie	Snacks/Desserts	1	250	25	Yellow
5						
6			All required information has been			
7			entered, ranking shows up.			

Figure 2-3. *Ranking automatically shows up*

So, how do we achieve our goal? The first step is to analyze the given sample ranking data shown in Figure 2-1. By doing so, we can realize that for an item to be Green, its saturated fat, sodium, and sugar levels are always all below certain thresholds. On the contrary, the saturated fat, sodium, and sugar levels for a Red food item are always above certain values. Certainly, if a food item does not belong to either Green or Red, it must be ranked Yellow. This understanding is critical.

Today's nutrition knowledge tells us that many chronic health problems result from excessive intake of saturated fat, sodium, and/or sugar. Healthy foods have lower levels of saturated fat, sodium, and sugar. That is why the amounts per serving of Green food items are always below certain levels. In contrast, unhealthy food items always have the amounts per serving above certain levels. When we develop our worksheet, we do not need to worry about the levels of Yellow ranking.

Before we step into the project, let's get ourselves familiar with some Excel functions that are needed in this project.

Functions to Learn

We are going to learn the new functions AND, OR, VLOOKUP, and ISBLANK. In addition, we need to revisit the IF function since we are going to make use of nested IF function in this chapter.

In Office 365, Excel has a few new functions such as XLOOKUP and XMATCH which are supposed to be more powerful than the classic VLOOKUP and MATCH functions. However, as this textbook also targets other versions of Excel, functions unique to Office 365 are not discussed.

IF

In Excel, several functions such as SUM, AVERAGE, COUNT, MAX, and MIN might be used the most. Excluding them, the IF function and its siblings become the most used function set. Nevertheless, IF statement is the most used statement in programming.

Take a look at Figure 2-1 again. Assume that foods are ranked only based on saturated fat level. Thus, for any fruit, we can say, "if its saturated fat level is greater than or equal to 1.5 grams per serving, then it is red; else if its saturated fat level is less than or equal to 1 gram per serving, then it is green; otherwise, it is yellow." Just from this English statement, we know that we need to use the IF function.

The syntax of the IF function is

```
IF(logical-test, [value-if-true], [value-if-false])
```

The beauty of IF function is that it can be nested, that is, one or more IF functions can be inside another IF function. We might be confused at this moment. Let's think about the following scenario.

In an Excel worksheet, if the value in cell A1 is greater than or equal to 15, then "Red" is displayed in cell B1. However, if the value in cell A1 is less than or equal to 10, B1 displays "Green"; otherwise, B1 displays "Yellow."

Open a blank Excel worksheet, and then follow the given instructions:

1. In cell A1, enter 10.

2. In cell B1, enter the formula =IF(A1>=15, "Red", IF(A1<=10, "Green", "Yellow")).

The previous formula states that (1) when the logical test A1 >= 15 is true, that is, when A1 is indeed greater than or equal to 15, the value of B1 is "Red"; (2) when A1 >= 15 is false, the inner IF function IF(A1<=10, "Green", "Yellow") is executed.

In the inner IF function, the logical test is A1 <= 10. If this assertion is true, B1 has value "Green"; otherwise, "Yellow."

By now, we can change the value in cell A1, and then B1 will display a different color name accordingly. Let's select both cells A1 and B1 and autofill them together to row 7; we can then notice the changes of the values in cells B1:B7. This is shown in Figure 2-4. Take A2 as an example; since A2=11, both A2>=15 and A2<=10 fail; therefore, Yellow is displayed in B2.

	A	B
1	10	Green
2	11	Yellow
3	12	Yellow
4	13	Yellow
5	14	Yellow
6	15	Red
7	16	Red

Figure 2-4. *The nested IF function*

ISBLANK

In the previous example, if we clear the integers inside cells A1:A7, that is, A1:A7 all become blank, we will notice that cells B1:B7 all display the same text "Green." This is because when a cell is blank, it is treated as 0. It is desirable that when A1 is blank, correspondingly, B1 displays nothing, that is, B1 should be blank, too. To achieve this aim, we need to use the ISBLANK function and nest our IF function deeper.

Function ISBLANK has the following syntax:

ISBLANK(VALUE)

The value can be numerical or non-numerical, can be a cell reference, and can be an expression. If the value is blank, the function returns true; otherwise, it returns false.

Back to our cells A1 and B1. The logic can be explained as the following: if A1 is blank, then B1 displays nothing; otherwise, B1 displays a color name according to the value in A1.

Based on this logic, please revise the formula in B1 to be

```
=IF(ISBLANK(A1), "", IF(A1>=15, "Red", IF(A1<=10, "Green", "Yellow")))
```

Autofill from B1 to B7, what will we see? Now, if we enter some integers in cells A1:A7, we can notice the corresponding changes in cells B1:B7.

Be aware that an empty string is not treated as blank by the function ISBLANK. The formula `=ISBLANK("")` returns false. However, the function COUNTBLANK treats an empty string as blank. Ideally, the two functions ISBLANK and COUNTBLANK should treat an empty string the same. The function COUNTBLANK is not used in this book and, therefore, is not explained in this book.

AND, OR

The syntax of function AND is

```
AND(logical1, [logical2], ...)
```

From the syntax, we can tell that the AND function must have at least one logical test, but it can have two or more logical tests, too. The AND function returns true only when all logical tests are true; otherwise, it returns false.

Similarly, the syntax of the OR function is

```
OR(logical1, [logical2], ...)
```

Function OR always returns true as long as at least one logical test is true. It returns false only when all logical tests are false.

Let's conduct an experiment:

1. In cells A1, A2, A3, and A4, enter "Data," 10, 20, and 30, respectively.

2. In cell B1, enter the text "AND" (without the quotation marks).

3. In cell B2, enter the formula =AND(A2>=10, A3>=10, A4>=10). All logical tests are true. What will be displayed in cell B2? We should ask ourselves the same question for the following formulas, too.

4. In cell B3, enter the formula =AND(A2>=20, A3>=20, A4>=20). One logical test is false.

5. In cell B4, enter the formula =AND(A2>30, A3>30, A4>30). Note that the logical operator is ">" instead of ">=". All logical tests are false.

6. In cell C1, enter the text "OR" (without the quotation marks).

7. In cell C2, enter the formula =OR(A2>=10, A3>=10, A4>=10). All logical tests are true.

8. In cell C3, enter the formula =OR(A2>=20, A3>=20, A4>=20). Two logical tests are true.

9. In cell C4, enter the formula =OR(A2>30, A3>30, A4>30). All logical tests are false.

Our worksheet should look like Figure 2-5.

	A	B	C	D
1	Data	AND	OR	
2	10	TRUE	TRUE	
3	20	FALSE	TRUE	
4	30	FALSE	FALSE	

Figure 2-5. *Functions AND plus OR*

Hope this experiment can earn us a clear understanding of these two functions.

VLOOKUP

Excel has several functions with searching or matching ability including INDEX, MATCH, LOOKUP, VLOOKUP, HLOOKUP, SEARCH, and FIND. We have learned and used LOOKUP in the last chapter. In this chapter, we are going to learn and use VLOOKUP which is used more commonly than LOOKUP. However, I personally prefer using LOOKUP because it provides more flexibility.

The syntax of VLOOKUP is VLOOKUP(lookup-value, table-array, col-index-number, [range-lookup]).

The syntax can get us lost. Fortunately, Excel has excellent help-pages available for all its functions. Such help-pages used to be available locally on our computer, but now, they are stored online. The reason why I am talking about Excel help-pages is because I have attained much knowledge from them and I would encourage everyone to make use of them.

There are several ways to access Excel help-pages, and these ways might look different on different Excel versions. Here, I will show three ways to access the help-page of the VLOOKUP function.

Way 1. Open a blank worksheet. In cell A2 (we can do so in any cell), type "=VLOOKUP(", and pause there (without the quotation marks). A hint to VLOOKUP shows up as illustrated in Figure 2-6. Double-click on the link as shown in Figure 2-6, and a help-page will show up as illustrated in Figure 2-7. Be aware that I am using Excel 2016 to illustrate this process, but I have tried this approach successfully on Excel 2019 and Office 365.

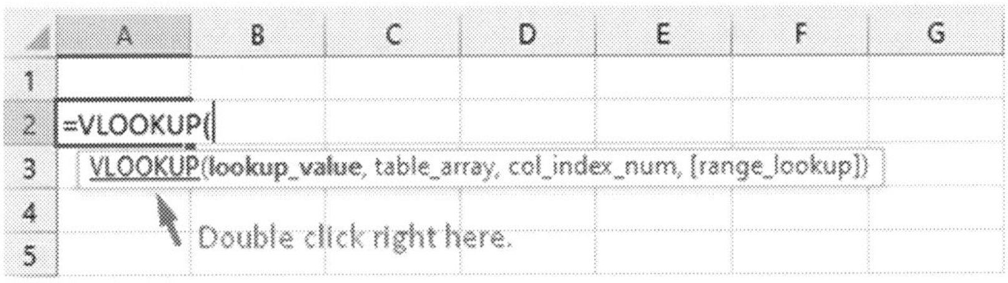

Figure 2-6. *A hint to the VLOOKUP function shows up*

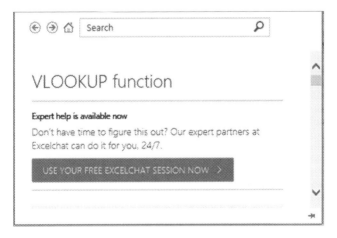

Figure 2-7. *Excel help page for VLOOKUP function*

The help-page available has several practical examples for the use of VLOOKUP together with a video. I am not going to show those examples or the video here since I will use another example to demonstrate the use of VLOOKUP later.

Way 2 is classic. Click the Home tab in our worksheet. On the right side of the top menu, click the small arrow right to the function symbol AutoSum ➤ on the upcoming small menu, select More Functions. This procedure is explained in Figure 2-8.

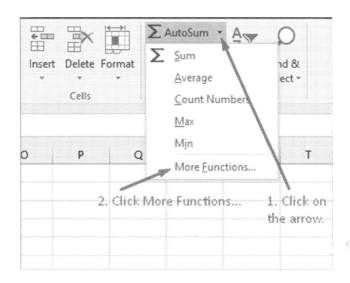

Figure 2-8. *Access More Functions*

The Insert Function window shows up which looks like Figure 2-9. Follow the instructions in Figure 2-9 to access the help-page.

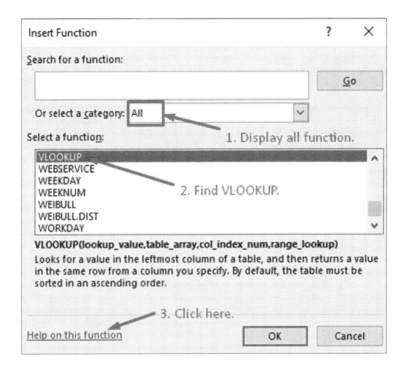

Figure 2-9. *The classic way to access Excel Help*

Way 3 is not available in early versions of Excel. However, this should not be a problem as most people are using Excel 2016 or later. Inside our worksheet, click the Formulas tab ➤ follow the instructions in Figure 2-10.

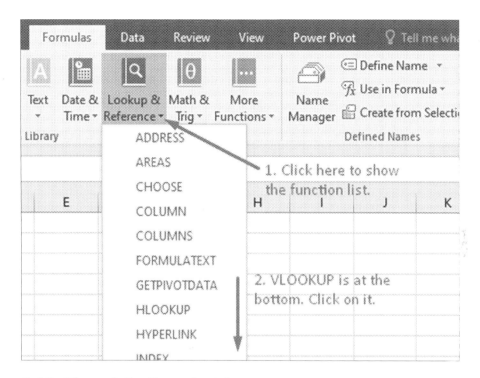

Figure 2-10. *Through the Formulas tab*

After clicking the VLOOKUP function as instructed in Figure 2-10, the Function Arguments window shows up. On this window, click the link "Help on this function" as explained in Figure 2-11 to display the help-page for VLOOKUP.

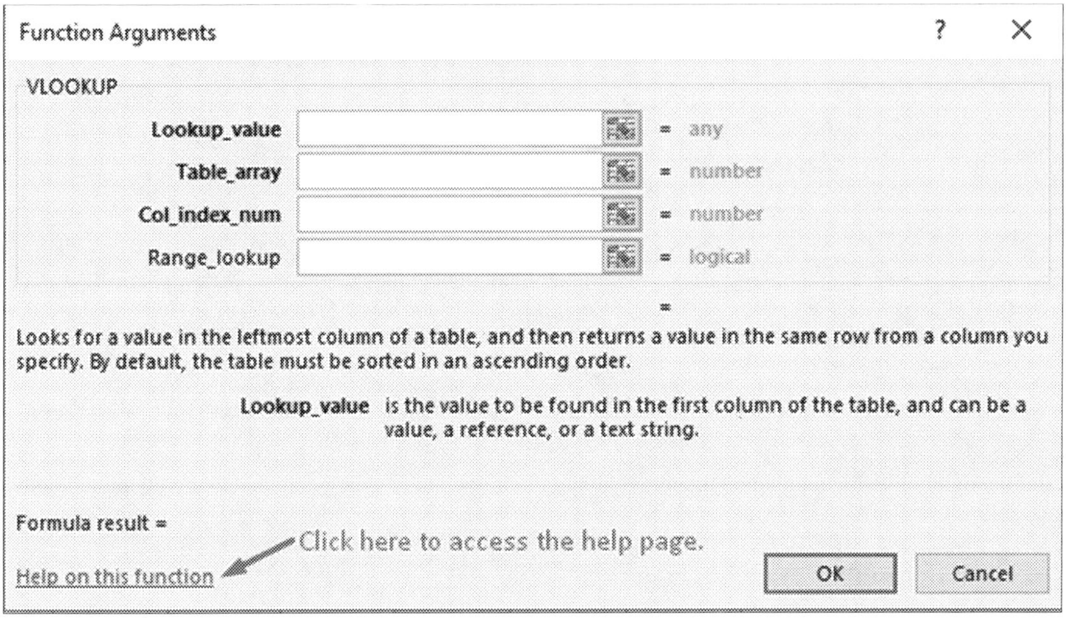

Function Arguments		? ☓
VLOOKUP		
Lookup_value		= any
Table_array		= number
Col_index_num		= number
Range_lookup		= logical

Looks for a value in the leftmost column of a table, and then returns a value in the same row from a column you specify. By default, the table must be sorted in an ascending order.

Lookup_value   is the value to be found in the first column of the table, and can be a value, a reference, or a text string.

Formula result =

Help on this function

Click here to access the help page.

OK   Cancel

Figure 2-11. *Access the help-page through Function Arguments*

Now, it's time to learn the use of VLOOKUP through our own example. Open an Excel worksheet, and enter values as shown in Figure 2-12. The first row is just the heading; the real data is stored in table A2:D5.

	A	B	C	D
1	category	fat	sodium	sugar
2	Plant	1	32	12
3	Grains	2	230	6
4	Fruit	2	200	5
5	Vegetables	1	140	4

Figure 2-12. *Sample data to learn VLOOKUP*

Look at Figure 2-12. The first column (column A) contains the lookup-values, while B2:D5 contains the targeted values. That means if we want to find the sodium standard for Plant, "Plant" is the lookup-value, and 32 is the wanted target. Note that the lookup-values must be in the first column for the VLOOKUP function.

Recall that the syntax of VLOOKUP is

`VLOOKUP(lookup-value, table-array, col-index-number, [range-lookup]).`

Table A2:D5 has four columns. The first column is column A, while the second, third, and fourth columns are B, C, and D. If we want to find the sodium value for Plant, the result is in the third column. Thus, we can write our formula as =`VLOOKUP("plant", A2:D5, 3)`, where lookup-value is "plant," table-array is A2:D5, and col-index-number is 3.

Unfortunately, the answer we get is not 32 but 200. We do not obtain the correct answer. What happened?

The texts on both Figure 2-9 and Figure 2-11 state that "By default, the table must be sorted in an ascending order." What does this mean?

This means that the lookup-values in the first column should better be sorted in ascending order from top-down by default. Why? Because by default, the optional argument range-lookup is TRUE for VLOOKUP. When range-lookup is TRUE, VLOOKUP's internal search is "Approximate" instead of "Exact match." Approximate search requires that the lookup-values be sorted in ascending order. If the lookup-values are not sorted, which is our case, we must specify the range-lookup to be false.

So, we need to revise our formula to be =`VLOOKUP("plant", A2:D5, 3, `**`false`**`)`.

Test Yourself: if we want to find the sugar value for Fruit, what should be the correct formula?[1]

Work on the Project

When we open chapter-2-1a.xlsx, we will notice that the data shown in Figure 2-1 is already reorganized in table H1:Q14 as demonstrated in Figure 2-13. The ranking standards are grouped into Green, Yellow, and Red as specified in the table for each food category.

In the last chapter, we experienced a little bit of table setup in Excel. Yes, how to set up our data in Excel worksheets is another important skill. The table setup in this project is for the use of the VLOOKUP function; thus, the category names are in the first column in H1:Q14. In addition, in the worksheet, the ranking standards are placed on the right

---

[1] The formula can be either =VLOOKUP("Fruit", A2:D5, 4, false) or =VLOOKUP(A4, A2:D5, 4, false).

side, and the user-interactive portion is on the left side. It is better to place the ranking standards on the right because if later, we want to hide the standards from users, our worksheet won't leave the first several columns blank.

As mentioned before, for an item to be Green, its saturated fat, sodium, and sugar levels are always less than or equal to the Green ranking standards, and for an item to be ranked Red, its saturated fat, sodium, and sugar levels must all be greater than or equal to the Red ranking standards. If an item is neither Green nor Red, it must be Yellow. Therefore, we will only make use of the Green and Red ranking standards, but leave those of Yellow as records only in the table. As shown in Figure 2-13, we intentionally leave four rows unoccupied in table H1:Q14 so that users can easily add four more categories. Note that if a new category must be created, this new category needs to be inserted inside table H3:Q14.

Food name	Category	Saturated Fat(g)	Sodium(mg)	Sugar(g)	Color Ranking		Category	Green			Yellow			Red		
								Fat(g)	Sodium(mg)	Sugar(g)	Fat(g)	Sodium(mg)	Sugar(g)	Fat(g)	Sodium(mg)	Sugar(g)
							Fruit	1	32	12	<=1	33-50	13-25	1.5	51	26
							Grains	2	230	6	2g	231-400	7 to 12	2.5	401	13
							Protein: plant	2	200	5	2.5 - 5	201-480	6 to 9	5.5	481	10
							vegetables	1	140	4	<=1	141-230	5 to 7	1.5	231	8
							Protein: Animal	2	200	0	2.5-5g	201-480mg	1g	5.5	481	2
							Dairy	1.5	180	12	2.0-3g	181-200mg	13-22g	3.5	201	23
							Beverages	0	0	0	0g	1-160mg	1-11g	0	161	12
							Snacks/Desserts	2	230	6	<=2g	231-400mg	7-12g	2.5	401	13

Figure 2-13. *Ranking standards are reorganized and placed on the right*

The user-interactive portion, table A2:E51, is left for entering food items and their relevant data. Once the required data for a food item has been entered, we want the ranking result to show up automatically in column F.

Name Manager and Data Validation

Since we are going to reference table H1:Q14 frequently, it is a good idea to name this table. Be aware that we only need to reference H3:Q14 (the first two rows are headings only); therefore, we are going to name H3:Q14 only.

In our worksheet, select cells H3:Q14, then click the Formulas tab on the top menu ➤ then click Name Manager ➤ the Name Manager window shows up. This procedure is demonstrated in Figure 2-14. Follow the instructions in Figure 2-14 to click "New."

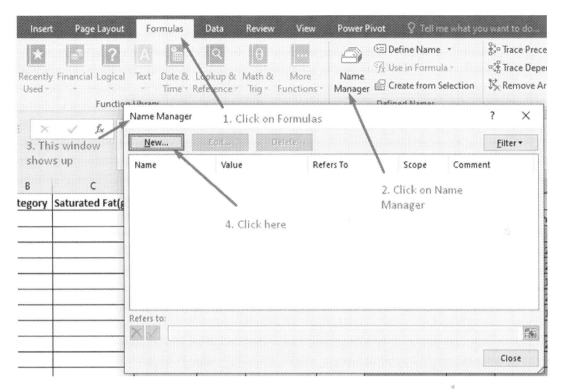

Figure 2-14. *Access Name Manger*

We will get a small window looking exactly like Figure 2-15. For simplicity, let's give table H3:Q14 the name T as shown in Figure 2-15. Be advised that it is a good practice to use a more meaningful name such as "NutritionData" for the table. Notice that the Scope is Workbook and the "Refers to" has the formula =Sheet1!$H$3:$Q$14. Click OK to close the window.

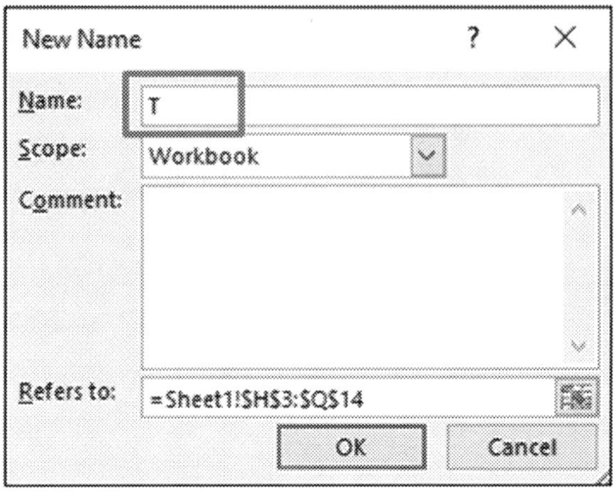

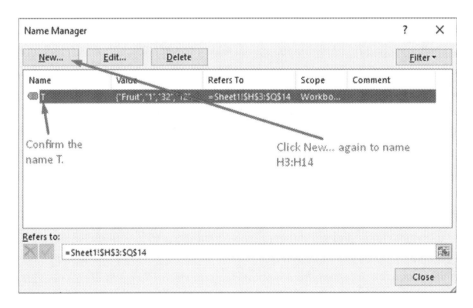

Figure 2-15. *Name the table T*

The Name Manager window comes back with the name T highlighted as shown in Figure 2-16. Do not close the Name Manager window; instead, click New again to name the array H3:H14.

Figure 2-16. *Confirmation of table T*

We are going to reference H3:H14 frequently, too. So, let's give H3:H14 the name L as shown in Figure 2-17. Make sure that the name is L and the "Refers to" has the formula =Sheet1!$H$3:$H$14 as illustrated in Figure 2-17.

Once we click OK, as shown in Figure 2-17, the Name Manager window comes back again. Please close it.

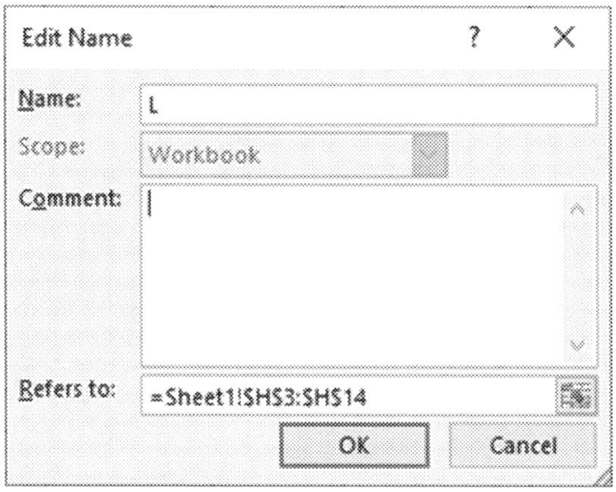

Figure 2-17. *Name the array H3:H14*

From now on, we can use T to represent table H3:Q14 and L to represent the array H3:H14. Be advised that if later the list of food categories must go beyond table H3:Q14, then both T and L must be updated accordingly.

An important feature we want is when a food item is entered in cell A2; its destination category in cell B2 must be selected from the available categories stored in H3:H14 (named L). This can be achieved by making use of another Excel built-in feature called Data Validation which can give us a drop-down list.

On our worksheet, click inside the cell B2, and then click the Data tab on the top menu ➤ click Data Validation as shown in Figure 2-18. Follow the instructions in Figure 2-18 to select Data Validation.

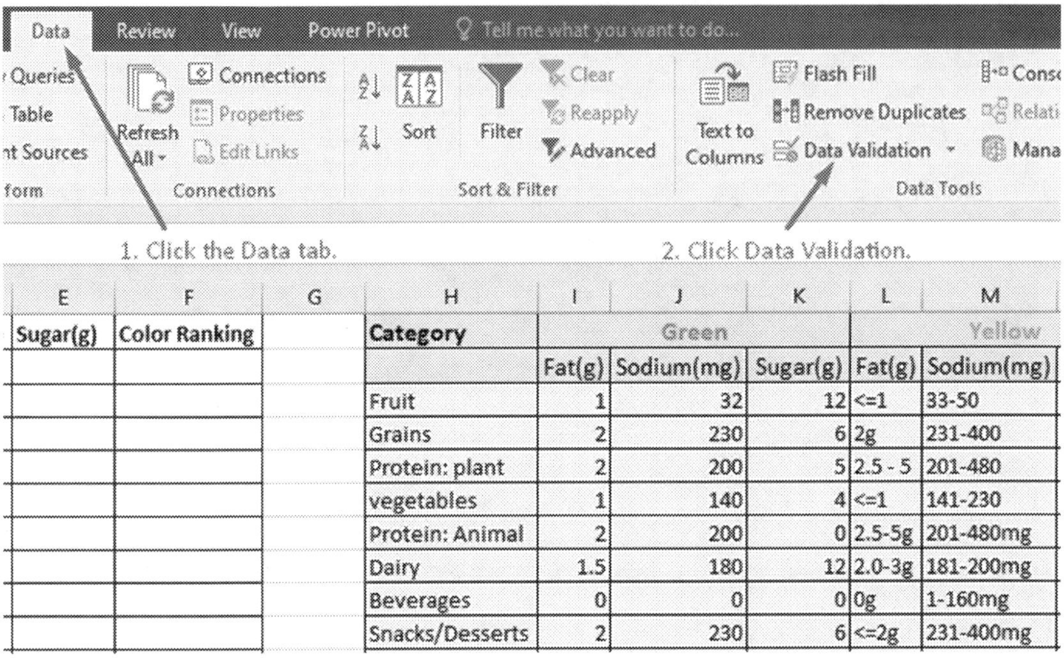

Figure 2-18. *Access Data Validation*

A small window named Data Validation shows up. On this window, in the drop-down list under the label Allow, select List as instructed in Figure 2-19. Follow the instructions in Figure 2-19 to finish the setup of data validation.

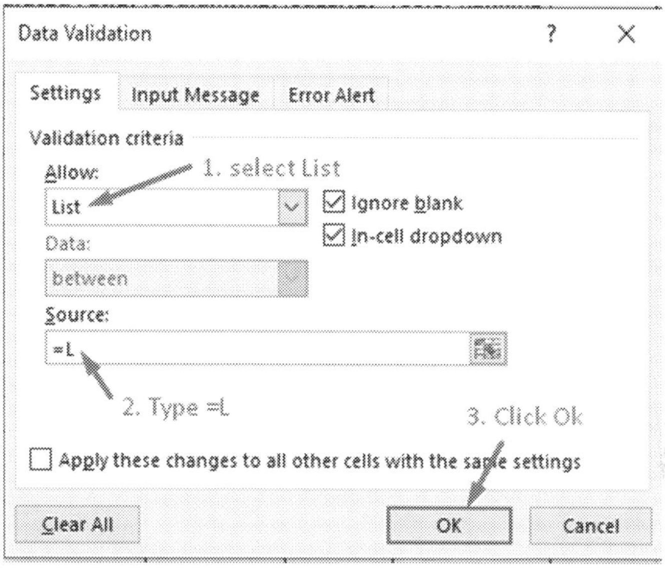

Figure 2-19. *Set up data validation*

Be sure to type "=L" immediately under the label Source. Missing the = operator will disable our data validation feature. If we happen to enter "L" instead of "=L", we need to select cell B2 and correct it in the Data Validation window.

After the data validation setup, when we click inside cell B2, a drop-down list shows up to let us select a category as shown in Figure 2-20. Do not make any selection!

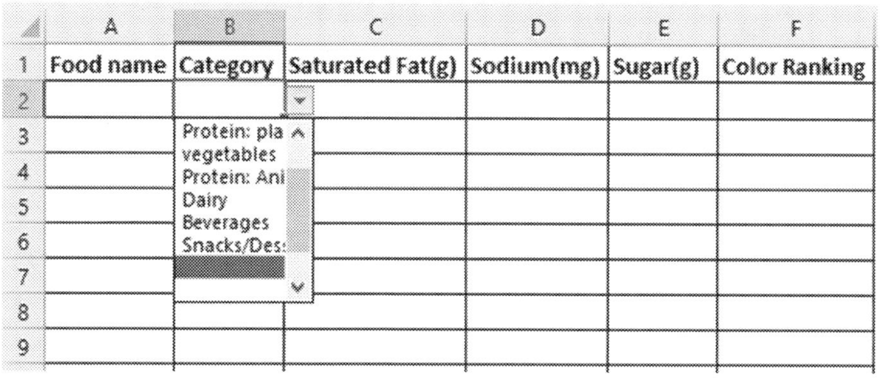

Figure 2-20. *The drop-down list in cell B2*

We would like this drop-down list feature to be true for all cells B2:B51. Therefore, autofill from B2 to B51. Remember to complete the autofill first before selecting anything from the drop-down list.

After the autofill, clicking any cell inside B2:B51 will make the drop-down list appear.

Instructions to Complete the Project

Follow the following instructions to finish up this project:

1. Enter "Toto apple" in cell A2.

2. Select Fruit in cell B2.

3. Enter 0, 1, and 10 inside cells C2, D2, and E2, respectively.

4. Inside cell F2, enter the following formula:

    ```
    =IF(OR(ISBLANK(B2), ISBLANK(C2), ISBLANK(D2),
    ISBLANK(E2)), "", IF(AND(C2 >= VLOOKUP(B2, T, 8, FALSE),
    D2 >= VLOOKUP(B2, T, 9, FALSE), E2 >= VLOOKUP(B2, T, 10,
    FALSE)), "Red", IF(AND(C2 <= VLOOKUP(B2, T, 2, FALSE),
    D2 <= VLOOKUP(B2, T, 3, FALSE), E2 <= VLOOKUP(B2, T, 4,
    FALSE)), "Green", "Yellow")))
    ```

    This formula may look scary at first. Let's break it down.

    1. *ISBLANK(B2)*: Tests if cell B2 is empty. The same test applies to cells C2, D2, and E2.

    2. *OR(ISBLANK(B2), ISBLANK(C2), ISBLANK(D2), ISBLANK(E2))*: If any cell between B2:E2 is empty, then the data entry for this food item is not complete. This requires nothing to show up in cell F2.

    3. *VLOOKUP(B2, T, 8, FALSE)*: Uses B2 as the lookup-value (in this case, Fruit) to find the corresponding value (in this case 1.5) in column O which is the 8th column in our table T.

    4. *VLOOKUP(B2, T, 9, FALSE) and VLOOKUP(B2, T, 10, FALSE)*: Find the corresponding values in column P and column Q, respectively (51 and 26).

    5. *C2 >= VLOOKUP(B2, T, 8, FALSE)*: Tests if C2 is >= 1.5 (in this case, false).

6. *AND(C2 >= VLOOKUP(B2, T, 8, FALSE), D2 >= VLOOKUP (B2, T, 9, FALSE), E2 >= VLOOKUP(B2, T, 10, FALSE))*: Returns TRUE if C2, D2, and E2 all meet the standards for being Red (above or equal to). Note, the ranking standards for being Red are stored in columns O, P, and Q which are columns 8, 9, and 10 in table T.

7. *IF(AND(C2 >= VLOOKUP(B2, T, 8, FALSE), D2 >= VLOOKUP (B2, T, 9, FALSE), E2 >= VLOOKUP(B2, T, 10, FALSE)), "Red"*: This IF expression asserts if cell F2 should display Red. If true, "Red" is displayed. If false (in this case), it goes to the next inner IF expression.

8. *VLOOKUP(B2, T, 2, FALSE)*: Uses B2 as the lookup-value to find the corresponding value in column I (in this case, 1).

9. *VLOOKUP(B2, T, 3, FALSE), VLOOKUP(B2, T, 4, FALSE)*: Find the corresponding values in columns J and K (in this case, 32 and 12).

10. *AND(C2 <= VLOOKUP(B2, T, 2, FALSE), D2 <= VLOOKUP (B2, T, 3, FALSE), E2 <= VLOOKUP(B2, T, 4, FALSE))*: Tests if C2, D2, and E2 all meet the ranking standards for being Green (below or equal to). Note that the ranking standards for being Green are stored in columns I, J, and K which are columns 2, 3, and 4 in table T.

11. *IF(AND(C2 <= VLOOKUP(B2, T, 2, FALSE), D2 <= VLOOKUP (B2, T, 3, FALSE), E2 <= VLOOKUP(B2, T, 4, FALSE)), "Green", "Yellow")*: This inner IF expression asserts if C2, D2, and E2 all meet the Green ranking standards. If true, "Green" will be displayed in cell F2; otherwise, "Yellow" will be.

12. After the preceding formula is entered, "Green" should show up inside cell F2.

5. Autofill from cell F2 to F51. Note that though cells F3:F51 have a formula inside, nothing is displayed in them at this moment.

6. Follow Figure 2-21 to enter two more food items.

⏴	A	B	C	D	E	F
1	Food name	Category	Saturated Fat(g)	Sodium(mg)	Sugar(g)	Color Ranking
2	Toto apple	Fruit	0	1	10	Green
3	cola A	Beverages	0	200	30	Red
4	USA cookie	Snacks/De	1	250	25	Yellow
5						
6						

Figure 2-21. *Enter more food items*

7. The next step is to apply conditional formatting to column F
    such that words are colored based on their meanings. Select cells
    F2:F51, then click the Home tab ➤ click Conditional Formatting
    ➤ click Highlight Cell Rules ➤ select Equal To ... as shown in
    Figure 2-22.

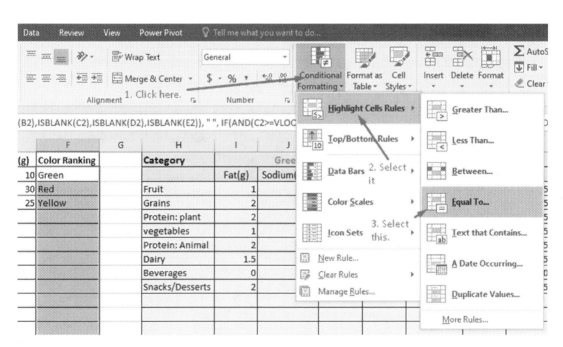

Figure 2-22. *Start conditional formatting and select Equal To*

8. Once we have clicked Equal To... as shown in Figure 2-22, the Equal To window shows up. Type Green in the box, and select Custom Format as shown in Figure 2-23.

    At this point, we can choose an easy route by selecting Green Fill with Dark Green Text, which will also highlight our cells in addition to coloring the text. Since in Figure 2-3, only words are colored, let's walk the harder road by selecting Custom Format.

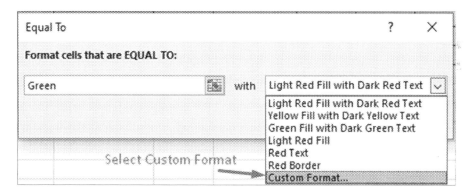

Figure 2-23. *Select Custom Format*

9. Once we have selected Custom Format, the Format Cells window appears. On this window, select a green color as shown in Figure 2-24, and then click OK.

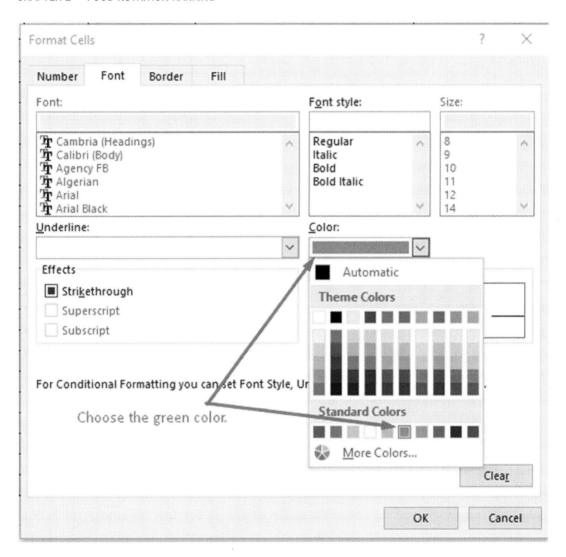

Figure 2-24. *Select a green color*

10. The Equal To window shows up again as exhibited in Figure 2-25. Click OK.

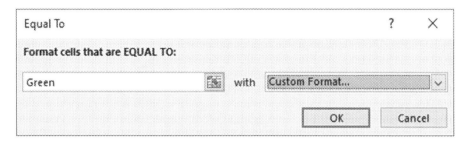

Figure 2-25. *Apply conditional format on Green*

11. Repeat steps 7–10 for Red and Yellow.

12. By now, part of our worksheet should have been completed, and
     our result should look like Figure 2-3.

     However, we should not allow users to modify the formulas inside
     cells F2:F51. Thus, it would be a good idea to make cells F2:F51
     password protected (such a procedure is explained in the last
     chapter).

13. Like mentioned before, we may want to hide table H1:Q14. In fact,
     we may also want to protect table H1:Q14. Let's just hide table
     H1:Q14 from the regular view. There are two ways to achieve so.

     One way is to change the text colors in table H1:Q14. We can select
     H1:Q14 ➤ click the Home tab ➤ Change the Font Color to be the
     same as the background color. Unfortunately, this approach does
     not work well since H1:Q14 has two different background colors.

     A better approach is to make use of the formatting style named
     Number, that is, we are going to treat the content in H1:Q14 as
     numbers. Note that by default, their format style is General.

     Select table H1:Q14 ➤ click the Home tab ➤ click the arrow in the
     Number group as shown in Figure 2-26.

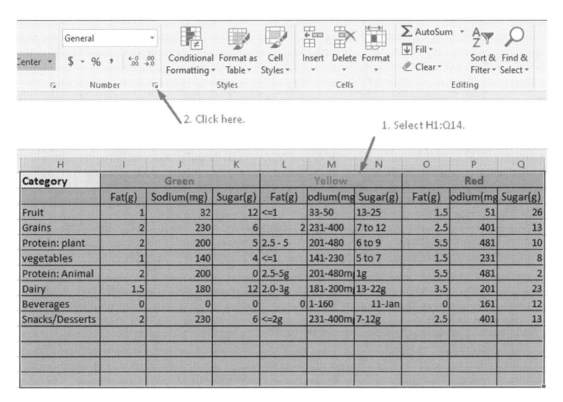

Figure 2-26. *Treat the content as numbers to hide them*

The Format Cells window comes up. On this window, select
Number ➤ click Custom ➤ under the label Type, enter exactly
three semicolons ";;;" (without quotation marks) ➤ click OK.
This is explained in Figure 2-27.

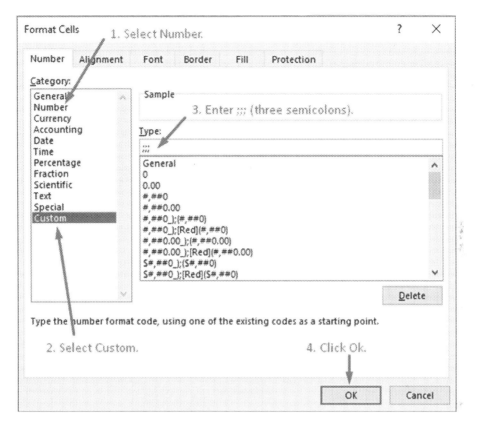

Figure 2-27. *Type ;;; to hide the content*

By now, our worksheet should look like Figure 2-28. Note that to avoid table H1:Q14 to be accidently modified, after hiding the content, it is always a good idea to protect the table by password.

	A	B	C	D	E	F	G	H	I	J	K	L	M	N	O	P	Q
1	Food name	Category	Saturated Fat(g)	Sodium(mg)	Sugar(g)	Color Ranking											
2	Toto apple	Fruit	0	1	10	Green											
3	cola A	Beverages	0	200	30	Red											
4	USA cookie	Snacks/Desserts	1	250	25	Yellow											
5																	
6																	
7																	
8																	
9																	
10																	
11																	
12																	
13																	
14																	
15																	

Figure 2-28. *The content inside table H1:Q14 is hidden*

The final result is available in chapter-2-1b.xlsx. Be aware that in chapter-2-1b.xlsx, neither the column F is protected nor is table H1:Q14 hidden. However, chapter-2-1c. xlsx is password protected, and its table T is hidden.

In chapter-2-1c.xlsx, the conditional formatting of column F is cell highlighting instead of text coloring. One reminder is that chapter-2-1c.xlsx can be delivered as a protected product to users who do not have the privilege to revise the category standards or the formulas in column F. The password for chapter-2-1c.xlsx is "Excel" (without the quotation marks).

My personal experience is when I want to make a worksheet as a deliverable product, I do a better job because I then want to automate the worksheet as much as possible. So, our goal is always to make the worksheet as automated as possible.

Chapter Tip

The tip of this chapter is to use Excel to find the weekday for any given dates since January 1, 1900 (expressed as month/day/year according to the US tradition). For instance, do you know the weekday of your birthday? Assume it is 5/20/2000; what is the weekday?

Open a blank worksheet, and enter 5/20/2000 in cell K1. Excel automatically detects that the content is of Date type. Click the small arrow as instructed in Figure 2-29.

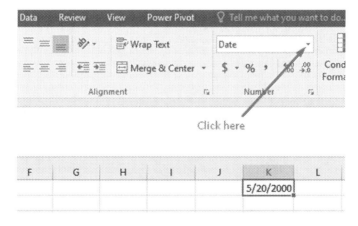

Figure 2-29. *Type Date detected*

The Format Cells window comes out. On this window, select the Long Date Format as shown in Figure 2-30. We will see that 5/20/2000 is Saturday.

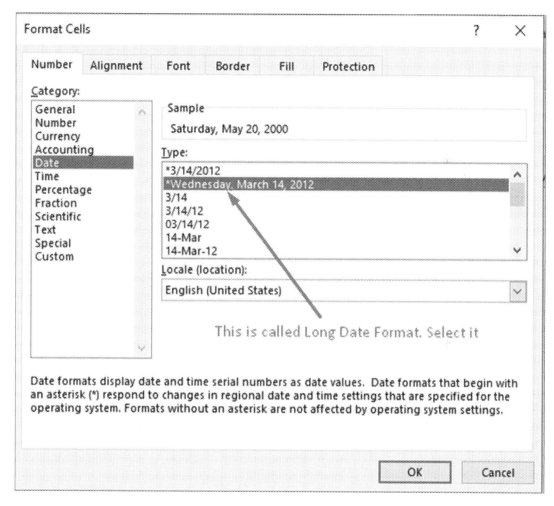

Figure 2-30. *Select the long date format*

Test Yourself: what is the weekday of 5/20/3000?[2]

---

[2] Tuesday.

Review Points

We have reached the end of Chapter 2. For this chapter, please review the following concepts and Excel skills:

1. Functions IF, ISBLANK, AND, OR, and VLOOKUP.

2. Access Excel help-pages for functions.

3. Name Manager.

4. Table setup for VLOOKUP function.

5. Data validation.

6. Conditional formatting.

7. Hide cell content.

CHAPTER 3

Payroll Calculation

Please download the sample Excel files from `https://github.com/hhohho/master-Excel-through-projects` for this chapter's exercises.

There are outstanding software systems and tools that can automate the payroll calculation process; Excel remains an essential tool for small business owners, however. Education-wise, Excel is not replaceable for accounting.

Payroll calculation is fairly complicated due to the fact that tax laws are evolving almost every year. Taking the United States as an example, there are federal tax laws that never stop being updated year after year, and each state has its own tax policies. For this reason, this chapter presents two projects so that we can experience more of payroll calculation. The first project explains 2021 US federal income tax withholding. The second project follows the first project but incorporates Connecticut state income tax withholding. In addition, the second project makes future calculation fully automatic.

Again, our goal is to automate the calculation as much as possible in Excel worksheets. In addition, as we will soon realize, table setup and name management become critical in this chapter.

Functions to Learn

Before we proceed to the payroll projects, we need to be familiar with several new Excel functions, including ROUND, SUBSTITUTE, INDEX, MATCH, and INDIRECT.

ROUND

In accounting, we need two decimal digits after the decimal point. The whole integers represent dollars, and the two decimal digits after the decimal point stand for pennies. For this purpose, we need to learn and use the ROUND function.

© Hong Zhou 2022
H. Zhou, *Mastering Excel Through Projects*, https://doi.org/10.1007/978-1-4842-7842-0_3

ROUND is a very simple function. As the name suggests, this function rounds a decimal number. It takes in two arguments: the first one is the number to round, and the second one specifies how many digits to keep after the decimal point.

For example, assume we want to round the number 3.1415926 stored in cell A1 such that only two digits after the decimal point are kept. We need to type in cell B1 the formula =ROUND(A1, 2).

To make a decimal number have only two digits after the decimal point, we can also make use of the Excel number formatting feature as presented in Figure 3-1. Be aware that this formatting, either Increase Decimal or Decrease Decimal, does not truly change the number's decimal digits; it just makes the number look like what we want. The ROUND function does change the number, however. For this reason, it is better to use the ROUND function in this chapter's projects.

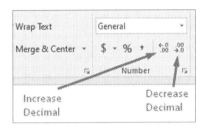

Figure 3-1. *Increase or decrease decimal*

SUBSTITUTE

The function SUBSTITUTE has the default syntax SUBSTITUTE(text, old-text, new-text). It can replace old-text with new-text within the first text argument. For instance, given a text string such as "Married Filing Jointly," we can make use of the function SUBSTITUTE to change it to be Married_Filing_Jointly or MarriedFilingJointly.

Assume cell A1 has the text "Married Filing Jointly"; to obtain Married_Filing_Jointly in cell B1, enter the formula =SUBSTITUTE(A1, " ", "_") in B1.

To obtain MarriedFilingJointly in cell C1, enter the formula =SUBSTITUTE(A1, " ", "") in C1.

INDEX

INDEX and MATCH are two powerful and popularly used functions. To become an experienced user of Excel, we must be skilled in both functions.

The syntax of INDEX is INDEX(`array, row-number, [column-number]`). Here, the array could be one- or two-dimensional. In a typical two-dimensional array, the use of the two parameters, row-number and column-number, can pinpoint a specific cell. Let's do the following experiment:

1. Open a blank Excel worksheet, and enter some data into cells A1:D5 as shown in Figure 3-2.

	A	B	C	D
1	Name	WorkingHours	HourRate	Wage
2	John	50	$22	$1,100
3	Mary	30	$25	$750
4	Rose	40	$30	$1,200
5	Ted	20	$20	$400

Figure 3-2. Sample data for function Index

2. Assume that we want to get the wage for Mary which is located at the third row and fourth column; we need to type in a target cell (e.g., cell E3) this formula =INDEX(A1:D5, 3, 4).

3. When the second parameter row-number = 0, INDEX fetches a column based on the third parameter column-number. For example, assume we want to pick the entire HourRate column, our formula should then be =INDEX(A1:D5, 0, 3). However, since no single cell can host a column, we cannot display this fetched column unless we make use of Excel's array formula.

   Select cells E1:E5. Type the formula =INDEX(A1:D5, 0, 3) in the formula bar, and then press the three keys CTRL + SHIFT + ENTER (by pressing down CTRL + SHIFT, and then press ENTER). The HourRate column is displayed in column E now. This is illustrated in both Figure 3-3 and Figure 3-4.

Figure 3-4 shows that after pressing CTRL + SHIFT + ENTER, the original formula =INDEX(A1:D5, 0, 3) is enclosed by { }, which reveals that the formula is now an array formula.

Note to never try to revise the formula(s) or change the content in the array generated by an array formula.

| INDIRECT | ▾ | ⋮ | × | ✓ | *fx* | =index(A1:D5, 0, 3) |

Press CTRL + SHIFT then hit ENTER

▲	A	B	C	D	E
1	Name	WorkingHours	HourRate	Wage	, 0, 3)
2	John	50	$22	$1,100	
3	Mary	30	$25	$750	
4	Rose	40	$30	$1,200	
5	Ted	20	$20	$400	

Figure 3-3. *Fetching a column by function Index*

| E5 | ▾ | ⋮ | × | ✓ | *fx* | {=INDEX(A1:D5, 0, 3)} |

The { } marks that this is an array formula. Do not type { } to create an array formula.

▲	A	B	C	D	E
1	Name	WorkingHours	HourRate	Wage	HourRate
2	John	50	$22	$1,100	22
3	Mary	30	$25	$750	25
4	Rose	40	$30	$1,200	30
5	Ted	20	$20	$400	20

Figure 3-4. *Array formula*

4. In a similar way, we can fetch a row. For example, if we want to get the fourth row, the row for Rose, we can use the formula =INDEX(A1:D5,4,0). The trick is when column-number = 0, INDEX fetches a row defined by the row-number argument.

5. INDEX function can be used to fetch a specific cell from a one-dimensional array, too. For instance, assume we want the working hours of Rose; we can apply this formula =INDEX(A4:D4,2). Here, A4:D4 is a one-dimensional array, and, therefore, the formula does not have the column-number argument.

MATCH

MATCH function has the syntax: MATCH(lookup-value, lookup-array, [match-type]). The default match-type is 1, that is, when there is no match-type explicitly given, Excel assumes match-type = 1.

The match-type argument is critical in the use of MATCH. When match-type = 1, the lookup-array must be sorted in ascending order, and MATCH returns the position of the found element in the lookup-array such that the element is immediately less than or equal to the lookup-value, that is, the position of the lower boundary of the bracket into which the lookup-value falls.

Now, let's try three experiments.

Experiment 1

In this experiment, match-type = 1.

Open a blank worksheet, and enter some data exactly as shown in Figure 3-5. Observe that the data in A2:A6 are sorted in ascending order. If the data is not sorted in ascending order, our formula may or may not work correctly.

	A	B	C	D
1	lookup-array	lookup-value	match-type	MATCH
2	0	-1	1	
3	10	0	1	
4	15	12	1	
5	16	18	1	
6	22	30	1	

Figure 3-5. *The table setup to learn MATCH function*

In cell D2, enter the formula =MATCH(B2, A$2:A$6, C2), then autofill from D2 to D6. We shall get the results as shown in Figure 3-6.

	A	B	C	D
1	lookup-array	lookup-value	match-type	MATCH
2	0	-1	1	#N/A
3	10	0	1	1
4	15	12	1	2
5	16	18	1	4
6	22	30	1	5

Figure 3-6. *MATCH function experiment 1, match-type = 1*

The following is the explanation of the results in the array D2:D6 when match-type = 1:

- What we get in cell D2 is #N/A; this is because when lookup-value = -1, there is no value in the array A2:A6 that is less than or equal to -1; thus, the MATCH function fails.

- When lookup-value = 0, A2 <= 0 and A2 is the first element in the array A2:A6; thus, 1 is returned in cell D3.

- When lookup-value = 12, A3 is the element that is immediately less than 12, and A3 is the second element in the array A2:A6; thus, 2 is returned.

- When lookup-value = 18, A5 is the element immediately less than 18 and the fourth element in the array A2:A6; thus, 4 is returned.

- When lookup-value = 30 which is larger than every element in A2:A6, the position of the last element A6 is returned. Notice that A6 is the fifth element in A2:A6.

Experiment 2

In this experiment, change the match-type to be 0; revise both the lookup-array and lookup-values as shown Figure 3-7.

	A	B	C	D
1	lookup-array	lookup-value	match-type	MATCH
2	10	-1	0	#N/A
3	0	0	0	2
4	0	12	0	#N/A
5	16	16	0	4
6	22	30	0	#N/A

Figure 3-7. *MATCH function experiment 2, match-type = 0*

When match-type = 0, MATCH finds the first value that is exactly equal to the lookup-value, and the values in the lookup-array can be in any order (do not need to be sorted).

As long as MATCH cannot find an exact match for the given lookup-value, #N/A is returned.

Experiment 3

When match-type = -1, MATCH finds the position of the element in the lookup-array that is immediately greater than or equal to the lookup-value. However, the lookup-array must be sorted in descending order.

Revise our worksheet exactly as shown in Figure 3-8. When lookup-value = -1 (B2), the element in A2:A6 that is immediately greater than or equal to -1 is A6, which is the 5th element in A2:A6; therefore, 5 is returned in cell D2.

	A	B	C	D
1	lookup-array	lookup-value	match-type	MATCH
2	22	-1	-1	5
3	16	0	-1	5
4	15	12	-1	3
5	10	16	-1	2
6	0	30	-1	#N/A

Figure 3-8. *MATCH function experiment 3, match-type = -1*

When lookup-value = 30 (B6), however, since there is no value in A2:A6 that is greater than or equal to 30, #N/A is returned in cell D6.

INDIRECT

INDIRECT function is very interesting in that it returns the reference specified by a text string. Its syntax looks like `INDIRECT(ref_text, [a1])`, where the second argument is optional.

Excel has two cell reference styles. The default one is named A1-style, that is, columns are marked by letters, while rows are numbered. Another is named R1C1-style in which both rows and columns are numbered (the numbers are prefixed by letter R and C, respectively). For example, R3C4 references the cell at the third row and fourth column, equally D3 in A1-style. To activate R1C1 style, we need to click File ➤ Options ➤ Formulas ➤ right under "Working with formula," check the box for "R1C1 reference style." See Figure 1-4 and Figure 1-5. We are going to stick to the default A1 reference style in this book.

Continue with the worksheet in Experiment 3 of the MATCH function. Enter the text string "B5" (without the quotation marks) inside cell A7. Assume cell A7 stores the name of a cell whose value needs to be placed in cell B7. For instance, because currently cell A7 stores "B5," we then need to place the value of cell B5 in cell B7. If A7 stores "B6," then we want to obtain the value in cell B6.

Enter in cell B7 this formula `=INDIRECT(A7)`. The text string "B5" inside A7 is converted into cell reference B5 by INDIRECT, and the original formula `=INDIRECT(A7)` becomes `=B5`, that is, `INDIRECT(A7)`, which gives us cell reference B5 indeed. This results in the outlook of our worksheet being the same as Figure 3-9.

	A	B	C	D
1	lookup_array	lookup_value	match_type	MATCH
2	22	-1	-1	5
3	16	0	-1	5
4	15	12	-1	3
5	10	16	-1	2
6	0	30	-1	#N/A
7	B5	16		

Figure 3-9. *Learn the INDIRECT function*

Excel has another function named ADDRESS that is related to INDIRECT. Given specified row and column numbers, ADDRESS creates a cell reference as text. For example, =ADDRESS(3, 2) will generate the text $B$3 (third row and second column). =ADDRESS(A5, B5) will result in the text string $P$10 because in Figure 3-9, A5 = 10, and B5 = 16.

We will use the ADDRESS function later.

Work on Project 1

Payroll calculation is a complicated job because not only does it relate to federal income tax withholding but also, it depends on state income tax withholding. As different states can have different tax withholding brackets, this project focuses only on 2021 USA federal income tax withholding.

USA 2021 Federal IRS Income Tax Withholding Methods is published at www.irs. gov/forms-pubs/about-publication-15-t, called Publication 15-T. This project follows the instructions on Publication 15-T regarding Percentage Method Tables for Automated Payroll Systems because our goal is to make the maximum use of Excel's automation capability. Also, this project assumes the default, that is, employees are US residents and have completed Form W-4 of 2021 or something equivalent, except for step 2 in Form W-4.

The 2021 W-4 has five steps to complete. Step 1 requires a name, social security number, and address. In addition, step 1 requires employees to select federal income tax filing status which can be one of the three: Single or Married Filing Separately, Married Filing Jointly or Qualifying Widow(er), or Head of Household. Steps 2, 3, and 4 are used to claim dependents and adjustments. Step 5 is for signature. We will incorporate steps 3 and 4 from the W-4 into our worksheet, but ignore step 2 so as to simplify this project.

Federal Tax Withholding Explanation and Worksheet Setup

Federal income tax withholding depends on several factors including income, payroll period type (also called payment period type in this book), tax filing status, deduction, and additional withholding. Be aware that tax filing is for a fiscal year, not for a payroll period. Thus, in the standard approach explained in Publication 15-T, employees are assumed to make the same amount of money for each period such that an Adjusted

Annual Wage Amount can be calculated based on the given period. Withholding is then calculated based on this Adjusted Annual Wage Amount first and then transformed into period withholding. Table 3-1 presents the seven period types and their numbers of payments in a year defined by Publication 15-T.

Table 3-1. *Yearly number of payments for each payroll period type*

Semiannually	Quarterly	Monthly	Semimonthly	Biweekly	Weekly	Daily
2	4	12	24	26	52	260

Figure 3-10 presents a slice of 2021 Percentage Method Tables from Publication 15-T. Every method table has two versions; which version to apply depends on whether or not an employee has checked step 2 in Form W-4. To simplify our project, we are going to take the left-side versions, which are for standard withholding, that is, we are going to skip step 2 on Form W-4. Step 2 on Form W-4 is for taxpayers who claim more than one job, either because the spouse also has a job or the taxpayer has more than one job. It can be ignored if each job has its own tax withholding independently.

2021 Percentage Method Tables for Automated Payroll Systems

STANDARD Withholding Rate Schedules (Use these if the Form W-4 is from 2019 or earlier, or if the Form W-4 is from 2020 or later and the box in Step 2 of Form W-4 is NOT checked)					Form W-4, Step 2, Checkbox, Withholding Rate Schedules (Use these if the Form W-4 is from 2020 or later and the box in Step 2 of Form W-4 IS checked)				
If the Adjusted Annual Wage Amount (line 2a) is:		The tentative amount to withhold is:	Plus this percentage—	of the amount that the Adjusted Annual Wage exceeds—	If the Adjusted Annual Wage Amount (line 2a) is:		The tentative amount to withhold is:	Plus this percentage—	of the amount that the Adjusted Annual Wage exceeds—
At least—	But less than—				At least—	But less than—			
A	B	C	D	E	A	B	C	D	E
Married Filing Jointly					Married Filing Jointly				
$0	$12,200	$0.00	0%	$0	$0	$12,550	$0.00	0%	$0
$12,200	$32,100	$0.00	10%	$12,200	$12,550	$22,500	$0.00	10%	$12,550
$32,100	$93,250	$1,990.00	12%	$32,100	$22,500	$53,075	$995.00	12%	$22,500
$93,250	$184,950	$9,328.00	22%	$93,250	$53,075	$98,925	$4,664.00	22%	$53,075
$184,950	$342,050	$29,502.00	24%	$184,950	$98,925	$177,475	$14,751.00	24%	$98,925
$342,050	$431,050	$67,206.00	32%	$342,050	$177,475	$221,975	$33,603.00	32%	$177,475
$431,050	$640,500	$95,686.00	35%	$431,050	$221,975	$326,700	$47,843.00	35%	$221,975
$640,500		$168,993.50	37%	$640,500	$326,700		$84,496.75	37%	$326,700
Single or Married Filing Separately					Single or Married Filing Separately				
$0	$3,950	$0.00	0%	$0	$0	$6,275	$0.00	0%	$0
$3,950	$13,900	$0.00	10%	$3,950	$6,275	$11,250	$0.00	10%	$6,275
$13,900	$44,475	$995.00	12%	$13,900	$11,250	$26,538	$497.50	12%	$11,250
$44,475	$90,325	$4,664.00	22%	$44,475	$26,538	$49,463	$2,332.00	22%	$26,538
$90,325	$168,875	$14,751.00	24%	$90,325	$49,463	$88,738	$7,375.50	24%	$49,463
$168,875	$213,375	$33,603.00	32%	$168,875	$88,738	$110,988	$16,801.50	32%	$88,738
$213,375	$527,550	$47,843.00	35%	$213,375	$110,988	$268,075	$23,921.50	35%	$110,988
$527,550		$157,804.25	37%	$527,550	$268,075		$78,902.13	37%	$268,075
Head of Household					Head of Household				
$0	$10,200	$0.00	0%	$0	$0	$9,400	$0.00	0%	$0
$10,200	$24,400	$0.00	10%	$10,200	$9,400	$16,500	$0.00	10%	$9,400
$24,400	$64,400	$1,420.00	12%	$24,400	$16,500	$36,500	$710.00	12%	$16,500
$64,400	$96,550	$6,220.00	22%	$64,400	$36,500	$52,575	$3,110.00	22%	$36,500
$96,550	$175,100	$13,293.00	24%	$96,550	$52,575	$91,850	$6,646.50	24%	$52,575
$175,100	$219,600	$32,145.00	32%	$175,100	$91,850	$114,100	$16,072.50	32%	$91,850
$219,600	$533,800	$46,385.00	35%	$219,600	$114,100	$271,200	$23,192.50	35%	$114,100
$533,800		$156,355.00	37%	$533,800	$271,200		$78,177.50	37%	$271,200

Figure 3-10. *A slice of 2021 Percentage Method Tables for Automated Payroll Systems*

Take a close look at the method table for Married Filing Jointly on the left in Figure 3-10. Assume our adjusted annual wage amount (do not worry how to get such a number; we are going to learn it soon) is $100000 and our tax filing status is Married Filing Jointly. We should discover the following:

- Look up inside columns A and B. $100000 is at least $93250 but less than $184950; thus, $100000 falls into the bracket of $93250–184950 and should be matched to the fourth row ($93250) in column A.

- Column C shows the withholding amount ($9328) based on wage amount of $93250.

- Columns D and E instruct us that the amount over $93250 should be withheld 22%.

Thus, the withholding for $100000 = 9328+(100000–93250)*22%. The question to ask is how $9328 is obtained.

Well, 9328 = 1990 + (93250 - 32100) * 12%, where 1990 is the withheld amount right before 9328 in column C, 32100 is the number right before 93250 in column A, and 12% is the number right before 22% in column D.

We can then ask another question: How is $1990 in column C obtained? Without any doubt, we can figure out that 1990=0+(32100-12200)*10%, where 0 is the withheld amount right before 1990 in column C, 12200 is the number right before 32100 in column A, and 10% is the number right before 12% in column D.

Thus, we can conclude that as long as we have column A and column D, we can generate column C from top to bottom.

A careful examination on the Percentage Method Tables also discloses that every table has the same percentage column. This is good news because we can then significantly simplify these tables in our worksheet. Let's experience how we can build up our own tables based on Publication 15-T.

Open a blank worksheet, and enter the data exactly like what is shown in Figure 3-11. We can notice that column A in Figure 3-11 is dedicated to percentages and columns B, D, F match, respectively, to column A of Married Filing Jointly table, the column A of Single or Married Filing Separately table, and the column A of Head of Household table from Publication 15-T.

	A	B	C	D	E	F	G
1		Married Filing Jointly		Single or Married Filing Separately		Head of Household	
2	Plus Percentage	At least	Withhold	At least	Withhold	At least	Withhold
3	0%	0	0	0	0	0	0
4	10%	12200		3950		10200	
5	12%	32100		13900		24400	
6	22%	93250		44475		64400	
7	24%	184950		90325		96550	
8	32%	342050		168875		175100	
9	35%	431050		213375		219600	
10	37%	640500		527550		533800	

Figure 3-11. *Set up our tables*

Our task is to fill in columns C, E, and G. Certainly, we can fill in columns C, E, and G by copying those numbers from Publication 15-T, but that won't be a bright idea. Why? Though every year the tax law is revised, the revisions are often on the brackets and sometimes on the percentages, too. Thus, if columns C, E, and G are generated by formulas, when the numbers in columns A, B, D, and F are revised, columns C, E, and G are automatically updated.

We'd better enter zeros in cells C3, E3, and G3 since initially, there should be zero withholding. Note that if we do not enter zeros in these cells, Excel automatically assumes zeros of them. Explicitly placing zeros in those cells is always a good practice.

Cell C4 should store the withholding amount for taxable income up to $12200. Thus, the formula inside cell C4 is =C3 + (B4 - B3) * A3. Autofill from C4 to C10.

Test Yourself: work out the formulas inside cell E4 and G4 before reading on:

- The formula in cell E4 is =E3 + (D4 - D3) * A3. Autofill from E4 to E10.

- The formula in cell G4 is =G3 + (F4 - F3) * A3. Autofill from G4 to G10.

Our tables should look like Figure 3-12. Compare it with Figure 3-10 and Publication 15-T to confirm whether what we have obtained in Figure 3-12 is correct.

	A	B	C	D	E	F	G
1		Married Filing Jointly		Single or Married Filing Separately		Head of Household	
2	Plus Percentage	At least	Withhold	At least	Withhold	At least	Withhold
3	0%	0	0	0	0	0	0
4	10%	12200	0	3950	0	10200	0
5	12%	32100	1990	13900	995	24400	1420
6	22%	93250	9328	44475	4664	64400	6220
7	24%	184950	29502	90325	14751	96550	13293
8	32%	342050	67206	168875	33603	175100	32145
9	35%	431050	95686	213375	47843	219600	46385
10	37%	640500	168993.5	527550	157804.25	533800	156355

Figure 3-12. *Four method tables are set up*

Why should we set up the tables as shown in Figure 3-12? Let's use the expression = 9328 + (100000 - 93250) * 22% to explain. As we can see, the three numerical values 9328, 93250, and 22% in this expression are all stored in the same row. Therefore, given the adjusted annual wage amount $100000, once we have determined the lower boundary of its bracket is 93250, we can immediately find the corresponding base withholding 9328 and the percentage 22%.

There are three such method tables, one for Married Filing Jointly, one for Single or Married Filing Separately, and one for Head of Household. We need to name these tables. Naming them can allow us to reference them easily.

We need to consider the fact that when a filing status such as Married Filing Jointly is selected, we can use the selected filing status to find the right table. For example, status Married Filing Jointly can be matched to the table named Married Filing Jointly. Unfortunately, a name cannot have space(s). Thus, we can delete blank spaces when we name these tables. For instance, status Married Filing Jointly matches to the named reference MarriedFilingJointly.

Instructions to Complete Project 1

Please open the file chapter-3-1a.xlsx. There are two worksheets inside this Excel file. One is named Payroll, and the other is named Behind-Scene. Click the Behind-Scene worksheet; we will see that there are five tables and two arrays which are already set up and named as shown in Figure 3-13.

	A	B	C	D	E	F	G
1		MarriedFilingJointly		SingleOrMarriedFilingSeparately		HeadOfHousehold	
2	Plus_Percentage	At least	Withhold	At least	Withhold	At least	Withhold
3	0%	0	0	0	0	0	0
4	10%	12200	0	3950	0	10200	0
5	12%	32100	1990	13900	995	24400	1420
6	22%	93250	9328	44475	4664	64400	6220
7	24%	184950	29502	90325	14751	96550	13293
8	32%	342050	67206	168875	33603	175100	32145
9	35%	431050	95686	213375	47843	219600	46385
10	37%	640500	168993.5	527550	157804.25	533800	156355
11							
12	FilingStatus	SSM			numPay		
13	Married Filing Jointly	SSN Rate	6.20%		Semiannually	2	
14	Single or Married Filing Separately	SSN Cap	$142,800.00		Quarterly	4	
15	Head of Household	Medicare Rate	1.45%		Monthly	12	
16		Over rate	0.90%		Semimonthly	24	
17		Over limit	$200,000.00		Biweekly	26	
18					Weekly	52	
19					Daily	260	

Figure 3-13. *Table setup*

Table SSM is for Social Security tax and Medicare tax, which is cited from the following IRS website: www.irs.gov/taxtopics/tc751.

From table SSM, we understand that Social Security tax rate is 6.2% and the cap (also called base limit) is $142800, that is, income over the cap is not taxed for Social Security. The Medicare tax rate is 1.45% if the taxable income is not more than $200000. For any amount over $200000, the employers are required to withhold additional 0.9% Medicare tax.

Click the Formulas tab ➤ Name Manager; we can have a quick look at those names for the tables and arrays, as shown in Figure 3-14.

Name	Value	Refers To	Scope
FilingStatus	{"Married Filing Jointly";"Single or Marri...	="Behind-Scene'!S...	Workbook
HeadofHouseh...	{"0","0";"10200","0";"24400","1420";"64400...	="Behind-Scene'!SF...	Workbook
MarriedFilingJo...	{"0","0";"12200","0";"32100","1990";"93250...	="Behind-Scene'!SB...	Workbook
numPay	{"Semiannually","2";"Quarterly","4";"Mon...	="Behind-Scene'!SE...	Workbook
Plus_Percentage	{"0%";"10%";"12%";"22%";"24%";"32%";"35...	="Behind-Scene'!S...	Workbook
SingleorMarrie...	{"0","0";"3950","0";"13900","995";"44475","...	="Behind-Scene'!S...	Workbook
SSM	{"6.20%";" $132,900.00 ";"1.45%";"0.90%";...	="Behind-Scene'!S...	Workbook

Figure 3-14. *Names of the five tables and two arrays*

Notice that the three percentage tables are named:

- MarriedFilingJointly

- SingleorMarriedFilingSeparately

- HeadofHousehold

Once the tables and arrays are properly named and set up, this project is 75% completed. This truly shows that table setup is critical in this project. Follow the given instructions to complete this project:

1. In worksheet Payroll, enter "Employee1" and 3068.62 in cells A2 and B2, respectively.

2. Click cell C2 ➤ then click the Data tab ➤ Data Validation ➤ the Data Validation window shows up. Follow instructions on Figure 3-15 to set up the list for the payroll period types.

   The formula =INDEX(numPay, 0, 1) fetches the names of the payroll period types (the first column in the table numPay) as an array, which serves as the source list for the data validation.

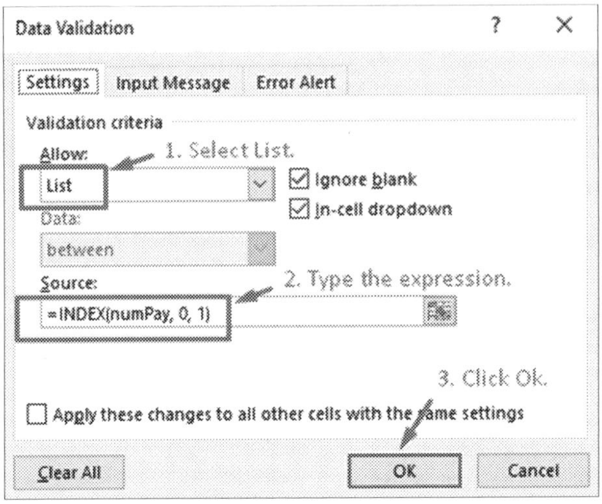

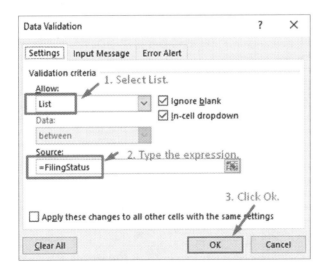

Figure 3-15. *Set the list for payroll period*

3. Autofill from C2 to C20. This autofill action enables the drop-down list in cells C2:C20.

    Select Biweekly for cell C2.

4. Click cell D2 ➤ click the Data tab ➤ Data Validation ➤ the Data Validation window shows up. Follow the instructions on Figure 3-16 to set up the list for filing status. Note that FilingStatus is a name defined in the worksheet Behind-Scene.

Figure 3-16. *Set up the list for filing status*

5. Autofill from D2 to D20.

   Select Married Filing Jointly for cell D2.

6. Enter formula =VLOOKUP(C2, numPay, 2, FALSE) in cell E2. Be aware that the last parameter in the VLOOKUP function is FALSE.

   Given the payroll period type in C2, E2 tries to obtain its matched number in the numPay table.

   A slight improvement can be made regarding the numPay table, which is to store the names of the payroll period types in ascending order. Once the names are in ascending order, we can then make use of the LOOKUP function.

   Part of our worksheet should look like Figure 3-17.

◢	A	B	C	D	E
1	Name	GrossPay	Payroll Period	Filing Status	EstimatedNumPay
2	Employee1	3068.62	Biweekly	Married Filing Jointly	26

Figure 3-17. *The first part of our worksheet*

7. Enter 142.12, 28.32, and 200 in cells F2, G2, and H2, respectively. Understand that "HSA" stands for Health Saving Account.

8. In cell I2, enter the formula =(B2 - SUM(F2:H2)) * E2. This formula computes the annualized taxable income for Social Security tax or Medicare tax. Note that health expenses are not taxable.

9. Cell J2 calculates Social Security tax. In cell J2, enter the formula

   =ROUND(IF(I2<INDEX(SSM, 2), I2 * INDEX(SSM, 1) / E2, INDEX(SSM, 2) * INDEX(SSM, 1) / E2), 2)

   I2 < INDEX(SSM, 2) assesses if the annualized taxable income in cell I2 is less than the cap of Social Security tax.

If yes, `I2*INDEX(SSM,1)/E2` is returned. Here

- `INDEX(SSM,1)` finds the Social Security tax rate.

- `I2*INDEX(SSM,1)` calculates the annualized Social Security tax.

- `I2*INDEX(SSM,1)/E2` is the Social Security tax of this payroll period.

If no, `INDEX(SSM,2)*INDEX(SSM,1)/E2` is returned:

- `INDEX(SSM,2)` fetches the cap of Social Security tax. When taxable amount is more than the cap, Social Security tax is calculated based on the cap.

- `INDEX(SSM,2)*INDEX(SSM,1)` calculates the annualized tax.

- `INDEX(SSM,2)*INDEX(SSM,1)/E2` is the Social Security tax of this payroll period.

Function ROUND is used to round up to only two decimal digits after the decimal point.

10. In cell K2, enter the formula `=ROUND(I2*INDEX(SSM,3)/E2,2)`. This formula calculates regular Medicare tax. We do not want to fabricate a complicated formula for both regular Medicare tax and additional Medicare tax. Instead, we would like to calculate them separately.

11. Cell L2 calculates the additional Medicare tax only when the taxable income in cell I2 is greater than the limit stored in the array SSM. The formula should be

`=ROUND(IF(I2>INDEX(SSM, 5), (I2 - INDEX(SSM, 5)) / E2 * INDEX(SSM,4), 0), 2)`

By now, part of our worksheet should look like Figure 3-18.

F	G	H	I	J	K	L
Medical Insurance	Dental Insurance	HSA	Annualized-SSM-pay	SS Tax	Medicare	Additional Medicare Tax
142.12	28.32	200	70152.68	167.29	39.12	0

Figure 3-18. *The second part of our worksheet*

12. Employers may provide a retirement plan which requires the employees to contribute a certain amount of money into their individual IRA accounts. Such a contribution is directly deducted from payroll. Cell M2 stores the percentage of her/his gross income that an employee chooses to contribute. Enter 5% in cell M2.

13. Enter the formula =ROUND(B2 * M2, 2) in cell N2. This formula calculates the dollar amount deducted from this payroll period into IRA.

14. Cell O2 calculates the taxable amount of this payroll period, which is the gross pay (B2) subtracted by the medical insurance expense (F2), dental insurance expense (G2), HSA (H2), and IRA deduction (N2). The formula inside cell O2 should be

    =IF((B2-SUM(F2:H2)-N2) <0, 0, ROUND(B2-SUM(F2:H2)-N2, 2))

    The reason to use the IF function here is to avoid negative numbers. If the result is negative, we should set it to be zero.

15. The formula =ROUND(IF(O2 * E2 <= 0, 0, O2 * E2), 2) computes the annualized taxable income in cell P2. Note that the IF function is to avoid a negative number (though it is unlikely to happen since we have already guarded this in cell O2).

16. Column Q records the "other income" from Form W-4. Some employees may have other income(s), and they would like to withhold tax on those income(s) through this employment. Step 4(a) on Form W-4 allows employees to enter such an income amount.

    Enter 0 in cell Q2.

17. Column R records the deduction amount from Form W-4 Step 4(b). Enter 0 in cell R2. At this point, the third part of our worksheet should look like Figure 3-19.

M	N	O	P	Q	R
IRA rate	IRA Deduction	Period Taxable Income	Annualized Taxable Income	W-4 Step 4(a)(other income)	W-4 Step 4(b)
5%	153.43	2544.75	66163.5	0	0

Figure 3-19. *The third part of our worksheet*

18. For 2021, the standard deduction is $12900 for Married Filing Jointly; otherwise, it is $8600. So, the formula inside cell S2 should be

    ```
    =IF(D2=INDEX(FilingStatus, 1), 12900, 8600)
    ```

    Note that it would be a good idea to store the standard deduction numbers (12900 and 8600) in a named table, too.

19. The Adjusted Annual Wage Amount in cell T2 is calculated by the formula =P2 + Q2 - R2 - S2.

20. Enter the following formula in cell U2:

    ```
    =MATCH(T2, INDEX(INDIRECT(SUBSTITUTE(D2, " ", "")), 0, 1), 1)
    ```

    `SUBSTITUTE(D2, " ", "")` transforms "Married Filing Jointly" to "MarriedFilingJointly."

    `INDIRECT(SUBSTITUTE(D2, " ", ""))` creates the reference MarriedFilingJointly which represents table B3:C10 in the Behind-Scene worksheet.

    `INDEX(INDIRECT(SUBSTITUTE(D2, " ", "")), 0, 1)` fetches the array B3:B10 from table B3:C10 (MarriedFilingJointly).

    This formula finds the position of a value in the array B3:B10 such that this value is immediately less than or equal to cell T2. In this specific case, because 32100 in B3:B10 (in the worksheet Behind-Scene) is immediately less than 53263.5 (the number in cell T2), its position (3 in this specific case) is returned.

The value in cell U2 will be used three times in cell V2; that is the reason why we need to calculate it first.

21. Cell V2 computes the tentative federal tax withholding. Based on the Adjusted Annual Wage Amount in cell T2 which is 53263.5 for Employee 1, we need to look into the table for Married Filing Jointly to calculate the tentative federal tax withholding. Mathematically, the expression is `1900 + (53263.5 - 32100) * 12%) / 26`. But what is the formula for this expression? Enter the following formula in cell V2:

```
=ROUND(((INDEX(INDIRECT(SUBSTITUTE(D2, " ", "")), U2, 2) + (T2 -
INDEX(INDIRECT(SUBSTITUTE(D2, " ", "")), U2, 1)) * INDEX(Plus_
Percentage, U2))/E2, 2)
```

`INDEX(INDIRECT(SUBSTITUTE(D2," ","")),U2,2)` fetches the base withholding amount. In this specific example, it is 1990.

`INDEX(INDIRECT(SUBSTITUTE(D2," ","")),U2,1)` fetches the lower boundary of a specific income bracket based on the filing status and taxable income. In this specific case, it is 32100.

`(T2 - INDEX(INDIRECT(SUBSTITUTE(D2, " ", "")), U2, 1))` calculates the amount over the lower boundary. In this specific instance, it is (53263.5 – 32100).

`INDEX(Plus_Percentage, U2)` finds the corresponding percentage rate for the specific tax bracket (12%).

Therefore, the formula in cell V2 can be interpreted as

```
=ROUND((1900 + (53263.5 - 32100) * 12%) / 26, 2)
```

At this point in time, part of our worksheet looks like Figure 3-20.

	S	T	U	V
1	Standard Deduction	Adjusted Annual Wage Amount	Table Pos	Tentative Withholding
2	12900	53263.5	3	174.22

Figure 3-20. *The fourth part of our worksheet*

22. Enter 0 inside cell W2, and enter 50 in cell X2.

23. Enter in cell Y2 the formula

    ```
    =IF(V2 - (W2 / E2) + X2 < 0, 0, V2 - (W2 / E2) + X2)
    ```

    The final federal income tax withholding is computed as V2 -
    (W2 / E2) + X2. Here, we again make use of the IF function to
    guarantee that the withholding won't be negative.

24. In cell Z2, the formula =B2-SUM(F2:H2)-SUM(J2:L2)-N2-Y2
    calculates the final pay. The last part of our worksheet should look
    like Figure 3-21.

W	X	Y	Z
W-4 Step 3(dependent duction)	W-4 Step 4(C)(Additional Withholding)	Final fed withholding	Final Period Pay
0	50	224.22	2114.12

Figure 3-21. *The last part of our worksheet*

The final result can be found in the file Chapter-3-1b.xlsx. Be aware that the final
period pay does not consider state income tax withholding in this project.

When we enter next employee's information in the third row (and in other rows
later), we do not need to re-enter the formulas. Instead, we can simply autofill the
formulas from the first employee.

We can rename the Payroll worksheet based the pay date. For example, assume that
everyone in our company is paid biweekly, and if our first biweekly payroll worksheet is
named 5-7-2021, for next biweekly pay, we can simply make a copy of the worksheet 5-7-
2021 and rename it 5-21-2021 so as to minimize the workload of the accountant.

Work on Project 2

Project 2 is a follow-up on project 1. In project 2, 2021 Connecticut state income tax
withholding is included.

There is one more upgrade in project 2. We want to set up the formulas for the first
employee in such a way that when we enter data of other employees, the calculated
results can automatically show up, that is, we do not even need to autofill formulas
anymore. For this purpose, we need to wrap some existing formulas with either the
IFERROR function or the IF function.

Table Setup and Naming

Connecticut state income tax withholding is more complicated than Federal income tax withholding because it does not provide percentage tables. Connecticut state income tax withholding calculation rules are published in document TPG-211 at the address `https://portal.ct.gov/-/media/DRS/Forms/2021/WTH/TPG-211_1220.pdf`.

TPG-211 gives a detailed procedure of tax withholding calculation which must go through five tables named A-E. But as we can find out, there is no percentage table for Connecticut income tax withholding calculation in the TPG-211 document. Retyping these five tables into our worksheet without error(s) is not an easy mission. Fortunately, if we pay close attention to the contents of these tables, we can find some rules that can help simplify those tables or enter them with minimum effort.

Connecticut has six withholding codes A-F. Depending on the code an employee has selected, a different column in the five tables is chosen at each calculation step. Therefore, not only do we need to reproduce the five tables in our worksheet, but also we need to establish a naming mechanism that can match a withholding code to a specific column in each table. This is why setup is also critical in this project.

Let's take a look at Table A which is displayed in Figure 3-22.

Table A - Personal Exemptions*

Withholding Code A			Withholding Code B			Withholding Code C			Withholding Code F		
Annualized Salary			Annualized Salary			Annualized Salary			Annualized Salary		
More than	Less Than or Equal to	Exemption	More than	Less Than or Equal to	Exemption	More than	Less Than or Equal to	Exemption	More than	Less Than or Equal to	Exemption
$ 0	$24,000	$12,000	$ 0	$38,000	$19,000	$ 0	$48,000	$24,000	$ 0	$30,000	$15,000
$24,000	$25,000	$11,000	$38,000	$39,000	$18,000	$48,000	$49,000	$23,000	$30,000	$31,000	$14,000
$25,000	$26,000	$10,000	$39,000	$40,000	$17,000	$49,000	$50,000	$22,000	$31,000	$32,000	$13,000
$26,000	$27,000	$ 9,000	$40,000	$41,000	$16,000	$50,000	$51,000	$21,000	$32,000	$33,000	$12,000
$27,000	$28,000	$ 8,000	$41,000	$42,000	$15,000	$51,000	$52,000	$20,000	$33,000	$34,000	$11,000
$28,000	$29,000	$ 7,000	$42,000	$43,000	$14,000	$52,000	$53,000	$19,000	$34,000	$35,000	$10,000
$29,000	$30,000	$ 6,000	$43,000	$44,000	$13,000	$53,000	$54,000	$18,000	$35,000	$36,000	$ 9,000
$30,000	$31,000	$ 5,000	$44,000	$45,000	$12,000	$54,000	$55,000	$17,000	$36,000	$37,000	$ 8,000
$31,000	$32,000	$ 4,000	$45,000	$46,000	$11,000	$55,000	$56,000	$16,000	$37,000	$38,000	$ 7,000
$32,000	$33,000	$ 3,000	$46,000	$47,000	$10,000	$56,000	$57,000	$15,000	$38,000	$39,000	$ 6,000
$33,000	$34,000	$ 2,000	$47,000	$48,000	$ 9,000	$57,000	$58,000	$14,000	$39,000	$40,000	$ 5,000
$34,000	$35,000	$ 1,000	$48,000	$49,000	$ 8,000	$58,000	$59,000	$13,000	$40,000	$41,000	$ 4,000
$35,000	and up	$ 0	$49,000	$50,000	$ 7,000	$59,000	$60,000	$12,000	$41,000	$42,000	$ 3,000
			$50,000	$51,000	$ 6,000	$60,000	$61,000	$11,000	$42,000	$43,000	$ 2,000
			$51,000	$52,000	$ 5,000	$61,000	$62,000	$10,000	$43,000	$44,000	$ 1,000
			$52,000	$53,000	$ 4,000	$62,000	$63,000	$ 9,000	$44,000	and up	$ 0
			$53,000	$54,000	$ 3,000	$63,000	$64,000	$ 8,000			
			$54,000	$55,000	$ 2,000	$64,000	$65,000	$ 7,000			
			$55,000	$56,000	$ 1,000	$65,000	$66,000	$ 6,000			
			$56,000	and up	$ 0	$66,000	$67,000	$ 5,000			
						$67,000	$68,000	$ 4,000			
						$68,000	$69,000	$ 3,000			
						$69,000	$70,000	$ 2,000			
						$70,000	$71,000	$ 1,000			
						$71,000	and up	$ 0			

* For *Withholding Code "D"*, the Personal Exemption is $0

Figure 3-22. *CT state income tax withholding table A*

What patterns can we find from this table? Using Withholding Code A as an example, we can tell that the Annualized Salary goes up by 1000; the corresponding Exemption goes down by 1000 until it reaches 0. The same applies to other codes in Table A. So, even though there is no percentage table for us to reproduce Table A, we can make use of autofill to quickly reproduce Table A without error. Figure 3-23 shows the array Filing Code and the reproduced table A in our worksheet.

For instance, to generate the numbers inside the array C3:C15 as shown in Figure 3-23, we can enter 0, 24000, and 25000 in cells C3, C4, and C5, respectively ➤ select both C4 and C5 ➤ autofill them to cell C15.

	A	B	C	D	E	F	G	H	I	J	K	L
1	Filing Code						Exemption-- Table A					
2	A		A		B		C		D, E		F	
3	B		0	12000	0	19000	0	24000	0	0	0	15000
4	C		24000	11000	38000	18000	48000	23000	0	0	30000	14000
5	D		25000	10000	39000	17000	49000	22000	0	0	31000	13000
6	E		26000	9000	40000	16000	50000	21000			32000	12000
7	F		27000	8000	41000	15000	51000	20000			33000	11000
8			28000	7000	42000	14000	52000	19000			34000	10000
9			29000	6000	43000	13000	53000	18000			35000	9000
10			30000	5000	44000	12000	54000	17000			36000	8000
11			31000	4000	45000	11000	55000	16000			37000	7000
12			32000	3000	46000	10000	56000	15000			38000	6000
13			33000	2000	47000	9000	57000	14000			39000	5000
14			34000	1000	48000	8000	58000	13000			40000	4000
15			35000	0	49000	7000	59000	12000			41000	3000
16					50000	6000	60000	11000			42000	2000
17					51000	5000	61000	10000			43000	1000
18					52000	4000	62000	9000			44000	0
19					53000	3000	63000	8000				
20					54000	2000	64000	7000				
21					55000	1000	65000	6000				
22					56000	0	66000	5000				
23							67000	4000				

Figure 3-23. *Table Filing Codes and Table A*

Similarly, to generate the numbers inside the array D3:D15, we can enter 12000 and 11000 in cells D3 and D4, respectively ➤ select both D3 and D4 ➤ autofill them to cell D15.

Be aware that because codes D and E are not included in Table A, we give them 0 in our reproduced table A.

Let's work on Table B which is shown in Figure 3-24. Though this is not a percentage table, its content is exactly a percentage table. Take a close look at the part for Code A, D, or F, for instance. We can find out the following:

- Up to 10000 is taxed 3%.

- Between 10000 and 50000 is 300 + 5% * (excess over 10000), where the base withholding 300 = 0 + 3% * 10000.

- Between 50000 and 100000 is 2300 + 5.5% * (excess over 50000), where the base withholding 2300 = 300 + 5% * (50000 - 10000).

Table B - Initial Tax Calculation

Withholding Code A, D, or F
If the amount from *Step 6* is:

Less than or equal to:	$ 10,000	3.00%
More than $10,000, but less than or equal to	$ 50,000	$300 plus 5.0% of the excess over $10,000
More than $50,000, but less than or equal to	$100,000	$2,300 plus 5.5% of the excess over $50,000
More than $100,000, but less than or equal to	$200,000	$5,050 plus 6.0% of the excess over $100,000
More than $200,000, but less than or equal to	$250,000	$11,050 plus 6.5% of the excess over $200,000
More than $250,000, but less than or equal to	$500,000	$14,300 plus 6.9% of the excess over $250,000
More than $500,000		$31,550 plus 6.99% of the excess over $500,000

Withholding Code B
If the amount from *Step 6* is:

Less than or equal to:	$ 16,000	3.00%
More than $16,000, but less than or equal to	$ 80,000	$480 plus 5.0% of the excess over $16,000
More than $80,000, but less than or equal to	$160,000	$3,680 plus 5.5% of the excess over $80,000
More than $160,000, but less than or equal to	$320,000	$8,080 plus 6.0% of the excess over $160,000
More than $320,000, but less than or equal to	$400,000	$17,680 plus 6.5% of the excess over $320,000
More than $400,000, but less than or equal to	$800,000	$22,880 plus 6.9% of the excess over $400,000
More than $800,000		$50,480 plus 6.99% of the excess over $800,000

Withholding Code C
If the amount from *Step 6* is:

Less than or equal to:	$ 20,000	3.00%
More than $20,000, but less than or equal to	$100,000	$600 plus 5.0% of the excess over $20,000
More than $100,000, but less than or equal to	$200,000	$4,600 plus 5.5% of the excess over $100,000
More than $200,000, but less than or equal to	$400,000	$10,100 plus 6.0% of the excess over $200,000
More than $400,000, but less than or equal to	$500,000	$22,100 plus 6.5% of the excess over $400,000
More than $500,000, but less than or equal to	$1,000,000	$28,600 plus 6.9% of the excess over $500,000
More than $1,000,000		$63,100 plus 6.99% of the excess over $1,000,000

Figure 3-24. *CT income tax withholding table B*

Can we see the pattern? Does this ring the bell on how we reproduced the Percentage Method Tables from Publication 15-T? We can also find out that the three calculation groups in Table B have the same percentage levels.

Assume we are going to reproduce Table B as shown in Figure 3-25 where columns C, E, and G store the brackets and columns D, F, and H record the initial tax amounts. We set the initial taxes to be zero in cells D31, F31, and H31. We can then enter the formula =D31 + $A31 * (C32 - C31) in cell D32 and autofill to D37. We can finish columns F and H in a similar way. Figure 3-26 shows the completed table B in our worksheet. Note that Code E has no initial tax in Connecticut.

	A	B	C	D	E	F	G	H	I	J
29						Initial Tax -- Table B				
30	Plus Percentage		A, D, F		B		C		E	
31	3.00%		0	0	0	0	0	0	0	0
32	5.00%		10000		16000		20000		0	0
33	5.50%		50000		80000		100000			
34	6.00%		100000		160000		200000			
35	6.50%		200000		320000		400000			
36	6.90%		250000		400000		500000			
37	6.99%		500000		800000		1000000			

Figure 3-25. *Reproduce Table B, code A, D, and F*

	A	B	C	D	E	F	G	H	I	J
29						Initial Tax -- Table B				
30	Plus Percentage		A, D, F		B		C		E	
31	3%		0	0	0	0	0	0	0	0
32	5%		10000	300	16000	480	20000	600	0	0
33	6%		50000	2300	80000	3680	100000	4600		
34	6.00%		100000	5050	160000	8080	200000	10100		
35	6.50%		200000	11050	320000	17680	400000	22100		
36	6.90%		250000	14300	400000	22880	500000	28600		
37	6.99%		500000	31550	800000	50480	1000000	63100		

Figure 3-26. *Table B and its matching percentage table in Excel worksheet*

I do not need to show how to analyze Tables C, D, and E. It is a good idea to leave them as an exercise. Anyhow, they are reproduced in the Excel file chapter-3-2a.xlsx by applying formulas and autofill. Chapter-3-2a.xlsx is a follow-up on the completed chapter-3-1b.xlsx from project 1, but it contains an additional worksheet named CT which stores all the tables for Connecticut state income tax withholding.

In this chapter, sometimes, we are mentioning the tables in TPG-211, and sometimes, we are referencing the reproduced tables in our worksheet. To differentiate them, whenever a table in TPG-211 is referenced, it is prefixed by "Table." The reproduced tables are prefixed by "table." For example, Table A means the one in TPG-211, but table A cites the reproduced counterpart in our worksheet.

As there are five tables and six codes, we need to create quite a few names for the tables in the CT worksheet. For example, for table A, we need to have names A_A, A_B, A_C, A_D, A_E, and A_F. In each name, the first letter references a reproduced table, and the second letter references a code. In the name A_B, A represents table A while, B represents code B. Thus, when code B is selected, we can use the name A_B to find the array dedicated for code B in table A.

Each name references an array in the CT worksheet. For instance, A_B references E3:F22 as shown in Figure 3-23 and Figure 3-27. Be aware that since both codes D and E share the same columns as shown in Figure 3-23, the two names A_D and A_E reference the same array I3:J5.

Similarly, for table B, we have names B_A, B_B, B_C, B_D, B_E, and B_F. Again, because codes A, D, and F share the same calculation procedure in Table B as shown in Figure 3-24, B_A, B_D, and B_F reference the same array C31:D37 in our table B as illustrated in Figure 3-26.

For other tables C, D, and E, the naming follows the same mechanism. Figure 3-27 displays some of the names related to these tables.

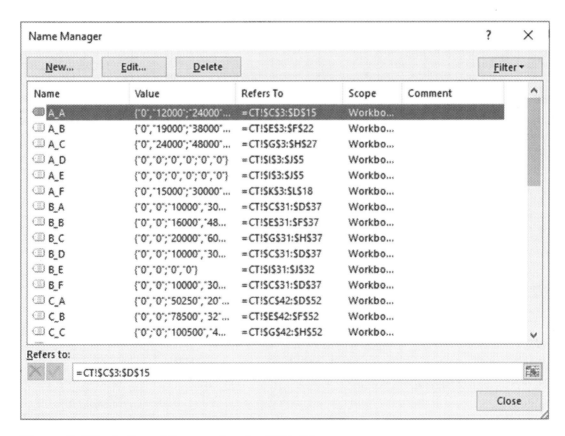

Figure 3-27. *A slice of the naming for CT tables*

Instructions to Complete Project 2

Like mentioned before, chapter-3-2a.xlsx is an upgraded version of chapter-3-1b.xlsx. So, let's first figure out some differences between chapter-3-2a.xlsx and chapter-3-1b.xlsx.

Open chapter-3-2a.xlsx and stay on the Payroll worksheet. Take column E as an example. Click cell E2; we see the following formula:

```
=IF(C2="", "", LOOKUP(C2, numPay))
```

This formula specifies that if C2 is blank, that is, if the payroll period type has not been selected, nothing will be displayed in cell E2. See the upgrade? Here, the IF function is used to make sure that the number of payment periods should be calculated only after C2 has a valid value.

This formula is also upgraded to make use of the LOOKUP function instead of VLOOKUP because the payroll period names in the numPay table have been sorted in ascending order. LOOKUP is slightly simpler than VLOOKUP.

Now, let's turn our eyes to cell E5. There is nothing showing up in cell E5, but when we click cell E5, we see the following formula:

```
=IF(C5="", "", LOOKUP(C5, numPay))
```

What happened? Well, in chapter-3-2a.xlsx, the existing formula in E2 is not only upgraded but also pre-copied (autofill) so that there is no need to re-enter or re-autofill it again. This happens to all other cells that inherit formulas from chapter-3-1b.xlsx.

We are going to continue our calculation of tax withholding from column Z, where the Connecticut state income tax withholding calculation starts. At this moment, part of our worksheet looks like Figure 3-28. Note that final period pay cannot be calculated until state tax withholding is completed in project 2.

	Y	Z	AA	AB	AC
1	Final fed withholding	CT filing code	CT-annualized sa	Table A Exemption	After Exemption
2	224.22				
3					
4					
5					
6					

Figure 3-28. *Start CT income tax withholding*

Follow the given instructions to complete this project:

1. We need to create a drop-down list in cell Z2 for Connecticut income tax filing codes A-F. Remember that these codes are stored in the CT worksheet and is referenced by the name CT_code. Thus, click cell Z2 ➤ click the Data tab ➤ select Data Validation. On the upcoming Data Validation window, set up the validation criteria as illustrated in Figure 3-29.

    Autofill from Z2 to Z20 so that we do not need to autofill again for other employees (assume we have maximum 19 employees).

    Select code C for cell Z2.

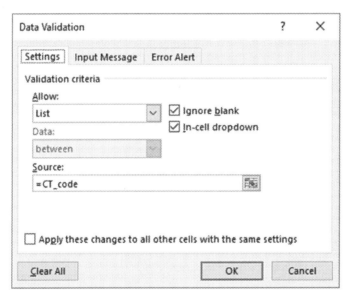

Figure 3-29. *Data validation for CT codes*

2. The annualized taxable salary for Connecticut is the same as that for federal IRS. So, enter the formula =P2 in cell AA2. Autofill from AA2 to AA20.

3. Remember we are following the instructions on TPG-211 which guide us through Tables A-E one by one. The first step is to determine the exemption amount from Table A. Cell AB2 calculates Table A exemption.

In cell AB2, enter the formula

`=IFERROR(LOOKUP(AA2, INDIRECT("A_"&Z2)), "")`

This formula needs some explanation.

"A_"&Z2 generates text "A_C" because the text inside cell Z2 is "C."

`INDIRECT("A_"&Z2)` transforms the text string "A_C" into the reference A_C which represents G3:H27 in the CT worksheet. G3:H27 is for code C in the reproduced table A.

`LOOKUP(AA2, INDIRECT("A_"&Z2))` finds the corresponding exemption in G3:H27 based on the taxable salary in cell AA2. In this case, it is 5000.

Since we are going to autofill from AB2 to AB20, the formulas in cells AB3:AB20 will have an error because their lookup-value is empty at this moment. The function IFERROR is used to make sure whenever an error occurs in a cell, nothing is displayed in that cell.

4. In cell AC2, enter the formula

    `=IFERROR(IF(AA2 - AB2<=0, 0, AA2 - AB2), "")`

    After exemption, the taxable amount is AA2 – AB2. However, our formula makes use of both IF and IFERROR functions to guarantee that the amount won't be negative after the exemption and nothing is displayed when an error happens.

    Autofill from AC2 to AC20. By now, part of our worksheet looks like Figure 3-30.

Y	Z	AA	AB	AC
Final fed withholding	CT filing code	CT-annual salary	Table A Exemption	After Exemption
224.22	C	66163.5	5000	61163.5

Figure 3-30. *Table A exemption calculated*

5. Our next step is to determine the initial tax amount from Table
    B. Based on the tax code in Z2 and the annualized taxable income
    after exemption in AC2, we can calculate the initial tax amount
    based on the reproduced table B and the percentage table (shown
    in Figure 3-26). In this specific case, because 61163.5 falls into the
    bracket 20000–1000000, the initial tax amount can be calculated
    by the expression

    ```
    600 + 5% * (61163.5 - 20000)
    ```

    To obtain the numbers 600 and 20000 from table B and the
    percentage 5% from the percentage table, we need to obtain the
    table B row position first. Be aware that the row position is the
    lower boundary of the bracket and it can be pinpointed by the tax
    code in cell Z2 and the taxable amount in cell AC2.

    In cell AD2, enter the formula

    ```
    =IFERROR(MATCH(AC2, INDEX(INDIRECT("B_"&Z2), 0, 1)), "")
    ```

    This formula matches the value in AC2 to a row position in table B
    for code C.

    Autofill from AD2 to AD20.

6. In cell AE2, enter the following formula

    ```
    =IFERROR(ROUND(IF(Z2="E", 0, INDEX(INDIRECT("B_"&Z2),
    AD2, 2) + INDEX(CT_percentage, AD2) * (AC2 -
    INDEX(INDIRECT("B_"&Z2), AD2, 1))), 2), "")
    ```

    This formula calculates the initial tax amount which is annualized.

    First of all, code E has no withholding in Connecticut. Thus, the IF
    function is used to treat code E differently. As long as Z2 has code
    E, the initial tax amount is 0.

    Again, in this specific case, the initial tax amount can be
    calculated by the expression 600 + 5% * (61163.5 - 20000).

    INDIRECT("B_"&Z2) generates the reference B_C which stands for
    G31:H37 in table B for code C. Recall we give every code in every
    table a unique name (see Figure 3-27).

`INDEX(INDIRECT("B_"&Z2), AD2, 2)` locates the base tax amount in table B. In this specific case, it is 600.

`INDEX(CT_percentage, AD2)` fetches the tax rate based on AD2. In this specific case, it is 5%.

`INDEX(INDIRECT("B_"&Z2), AD2, 1)` identifies the lower boundary of the tax bracket. In this specific case, it is 20000.

`(AC2 - INDEX(INDIRECT("B_"&Z2), AD2, 1))` calculates the excess amount that AC2 is over 20000. This expression equals to `(61163.5 - 20000)`.

Autofill from AE2 to AE20.

7. Table C determines the amount to add back if the 3% tax rate phase-out applies. In cell AF2, enter formula

    `=IFERROR(LOOKUP(AA2, INDIRECT("C_"&Z2)), "")`

    Note that the add back amount is calculated based on the value in cell AA2.

    Autofill from AF2 to AF20.

8. Table D is used to determine the tax recapture amount. In cell AG2, enter the formula

    `=IFERROR(LOOKUP(AA2, INDIRECT("D_"&Z2)), "")`

    Again, the tax recapture amount is calculated based on the value in AA2.

    Autofill from AG2 to AG20.

9. The formula `=IF(AG2<>"",ROUND(SUM(AE2:AG2),2),"")` in cell AH2 sums up the tentative tax withholding. Notice the use of the IF function which guarantees that before AG2 is calculated, nothing is displayed in AH2. Be aware the <> operator denotes "not equal to."

    Autofill from AH2 to AH20. By now, part of our worksheet should look like Figure 3-31.

AD	AE	AF	AG	AH
Table B Pos	Table B tax	Table C add back	Table D recapture	tentative withholding
2	2658.18	0	0	2658.18

Figure 3-31. *Tables B-D calculated*

10. Table E is used to determine Personal Tax Credits which is based on the CT annualized salary (in AA2) and the withholding code (in Z2). To calculate the Personal Tax Credits, the first step is to determine the decimal amount from table E. The higher the decimal amount, the higher the credit, because the final state tax withholding equals AH2 * (1 – decimal amount).

    In cell AI2, enter the formula

    ```
    =IFERROR(LOOKUP(AA2, INDIRECT("E_"&Z2)), "")
    ```

    Autofill from AI2 to AI20.

11. In cell AJ2, enter the formula

    ```
    =IF(AI2<>"", ROUND(AH2 * (1 - AI2), 2), "")
    ```

    This formula computes the annualized Connecticut tax withholding. Observe the use of the IF function that guarantees nothing will be displayed in AJ2 if AI2 is blank.

    Autofill from AJ2 to AJ20.

12. We need to convert the annualized tax withholding into period withholding. Enter formula =IFERROR(ROUND(AJ2/E2, 2), "") in cell AK2, then autofill from AK2 to AK20.

13. Enter 50 in cell AL2 and 0 in cell AM2. At this point, part of our worksheet should look like Figure 3-32.

AI	AJ	AK	AL	AM
Table E percentage	Annualized CT withholding	Period withholding	Additional withholding	Reduced withholding
0.1	2392.36	92.01	50	0

Figure 3-32. *Table E completed*

14. Enter the formula =IFERROR(AK2 + AL2 - AM2, "") in cell AN2. This is the final state income tax withholding.

    Autofill from AN2 to AN20.

15. Starting from 1/1/2021, Connecticut mandates Paid Family Leave Insurance which is 0.5% of the annualized income. The cap for 2021 is $142800 which is stored in cell AT2.

    Enter formula =I2 in cell AO2. This is the annualized income upon which the Paid Family Leave Insurance is calculated.

    Autofill from AO2 to AO20.

16. In cell AP2, enter the following formula:

    =IFERROR(ROUND(IF(AO2<=$AT$1, AO2 * 0.5% / E2, $AT$1 * 0.5% / E2), 2), "")

    If AO2 is larger than the cap stored in cell AT1, the insurance is calculated based on AT1; otherwise, it is calculated using AO2 directly.

    Note that the calculated amount is divided by E2 to obtain the periodical Paid Family Leave Insurance amount.

    Autofill from AP2 to AP20.

17. The final period payment is calculated by the following formula in cell AQ2:

    =IFERROR(ROUND(B2-SUM(F2:H2)-SUM(J2:L2)-N2-Y2-AN2-AP2,2),"")

    Autofill from AQ2 to AQ20. Part of our worksheet should look like Figure 3-33.

AN	AO	AP	AQ
Final CT period withholding	CT paid family annualized income	CT paid family leave insurance	Final Period Pay
142.01	70152.68	13.49	1958.62

Figure 3-33. *Final period payment calculated*

Since we autofill all formulas to row 20, we can now add more employees without entering formulas or autofill again. Try to add a few employees into the worksheet to experience how our worksheet works. The Excel file chapter-3-2b.xlsx contains several more employees.

In our current setting, one worksheet records the payments for all employees for a pay date. In reality, it might be better to allocate one worksheet for one employee.

Chapter Tip

Sometimes, we may want our numbers to keep their leading zeros. For example, we would like to have our numbers to be displayed as 001, 002, 003, ..., 100.

However, Excel automatically removes leading zeros. What can we do? A simple tip is to place a single quotation mark before the first zero.

In a blank worksheet, enter '001 in cell A1 and '002 in cell B1. Select both cells and autofill to the right until cell J1. We will see something like what is shown in Figure 3-34. What happened is that these numbers are stored as text.

	A	B	C	D	E	F	G	H	I	J
1	001	002	003	004	005	006	007	008	009	010
2										

Figure 3-34. *Numbers stored as text*

However, as we can notice in Figure 3-34, all numbers have a warning (or an error). To remove such warning, we need to click File ➤ select Options ➤ select Formulas. On the Excel Options window, uncheck the option "Numbers formatted as text or preceded by an apostrophe" as shown in Figure 3-35. After this, the numbers in cells A1:J1 have no warnings anymore.

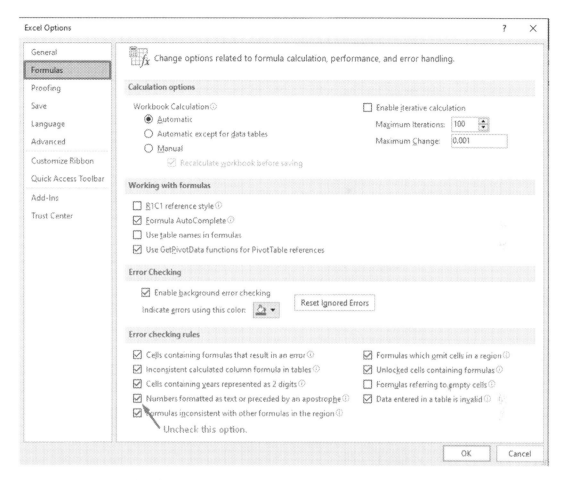

Figure 3-35. *Uncheck the option: Numbers formatted as text or preceded by an apostrophe*

A much better tip is presented by Mr. Kolyu Minevski, the book's technical reviewer. Please refer to his Excel blog at `https://excel-do.com/`. This tip is explained next.

In a blank worksheet, enter 1 in cell A1 and 2 in cell B1. Select both cells and autofill to the right until cell J1. Select cells A1:J1 ➤ click the Home tab ➤ click the small arrow in the Numbers group (refer to Figure 2-26).

On the upcoming Format Cells window, select Custom ➤ enter 000 inside the Type field ➤ click OK. This procedure is illustrated in Figure 3-36. Now, our numbers should be displayed as 001, 002, 003, …, 010.

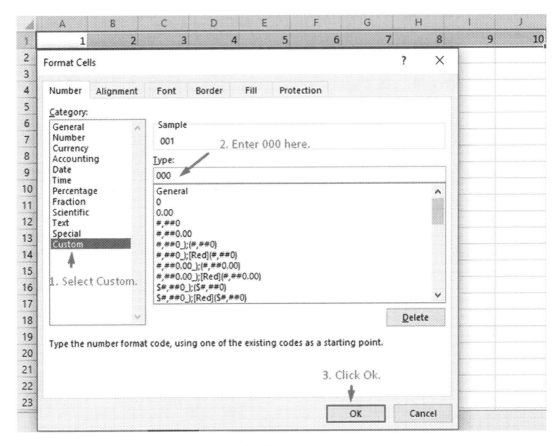

Figure 3-36. *Enter 000 in the Type field*

Review Points

1. Functions ROUND, SUBSTITUTE, INDEX, MATCH, and INDIRECT.

2. Understand the importance of table setup and name management.

3. Proper use of IF and IFERROR to automate future data entries.

4. Income tax withholding concepts and procedures.

5. Excel array formulas.

6. R1C1 reference style vs A1 reference style.

CHAPTER 4

Public and Private Key Cryptography

Please download the sample Excel files from `https://github.com/hhohho/master-Excel-through-projects` for this chapter's exercises.

Encryption techniques have been around for thousands of years. In today's digital world, encryption has become more sophisticated and challenging as the digital world is facing various malicious and smart hackers. To encrypt a digital message, we use a key (e.g., a password) to turn the message into a bit array via a specific algorithm or process, and then later, we can use another key, which might be the same as or different from the original key, to decrypt the bit array into the original message. If the key to decrypt is the same as the key to encrypt, it is called symmetric encryption, and the key in symmetric encryption is usually called a secret key. This is the traditional encryption approach. Its advantage lies in the fact that it can encrypt/decrypt an arbitrary length of data. Its disadvantage, however, lies in the fact that if we want to allow another user to decrypt our data, we must give the user our own key first – inconvenient when trying to share secure data. A workaround is achieved through the use of the public and private key algorithm, an asymmetric encryption in which the key to decrypt and the key to encrypt are different.

The public and private key cryptography is an ingenious innovation that has brought the world of cryptography significant breakthroughs. It is commonly known as RSA cipher, named after Ronald Rivest, Adi Shamir, and Leonard Adleman. The two terms, RSA and public and private key cryptography, are interchangeable in this book.

© Hong Zhou 2022
H. Zhou, *Mastering Excel Through Projects*, https://doi.org/10.1007/978-1-4842-7842-0_4

Public keys and private keys are paired entities; in other words, a public key has exactly one private key to match. Using a public and private key pair, a user can publish the public key for communal usage, keep the private key, and not worry about information leakage. The original challenge with symmetric keys, of course, is sending the secret key out safely. And additionally, there is never a guarantee that the users who obtain the secret key will use it securely and responsibly. The public and private key technology offers an inventive solution to these problems. Suppose user A wants to send user B a secret key. B would first create a public/private key pair and send the public key to A without any protection. A encrypts the secret key using B's public key and sends the encrypted data to B. This encrypted data can be decrypted by B only as B is the only person having the corresponding private key.

Confused at this moment? Do not worry. Please just remember that public key and private key are a key pair. Anything encrypted by the private key can only be decrypted by the public key, and anything encrypted by the public key can only be decrypted by the private key. We cannot use the same key to encrypt and decrypt. Therefore, as long the private key is safe, it does not matter who has access to the public key. Figure 4-1 visually illustrates the application of the public and private key cryptography.

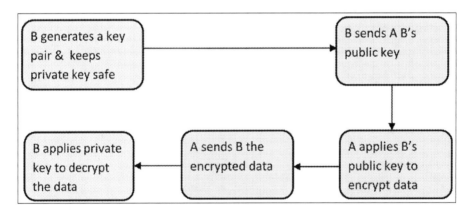

Figure 4-1. *Applying public key to encrypt and private key to decrypt*

By this point, we should have a pretty good idea why the secure transportation of secret keys is so important. But just in case you are not convinced, here is an example of the technique in action. Assume two entities, a client and a server, are starting up a secure network connection for data transportation. The client sends his public key to the server. The server randomly generates a secret key, utilizes the client's public key to encrypt the secret key, and gives it to the client. The client uses his own private key to decrypt the secret key. After this conversation, a secure connection has been established so that all messages between the server and the client are encrypted using the secret key. The beauty is, next time when the client logs in again, the secure connection is rebuilt with a different secret key, making the connection difficult to hack. This is one reason why after we have finished our transaction online, we should log out. If we stay logged in for too long, we are giving malicious hackers a better chance to figure out the secret key.

In this chapter, we are going to experience how the RSA cipher works. Be reminded that we are not going to present the mathematical proof of the RSA cipher.

Functions to Learn

We need to learn several new functions in this chapter, including CONCATENATE, LEN, MOD, QUOTIENT, GCD, INT, and COUNTIF.

CONCATENATE and the & Operator

The function CONCATENATE combines multiple text strings together as one text string. Its syntax is CONCATENATE(text1, [text2], ...), which indicates it can have one or more arguments. For example, the formula =CONCATENATE("Good", "Morning") generates a string "GoodMorning." If we want to have a space between the two words, we must explicitly add a space between. For example, we can revise our formula to be =CONCATENATE("Good", " ", "Morning").

Sometimes, people do not use the CONCATENATE function; instead, they use the operator & to combine text strings together. Assume cells A1 and B1 have the words Good and Morning, respectively; we can then write the formula =A1 & " " & B1 to combine the two words and leave a space between them.

In fact, the operator & is used more often than the function CONCATENATE.

LEN and INT

The LEN function has the syntax LEN(text). It returns the number of characters in the text string. For example, the formula =LEN("HELLO WORLD") returns 11. If the text string is stored in cell A1, the formula should then be =LEN(A1). Be advised that the space inside the text string " HELLO WORLD " is counted as a character. However, the empty string denoted by "" has length of zero. Please try the formulas =LEN(" ") and =LEN("") to see their difference.

The INT function simply rounds down a number to the nearest integer. In other words, it truncates off the digits after the decimal point if there are any. For example, =INT(9.99) returns 9, and =INT(8) returns 8.

MOD and Its Use in Encryption

Function MOD calculates the remainder after a number is divided by a divisor. We are familiar with remainders of integer divisions, but the Excel function MOD works on decimal numbers, too. The syntax of MOD is very simple: MOD(number, divisor). For example, the formula =MOD(11, 3) returns 2, and =MOD(2.3, 1.4) returns 0.9.

MOD can be used for encryption. The ancient Caesar cipher encrypts messages by changing each letter on the alphabet list to the one three places after. Taking the concept from Caesar cipher, letter A is encrypted into D, and X is encrypted into A. Let's assume A = 00, B = 01, ..., and Z=25. We can then use the formula =MOD(_M + 3, 26) to encrypt a letter denoted as _M (message) into the cipherText denoted as _C. Here, the key is 3.

To decrypt _C back to the original message _M, we need the formula =MOD(_C - 3, 26).

Note that MOD(_C - 3, 26) and MOD(_C - 3 + 26, 26) generate the same result in Excel.

Let's practice how to make use of the MOD function to encrypt and decrypt a simple message. Open the file chapter-4-1a.xlsx. There are two worksheets inside the file. The first worksheet is named encryption-example which demonstrates the encryption process. The second worksheet is named decryption-example which demonstrates the decryption process.

Worksheet encryption-example looks like Figure 4-2. Be aware that letters G–X are not shown.

	A	B	C	D	E	F	G
1				Message =	SEE YOU IN UNITED STATES	ciphertext =	
2							
3							
4	key=		6	message in letters	message in numbers	ciphertext in numbers	ciphertext in letters
5		10	1				
6	A	11	2				
7	B	12	3				
8	C	13	4				
9	D	14	5				
10	E	15	6				
11	F	16	7				
30	Y	35	26				
31	Z	36	27				

Figure 4-2. *Setup for encryption by using the MOD function*

Look at cell E1; our intended message contains spaces. We need to handle spaces in our encryption and decryption. Thus, we are not only dealing with 26 letters; we are dealing with the 26 letters plus the space character. That is why cell A5 contains a space character and is marked in red so that we won't delete the space character in A5 by accident. Be aware that this simple encryption and decryption example has two limitations. One is that the message in cell E1 can be composed of letters and spaces only. Another limitation is that the message in cell E1 cannot be longer than 27 characters because in this specific practice, dissected characters are stored only inside C5:C31, and C5:C31 can store maximum 27 characters. We can certainly allow a longer message.

The key is stored in cell B4 and is currently set to be 6. Once we have finished the task, we can change the key to any integer reasonable.

We once mentioned to let A = 00, B = 01, ..., Z = 25 such that every letter matches with a two-digit integer. However, Excel won't display an integer in the format of 00, 01, 02, ..., 25 by default. Thus, we would like to redefine the letters plus the space character. Let the space character = 10, A = 11, B = 12, ..., and Z = 36. In this case, the number must be subtracted by 10 first before its remainder can be calculated. Once the remainder is obtained, 10 is added back. Therefore, the formula to encrypt message _M would be

```
= MOD(_M + key - 10, 27) + 10
```

Similarly, the formula to decrypt the cipher text _C is

```
= MOD(_C - key - 10, 27) + 10
```

107

Follow the given instructions to complete the encryption and decryption tasks. Let's work on the encryption first inside the encryption-example worksheet:

1. The first step is to dissect the message into individual characters and store these characters in column D.

   In cell D5, enter the formula

   ```
   =IF(C5 <= LEN($E$1), MID($E$1, C5, 1), "")
   ```

   Cell E1 stores the message. The expression `MID($E$1, C5, 1)` fetches a character from E1. Which character to fetch is defined by C5. In this specific case, C5 = 1. Therefore, the first character is fetched. Since we need to autofill this formula from D5 to D31, it is possible that some numbers in column C are larger than the length of the message. When this happens, MID function will fail. IF function is used to safeguard such a case.

   Autofill from D5 to D31.

2. Enter `=IFERROR(LOOKUP(D5, $A$5:$B$31), "")` in cell E5. This formula translates a character to a number. Observe that table A5:B31 matches characters to numbers and vice versa.

   Since some cells in column D (D5:D31) have nothing inside, the LOOKUP function in the previous formula will fail for those cells. IFERROR is used to guarantee when errors happen; nothing is displayed.

   Autofill from E5 to E31.

3. Enter `=IFERROR(MOD(E5 + $B$4 - 10, 27) + 10, "")` in cell F5.

   Expression `MOD(E5 + $B$4 - 10, 27) + 10` encodes the character in E5 based on the key in B4. As some cells in column E (E5:E31) have nothing inside, IFERROR function is used to safeguard errors.

   Autofill from F5 to F31.

4. In cell G5, enter the formula `=IFERROR(LOOKUP(F5, $B$5:$B$31, $A$5:$A$31), "")`. This formula translates the encoded numbers into letters or space characters. Again, we use the function IFERROR.

   Autofill from G5 to G31.

5. In cell G1, enter the following formula:

```
=CONCATENATE(G5, G6, G7, G8, G9, G10, G11, G12, G13, G14,
G15, G16, G17, G18, G19, G20, G21, G22, G23, G24, G25, G26,
G27, G28, G29, G30, G31)
```

This function concatenates the encoded letters and spaces into a text string and stores the string inside cell G1. As mentioned before, the symbol & (called ampersand) is an operator to join text strings. Thus, the following formula can serve the same purpose:

```
=G5&G6&G7&G8&G9&G10&G11&G12&G13&G14&G15&G16&G17&G18&G19&G20
&G21&G22&G23&G24&G25&G26&G27&G28&G29&G30&G31
```

In some Excel versions, there is a much better function called TEXTJOIN. Office 365 has such a function, for example. I encourage you to look into TEXTJOIN on your own. So, if your Excel version has the TEXTJOIN function, enter the following formula inside G1:

```
=TEXTJOIN("", FALSE, G5:G31)
```

At this point, part of our worksheet encryption-example should look like Figure 4-3.

	A	B	C	D	E	F	G
1				Message =	SEE YOU IN UNITED STATES	ciphertext =	YKKFDU FOTF TOZKJFYZGZKY
2							
3							
4	key=	6		message in letters	message in numbers	ciphertext in numbers	ciphertext in letters
5		10	1 S		29		35 Y
6	A	11	2 E		15		21 K
7	B	12	3 E		15		21 K
8	C	13	4		10		16 F
9	D	14	5 Y		35		14 D
10	E	15	6 O		25		31 U
11	F	16	7 U		31		10
12	G	17	8		10		16 F
13	H	18	9 I		19		25 O
14	I	19	10 N		24		30 T

Figure 4-3. *Encryption example using MOD*

6. Switch to the second worksheet named decryption-example.

    In this worksheet, we are going to decode the encrypted message, that is, to decrypt the cipher text. Observe that cell E1 has the proper cipher text stored and the key in cell B4 is 6, the same as the key in the worksheet encryption-example.

    The decryption process is very similar to the encryption process with a couple differences. One difference is that the message in E1 is the cipher text.

7. Enter =IF(C5<=LEN($E$1), MID($E$1, C5, 1), "") in cell D5. This formula is the same as its counterpart in the encryption-example worksheet. Autofill from D5 to D31.

8. Enter =IFERROR(LOOKUP(D5, $A$5:$B$31), "") in cell E5. This formula translates the character in D5 back into a number. It is the same as its counterpart in the encryption-example worksheet. Autofill from E5 to E31.

9. In Cell F5, enter the formula =IFERROR(MOD(E5 - $B$4 - 10, 27) + 10, ""). Here, we are using the MOD function again to decode. This marks the second difference between the encryption process and the decryption process.

    Autofill from F5 to F31.

10. In cell G5, enter the formula =IFERROR(LOOKUP(F5, $B$5:$B$31, $A$5:$A$31), ""). This formula translates a number into a text character. Observe the use of the function IFERROR.

11. In cell G1, enter the formula

    =CONCATENATE(G5, G6, G7, G8, G9, G10, G11, G12, G13, G14, G15, G16, G17, G18, G19, G20, G21, G22, G23, G24, G25, G26, G27, G28, G29, G30, G31)

By now, part of our worksheet should look like Figure 4-4.

	A	B	C	D	E	F	G
1				ciphertext=	YKKFDU FOTF TOZKJFYZGZKY	message =	SEE YOU IN UNITED STATES
2							
3							
4	key=		6	cipher in letters	cipher in numbers	message in numbers	message in letters
5		10	1	Y		35	29 S
6	A	11	2	K		21	15 E
7	B	12	3	K		21	15 E
8	C	13	4	F		16	10
9	D	14	5	D		14	35 Y
10	E	15	6	U		31	25 O
11	F	16	7			10	31 U
12	G	17	8	F		16	10
13	H	18	9	O		25	19 I
14	I	19	10	T		30	24 N

Figure 4-4. *Decryption completed using MOD*

The completed result is in chapter-4-1b.xlsx. It is a good idea to protect the worksheets, but leave cells B4 and E1 unprotected. In chapter-4-1c.xlsx, both worksheets are password protected, and the password is again "Excel" (without the quotation marks).

Challenge: Try to modify chapter-4-1b.xlsx such that a message of size up to 36 characters can be encrypted and decrypted. This is a good exercise. The file chapter-4-1d.xlsx shows how to achieves this.

QUOTIENT and GCD

As the name suggests, function QUOTIENT calculates the quotient of a number divided by a divisor. Specifically, it returns the integer portion of a division. Its syntax is QUOTIENT(numerator, denominator). For example, =QUOTIENT(31, 2) returns 15, and =QUOTIENT(3.1, 2) returns 1.

GCD stands for Greatest Common Divisor. This function takes one or more arguments and finds the greatest common divisor among them. For example, =GCD(24, 16) returns 8, and =GCD(16, 25) returns 1. Note that when two numbers are relatively prime to each other, their greatest common divisor is 1. In the case of 16 and 25, though none of them is prime, their greatest common divisor is 1.

COUNTIF

COUNTIF counts within a range the number of cells that meet the given condition. Its syntax is COUNTIF(range, condition). Let's open a blank worksheet and enter some numbers and text strings like Figure 4-5.

◢	A	B	C	D	E	F
1	1	2	3	4	5	6
2	M	F	F	F	M	F
3						

Figure 4-5. *Learn function COUNTIF*

Assume we want to count in A1:F2 how many cells are larger than or equal to 3. Our formula should then be =COUNTIF(A1:F2, ">=3"). Be aware that the condition is presented as a text string.

If the question is changed to be: how many cells in A1:F2 are larger than or equal to C1? We know C1 has the number 3, but it can change, so this formula =COUNTIF(A1:F2, ">=3") does not apply anymore.

Again, the condition ">=3" is a text string. To obtain a similar text string, we can revise the condition to be ">=" & C1. Yes, that is the trick. Thus, our new formula should be =COUNTIF(A1:F2, ">=" & C1).

If we want to count how many cells in A2:F2 contain the letter "F," we should write our formula as =COUNTIF(A2:F2, "=F"). Excel allows to omit the = operator in such occasions. Thus, our formula can also be =COUNTIF(A2:F2, "F").

Again, what if the question is changed to be: how many cells in A2:F2 have the same content as cell B2? Well, our formula can then be =COUNTIF(A2:F2, B2).

Knowledge to Learn

Before we can work on the project, we need to develop some mathematical understanding about RSA. Such understanding is extremely important for us to understand the project.

RSA cryptography makes use of modular arithmetic. It encodes the message M to cipher text C via this expression: C = MOD(M^e, divisor). Recall ^ is the exponent operator, and be aware that we are now using M instead of _M and C instead of _C to denote "message" and "cipher text."

The expression MOD(M^e, divisor) is fairly simple. The challenge lies in the fact that its divisor is huge and e is not small either. Here, the divisor and e are the public key. We may have heard of RSA-1024 or RSA-2048. What are they? RSA-2048 means that the length of the divisor is of 2048 bits, that it, the divisor used in the MOD function is so large that it contains 2048 bits. In general, when we talk about the key size in RSA, we mean the size of the divisor.

To be the divisor in a public key, the integer must be semi-prime, that is, it must have exactly two prime factors. Assume divisor = p * q, where both p and q are prime integers and their sizes are close to each other. Because the key (the divisor) is so large, even it is publicly known, there isn't enough computational power to factor it to find p and q which are the private key. That is why the private key is safe.

In RSA cryptography, the message size must be smaller than the key size. However, when the message size is too small, for security reasons, it will be padded to be large enough so that it is of a size close to the key size. The challenge is M^e can become a number too large to calculate its modulus. This is where modular arithmetic comes to the play. We need to be clear of the following two modular arithmetic operations:

- MOD(M^e, divisor) = MOD((MOD(M, divisor))^e, divisor)

- MOD(M * N, divisor) = MOD(MOD(M, divisor) * MOD(N, divisor), divisor)

For example, the following formula =MOD(123456789 * 987654321, 32657) will fail in our worksheet. It fails because the numerator is too large compared to the divisor. The workaround is to modify the formula to be

=MOD(MOD(123456789, 32657) * MOD(987654321, 32657), 32657)

The revised formula returns the correct result 21964.

A workaround is needed more often for the expression C = MOD(M^e, divisor) because M^e can easily become too large. Formula =MOD(1712^8, 32657) will fail in our worksheet, too. The workaround is to revise it to be =MOD(MOD(1712^4, 32657)^2, 32657). The workaround gets the correct result 9349. Be advised that 1712^8 = (1712^4)^2.

In the project of this chapter, we need to make use of such workarounds often.

To use the private key to decode the cipher text C, the expression is M = MOD(C^d, divisor). What is d? d must satisfy the following requirement:

d * e + (p - 1) * (q - 1) * t = 1

where, d is a positive integer and t is an integer.

Certainly, there can be more than one (d, t) pair that can satisfy the given equation. But we want the smallest positive d. In real applications, we must find the smallest positive d; otherwise, it would be too large to work with.

We should realize that, in fact, d is the bona fide private key. However, because d can be figured out with the knowing of p and q, usually p and q are considered the private key.

With the above mathematical understanding, we are ready to work on our project in this chapter.

Work on the Project

Since we are using Excel to simulate the encryption and decryption process of RSA, we won't be able to try on large numbers. To simplify the demonstration, we are going to use a smaller integer as the message, too. Note that in real RSA encryption and decryption, a message is an integer (a huge one).

Assume A = 10, B = 11, ..., H = 17, I = 18, ..., Z=35. Our message is "HI," which equals 1718.

Open chapter-4-2a.xlsx. There is only one worksheet named public-key. In this worksheet, we are going to experience how to use a given public key to encode the message 1718, and then use the private key to confirm that the encryption is correct. Our worksheet should look like Figure 4-6.

	A	B	C	D	E	F	G	H	I	J
1	private key	p					Encoding			
2		q				remainder			IF	mod
3	public key	pq (divisor)								
4		e								
5		(p-1)(q-1)								
6		message								
7		encoded								
8		d								
9		decoded								
10										
11										
12										
13										
14										
15										
16										
17										
18										
19										
20							Decoding			
21						remainder			IF	mod
22										
23										

Figure 4-6. *RSA encryption setup*

Take a close look at this worksheet. The table Encoding is set up for the encryption process, and the table Decoding is for the decryption process. As shown on the left side of Figure 4-6, we need to set up the private and public keys. Please follow the given instructions:

1. Always define the private key first. Enter 139 and 137 in cells C1 and C2, respectively. Both 139 and 137 are prime numbers (the tip of this chapter shows how to verify if an integer is prime).

2. Enter the formula =C1 * C2 in cell C3. This computes the divisor in the public key (p*q).

3. Enter the formula =(C1 - 1) * (C2 - 1) in cell C5. This is for (p-1)*(q-1).

115

4. Enter 91 in cell C4.

    The exponent e must meet two requirements. First, it must be
    less than both p and q. Second, it must be relatively prime to
    (p-1)*(q-1). To verify whether 91 is prime to 18768 (C5), enter the
    formula =GCD(C4, C5) in cell A12. We should obtain 1 in cell A12,
    which confirms that e and (p-1)*(q-1) are prime to each other.

5. Enter 1718 in cell C6. Remember that "HI" = 1718. At this moment,
    part of our worksheet should look like Figure 4-7.

	A	B	C	D	E	F
1	private key	p	139			
2		q	137			remainder
3	public key	pq (divisor)	19043			
4		e	91			
5		(p-1)(q-1)	18768			
6		message	1718			
7		encoded				
8		d				
9		decoded				

Figure 4-7. *Set up private key, public key, and the message*

6. Our next job is to encrypt 1718 into another integer using the
    given public key. In this specific case, the encryption formula is
    =MOD(1718^91, 19043) which will certainly fail in our worksheet.
    To make the encryption a success and automate it, I will
    demonstrate the encryption process inside the table Encoding.
    Enter formula =C4 in cell E2. We are going to find the binary digits
    of e (at this moment, e = 91) in cells E2:F18.

7. Enter the formula =QUOTIENT(E2, 2) in cell E3 and the formula
    =MOD(E2, 2) in cell F3.

8. Autofill E3 and F3 together to E18:F18. The digits inside F3:F18
    delineate the binary form of the integer 91. Reading from cell F18
    up to F3, 0000000001011011 is the binary representation of 91. The
    leading zeros can be truncated. Remember that binary numbers
    are base 2.

Why should we calculate the binary representation of the decimal number 91? We are going to use it to help achieve automation of the encryption and decryption process. Right now, we should understand that every digit in a binary number such as 1011011 has a place value. The place value determines the exponent as shown in Figure 4-8. Figure 4-8 demonstrates how to convert the binary number 1011011 to the decimal number 91.

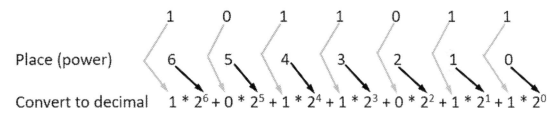

Figure 4-8. *Convert a binary number into decimal*

9. Enter 1 in cell G3 and the formula =G3 * 2 in cell G4. Autofill from G4 to G18.

Part of our worksheet should look like Figure 4-9. As shown inside the rectangle in Figure 4-9, each digit in the binary format has a place value matching to a decimal integer. Column G is used to help on explanation.

E	F	G	H	I	J
		Encoding			
91	remainder			IF	mod
45	1	== 1			
22	1	== 2			
11	0	== 4			
5	1	== 8			
2	1	== 16			
1	0	== 32			
0	1	== 64			
0	0	128			
0	0	256			
0	0	512			
0	0	1024			
0	0	2048			
0	0	4096			
0	0	8192			
0	0	16384			
0	0	32768			

Figure 4-9. *Explanation of the binary number*

10. In cell H3, enter the formula =MOD(C$6^G3, C$3). As G3 = 1, this is
     in fact =MOD(1718, 19043). Do not autofill.

11. In cell H4, enter the formula =MOD(H3^2, C$3), and then autofill
     from H4 to H18.
     Because H3 =MOD(1718, 19043), the formula in cell H4 in fact
     fulfills the following:

     =MOD(MOD(1718, 19043)^2, 19043), i.e. =MOD(1718^2, 19043)

     In cell H5, the formula is =MOD(H4^2, C$3). Substituting MOD(1718^2, 19043)
     for H4, the formula in cell H5 becomes =MOD((MOD(1718^2, 19043))^2,
     19043) which fulfills =MOD(1718^4, 19043).

We can then deduce that the formula in cell H6 fulfills =MOD(1718^8, 19043), ... and the formula in cell H9 fulfills = MOD(1718^64, 19043).

Be aware that =MOD(1718^8, 19043), MOD(1718^16, 19043), MOD(1718^32, 19043), and MOD(1718^64, 19043) are to fail if they were computed directly. At this moment, part of our worksheet should look like Figure 4-10.

	A	B	C	D	E	F	G	H	I	J
1	private key	p	139			Encoding				
2		q	137		91	remainder			IF	mod
3	public key	pq (divisor)	19043		45	1	1	1718		
4		e	91		22	1	2	18902		
5		(p-1)(q-1)	18768		11	0	4	838		
6		message	1718		5	1	8	16696		
7		encoded			2	1	16	4982		
8		d			1	0	32	7295		
9		decoded			0	1	64	10883		
10					0	0	128	11272		
11					0	0	256	3088		
12					0	0	512	14244		
13					0	0	1024	7414		
14					0	0	2048	9298		
15					0	0	4096	16627		
16					0	0	8192	9898		
17					0	0	16384	13212		
18					0	0	32768	8806		

Figure 4-10. *Individual modulus terms are calculated*

12. In cell I3, enter the formula =IF(F3 = 1, H3, 1). Autofill from I3 to I18. Recall that when we convert a binary number into a base-10 decimal number, only those digits of value 1 in the binary number can make the contribution (this saying may not be precisely correct).

13. In cell J3, enter the formula =I3. Do not autofill.

14. In cell J4, enter the formula =MOD(J3 * I4, C$3). Autofill from J4 to J18. Detailed explanation is required at this point.

The encryption expression is MOD(1718^91, 19043). Because 1718^91 is too large, this expression is bound to fail in our worksheet. Fortunately, we know that

91 = 64 + 0 + 16 + 8 + 0 + 2 + 1

= 1 + 2 + 0 * 4 + 8 + 16 + 0 * 32 + 64

Thus, MOD(1718^91, 19043) can be calculated by the following expression:

MOD(1718^91, 19043) = MOD(MOD(1718, 19043) * MOD(1718^2, 19043) * 1 * MOD(1718^8, 19043) * MOD(1718^16, 19043) * 1 * MOD(1718^64, 19043), 19043)

Notice that wherever the digit in the binary form of 91 is 0, we need to replace the corresponding modulus term with 1 in this multiplication expression (which is the purpose of Step 12). Since 91 = 1 + 2 + 0 * 4 + 8 + 16 + 0 * 32 + 64, both MOD(1718^4, 19043) and MOD(1718^32, 19043) are replaced with 1 in the previous multiplication expression.

Because each individual modulus term in the given expression is recorded in I3:I9, then

MOD(1718^91, 19043) = MOD(I3*I4*I5*I6*I7*I8*I9, 19043)

Unfortunately, this formula is bound to fail in our worksheet because the product of I3:I9 is still too large. How can we overcome this obstacle?

What we did in J4 to J18 is to make use of the associative property of modular arithmetic iteratively:

- J3 = I3.

- Cell J4 computes MOD(J3*I4, 19043) which is in fact MOD (I3*I4, 19043).

- Cell J5 computes MOD(J4*I5, 19043) which is in fact MOD(I3*I4*I5, 19043).

- Cell J6 computes MOD(J5*I6, 19043) which is in fact MOD(I3*I4*I5*I6, 19043).

- Similarly, cell J7 computes MOD(I3*I4*I5*I6*I7, 19043).

- Certainly, cell J8 computes MOD(I3*I4*I5*I6*I7*I8, 19043).

- Finally, cell J9 computes MOD(J8*I9, 19043) which is in fact MOD(I3*I4*I5*I6*I7*I8*I9, 19043), and this, in turn, is MOD(1718^91, 19043).

By means of the iterative modular arithmetic, every numerator in cells J4:J9 is not too large compared to the divisor. Therefore, all the formulas in cells J4:J9 work smoothly.

In this specific case, because I10:I18 are all 1s, therefore, J18 has the same result as J9.

15. In cell C7, enter the formula =J18.

By now, we have finished the encryption by using the public key. Part of our worksheet should look like Figure 4-11.

	A	B	C	D	E	F	G	H	I	J
1	private key	p	139				Encoding			
2		q	137		91	remainder			IF	mod
3	public key	pq (divisor)	19043		45	1	1	1718	1718	1718
4		e	91		22	1	2	18902	18902	5321
5		(p-1)(q-1)	18768		11	0	4	838	1	5321
6		message	1718		5	1	8	16696	16696	3821
7		encoded	7608		2	1	16	4982	4982	12265
8		d			1	0	32	7295	1	12265
9		decoded			0	1	64	10883	10883	7608
10					0	0	128	11272	1	7608
11					0	0	256	3088	1	7608
12					0	0	512	14244	1	7608
13					0	0	1024	7414	1	7608
14					0	0	2048	9298	1	7608
15					0	0	4096	16627	1	7608
16					0	0	8192	9898	1	7608
17					0	0	16384	13212	1	7608
18					0	0	32768	8806	1	7608

Figure 4-11. *Encryption completed by using public key*

16. To use the given private key to decode the cipher text (in this case, the integer 7608), the expression is MOD(7608^d, 19043). The first job is to find the magic positive integer d which satisfies the equation d * e + (p-1) * (q-1) * t = 1.

From the equation, we can solve for t as

t = (1 - d * e)/ ((p-1) * (q-1))

The idea is since d and t must be integers and there must be such a d between 1 and (p-1)*(q-1), we just need to find out this d when its corresponding t is also an integer.

Thus, enter 1 in cell L1.

17. Click cell L1 to select it ➤ click the Home tab ➤ click Fill ➤ select Series as shown in Figure 4-12.

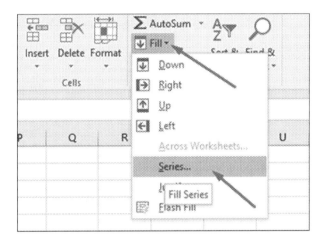

Figure 4-12. *Click Fill*

18. On the upcoming Series window, choose Columns, and set Step value = 1 and Stop value = 20000. Click OK as shown in Figure 4-13. After that, cells L1:L20000 contain the series 1 to 20000. Certainly, we can make use of the autofill feature to create such a series, too. Note that if we want to work with a larger divisor, we can fill the series to L1000000.

Troubleshoot: if your worksheet fails to generate such a series, it is likely you didn't enter 1 in cell L1 first (step 16).

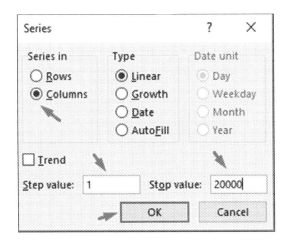

Figure 4-13. *Create the series*

19. In cell M1, enter the formula =(1 - L1 * C$4) / C$5. This formula calculates t when d = 1. Autofill with the double-click skill.

    Since (p-1) * (q-1) is less than 20000, there must be such an integer t. We need to find the first d when its matched t is an integer.

20. In cell N1, enter the formula =M1 - INT(M1). This formula calculates the expression t - INT(t).

    Autofill by double-clicking on the little square after moving the mouse cursor to the bottom-right corner of cell N1.

21. If t is an integer, we know that t - INT(t) = 0. Thus, in cell C8, enter the formula =INDEX(L:L, MATCH(0, N:N, 0)). This formula finds the smallest positive integer d when t is an integer. In this specific case, d = 12787.

22. Now, we need to move into the table Decoding. Soon, we will realize that the decoding process is almost the same as the encoding process. The first step is to find the binary form of d (which is 12787 in this specific example).

    Enter the formula =C8 in cell E21.

23. In cell E22, enter the formula =QUOTIENT(E21, 2). Autofill from E22 to E37.

24. In cell F22, enter the formula =MOD(E21, 2). Autofill from F22 to F37.

25. In cell G22 enter 1, and then in cell, G23 enter formula = 2 * G22.
    Autofill from G23 to G37. By now, part of our worksheet should
    look like Figure 4-14.

	B	C	D	E	F	G	H	I	J	K	L	M	N
7	encoded	7608		2	1	16	4982	4982	12265		7	-0.03389	0.966113
8	d	12787		1	0	32	7295	1	12265		8	-0.03874	0.961264
9	decoded			0	1	64	10883	10883	7608		9	-0.04358	0.956415
10				0	0	128	11272	1	7608		10	-0.04843	0.951566
11				0	0	256	3088	1	7608		11	-0.05328	0.946718
12				0	0	512	14244	1	7608		12	-0.05813	0.941869
13			'	0	0	1024	7414	1	7608		13	-0.06298	0.93702
14				0	0	2048	9298	1	7608		14	-0.06783	0.932172
15				0	0	4096	16627	1	7608		15	-0.07268	0.927323
16				0	0	8192	9898	1	7608		16	-0.07753	0.922474
17				0	0	16384	13212	1	7608		17	-0.08237	0.917626
18				0	0	32768	8806	1	7608		18	-0.08722	0.912777
19											19	-0.09207	0.907928
20						Decoding					20	-0.09692	0.90308
21				12787	remainder		IF		mod		21	-0.10177	0.898231
22				6393	1	1					22	-0.10662	0.893382
23				3196	1	2					23	-0.11147	0.888534
24				1598	0	4					24	-0.11632	0.883685
25				799	0	8					25	-0.12116	0.878836
26				399	1	16					26	-0.12601	0.873988

Figure 4-14. *Working on the decryption*

26. In cell H22, enter the formula =MOD(C$7, C$3). Do not autofill.

27. In cell H23, enter the formula =MOD(H22^2, C$3). Autofill from
    H23 to H37.

28. In cell I22, enter the formula =IF(F22=1, H22, 1). Autofill from
    I22 to I37.

29. In cell J22, enter the formula =I22. Do not autofill.

30. In cell J23, enter the formula =MOD(I23 * J22, C$3). Autofill from
    J23 to J37.

31. In cell C9, enter the formula =J37. The decryption process is
    completed. Part of our worksheet should look like Figure 4-15.

	E	F	G	H	I	J	K	L	M	N
20			Decoding					20	-0.09692	0.90308
21	12787	remainder			IF	mod		21	-0.10177	0.898231
22	6393	1	1	7608	7608	7608		22	-0.10662	0.893382
23	3196	1	2	9987	9987	18569		23	-0.11147	0.888534
24	1598	0	4	11978	1	18569		24	-0.11632	0.883685
25	799	0	8	2522	1	18569		25	-0.12116	0.878836
26	399	1	16	122	122	18344		26	-0.12601	0.873988
27	199	1	32	14884	14884	12605		27	-0.13086	0.869139
28	99	1	64	6237	6237	7881		28	-0.13571	0.86429
29	49	1	128	14363	14363	3211		29	-0.14056	0.859442
30	24	1	256	2950	2950	8079		30	-0.14541	0.854593
31	12	0	512	18892	1	8079		31	-0.15026	0.849744
32	6	0	1024	3758	1	8079		32	-0.1551	0.844896
33	3	0	2048	11701	1	8079		33	-0.15995	0.840047
34	1	1	4096	13274	13274	9513		34	-0.1648	0.835198
35	0	1	8192	13240	13240	1718		35	-0.16965	0.83035
36	0	0	16384	6785	1	1718		36	-0.1745	0.825501
37	0	0	32768	9294	1	1718		37	-0.17935	0.820652

Figure 4-15. *Decryption completed*

32. To experience encryption by private key but decryption by public key, we can make a copy of the public-key worksheet and rename the new worksheet private-key. Please do so.

33. In the private-key worksheet, change the formula inside cell E2 to be =C8. This means that the encryption expression is MOD(M^d, p*q), that is, we are encoding our message by using the private key.

34. In cell E21, change the formula to be =C4. This means that the decryption expression is MOD(C^e, p*q), that is, we are decoding the cipher text by using the public key.

Part of the worksheet private-key should look like Figure 4-16.

It would be fun to change the message to be another two letters. Remember that the message should be less than the divisor. If not, the decoding process won't work correctly.

The complete result can be found in the file chapter-4-2b.xlsx.

	B	C	D	E	F	G	H	I	J	K	L	M	N
1	p	139		Encoding							1	-0.0048	0.995205
2	q	137		12787	remainder			IF	mod		2	-0.00964	0.990356
3	pq (divisor)	19043		6393	1	1	1718	1718	1718		3	-0.01449	0.985507
4	e	91		3196	1	2	18902	18902	5321		4	-0.01934	0.980659
5	(p-1)(q-1)	18768		1598	0	4	838	1	5321		5	-0.02419	0.97581
6	message	1718		799	0	8	16696	1	5321		6	-0.02904	0.970961
7	encoded	10527		399	1	16	4982	4982	1366		7	-0.03389	0.966113
8	d	12787		199	1	32	7295	7295	5481		8	-0.03874	0.961264
9	decoded	1718		99	1	64	10883	10883	7047		9	-0.04358	0.956415
10				49	1	128	11272	11272	5431		10	-0.04843	0.951566
11				24	1	256	3088	3088	13088		11	-0.05328	0.946718
12				12	0	512	14244	1	13088		12	-0.05813	0.941869
13				6	0	1024	7414	1	13088		13	-0.06298	0.93702
14				3	0	2048	9298	1	13088		14	-0.06783	0.932172
15				1	1	4096	16627	16627	9815		15	-0.07268	0.927323
16				0	1	8192	9898	9898	10527		16	-0.07753	0.922474
17				0	0	16384	13212	1	10527		17	-0.08237	0.917626
18				0	0	32768	8806	1	10527		18	-0.08722	0.912777
19											19	-0.09207	0.907928
20				Decoding							20	-0.09692	0.90308
21				91	remainder			IF	mod		21	-0.10177	0.898231
22				45	1	1	10527	10527	10527		22	-0.10662	0.893382
23				22	1	2	6512	6512	16067		23	-0.11147	0.888534

Figure 4-16. *Encryption by private key*

Chapter Tip

This chapter's tip is about how to use Excel to determine if an integer is prime. Given an integer N, if there is no integer from 2, 3, ..., N/2 that can divide N, then N is a prime integer; otherwise, N is not prime.

Be aware that there are faster algorithms. The previous definition is simple and straightforward but not efficient at all.

Use 139 as the example. The quotient of 139/2 = 69. Thus, as long as no integers from 2 – 69 can divide 139, then 139 is prime; otherwise 139 is not prime.

Let's follow the given instructions to evaluate the number 139.

1. Open a blank worksheet, enter 139 in cell A1.

2. Enter 2 and 3 in cells B1 and B2, respectively.

3. Select both cells B1 and B2; autofill to cell B68 such that the series 2, 3, 4, 5, ..., 69 are in cells B1:B68. The reason to stop at B68 is because the quotient of 139/2 = 69 (Note, B68 = 69).

4. Enter =A\$1/B1 cell C1. Autofill from C1 to C68.

5. Enter =C1 - INT(C1) in cell D1. Autofill from D1 to D68.

6. If there is a number between 2 and 69 that can divide 139, then there must be a zero in D1:D68. Our next task is to count how many zeros there are in D1:D68. This requires us to use the function COUNTIF.

    Enter the formula =COUNTIF(D:D, 0) in cell E1. Note that the condition in this formula is "=0." Since 0 is a number and the relational operator is =, this condition can be simplified as just 0. Because E1 = 0, we are sure that 139 is prime. Part of our worksheet should look like Figure 4-17.

	A	B	C	D	E
1	139	2	69.5	0.5	0
2		3	46.33333	0.333333	
3		4	34.75	0.75	
4		5	27.8	0.8	

Figure 4-17. *Determine if a number is prime*

Change A1 to be 138; what do you see? You shall see something similar to Figure 4-18.

	A	B	C	D	E
1	138	2	69	0	6
2		3	46	0	
3		4	34.5	0.5	
4		5	27.6	0.6	
5		6	23	0	

Figure 4-18. *138 is not prime*

Test Yourself: can we make use of the function GCD to evaluate if 139 is prime?[1]

---

[1] The answer is yes. This would be a nice exercise.

Challenge: How can we make this prime-evaluation process automatic for integers less than or equal to 100000000? This is an excellent exercise which we all should try. Be aware that integer 2 is also a prime number.

The Excel file chapter-4-3b.xlsx presents such a product. This file makes use of a much more efficient algorithm to determine if an integer is prime. Please take a look. It is password-protected, and the password is "Prime" (without the quotation marks). Observe that the formulas inside this file are hidden, too.

Review Points

1. Functions CONCATENATE, LEN, MOD, QUOTIENT, GCD, INT, COUNTIF, and probably TEXTJOIN.

2. The operator &.

3. Symmetric encryption.

4. Concepts regarding RSA encryption by public and private keys.

5. Modular arithmetic properties.

6. Conversion between binary and decimal numbers.

7. Skills related to RSA encryption and decryption.

8. Assess whether an integer is prime or not in Excel.

CHAPTER 5

Two-Way Table and Chi-Square Test

Please download the sample Excel files from `https://github.com/hhohho/master-Excel-through-projects` for this chapter's exercises.

In statistics, a two-way table describes the relationship between two categorical variables. Here is a scenario. A medical study compared the assessment of emotional control of patients from two regions A and B to examine if there is any significant regional difference. These patients once had issues with emotional control and have gone through certain treatment procedures that are somewhat different between the two regions. Their emotional control was assessed relative to what it had been before the treatment. The data is shown in Figure 5-1. Here, the two categorical variables are Region which is the explanatory variable with two denominations A and B, and Emotional Control Assessment which is the dependent variable with five outcomes.

	A	B	C
1	**Emotional control Assessment**	**Region A**	**Region B**
2	Much better	85	441
3	Somewhat better	81	398
4	About the same	69	579
5	Somewhat worse	46	292
6	Much worse	21	70

Figure 5-1. *Sample data in a two-way table*

© Hong Zhou 2022

H. Zhou, *Mastering Excel Through Projects*, https://doi.org/10.1007/978-1-4842-7842-0_5

The commonly used statistical method for a two-way table is chi-square method. To apply chi-square method, we must calculate the expected count for each denomination and outcome. By comparing the expected counts against the observed counts (also called the actual counts in this book), we can then determine if there is any statistically significant difference among the outcomes of the denominations. The difference can be a result of random chance. Chi-square method calculates the probability of the random chance. For something to be statistically significant, such a probability generally has to be less than 0.05.

CHITEST, one function for chi-square analysis in Excel, does not automatically compute the expected counts, however. This means that we need to calculate the expected counts ourselves. As the numbers of denominations and outcomes vary in different datasets, we may want to create an Excel worksheet that can conduct chi-square test for any datasets as long as their numbers of denominations and outcomes are in a certain range. This is what this chapter's project is going to demonstrate.

Functions to Learn

There are a few new functions to learn including ISERROR, ADDRESS, and CHITEST. However, we will explain CHITEST when we need to use it. Note that there are two functions in Excel that can perform the chi-square test: CHISQ.TEST and CHITEST. They have the same syntax. We can use either one, but CHITEST has backward compatibility. If you are using a later version of Excel, it is better to use CHISQ.TEST.

ISERROR

Function ISERROR tests if an expression can result in an error. If the expression does, TRUE is returned; otherwise, FALSE is returned. For example, the formula =ISERROR(5/0) returns TRUE, while =ISERROR(3+2) returns FALSE.

ADDRESS

Function ADDRESS was once briefly explained in Chapter 3. It has the syntax ADDRESS(row-number, column-number, [abs_num]). It creates a cell reference from the given row number and column number but treats the cell reference as a text string. Again, the generated cell reference is not a true cell reference; instead, it is a text string only. To convert the text string into a true cell reference, we need to use the function INDIRECT.

For example, =ADDRESS(4, 2) generates a cell reference in text for the cell at the fourth row and the second column: "$B$4". Recall columns A, B, C, … are numbered 1, 2, 3, …, etc.

Does the function ADDRESS only return an absolute cell reference? Not at all. The third optional argument abs_num is used to control the reference type:

- If abs_num = 1 or is not provided, an absolute reference string is generated.

- When abs_num = 2, only the row-index is absolute.

- If abs_num = 3, only the column-index is absolute.

- When abs_num = 4, a relative reference string is returned.

For instance, =ADDRESS(1, 4, 2) returns a text string "D$1", =ADDRESS(1, 4, 3) gives "$D1", and =ADDRESS(1, 4, 4) generates "D1".

Test Yourself: what will =ADDRESS(5, 5, 4) return?[1]

Work on the Project

Open the file chapter-5-1a.xlsx. We will see a worksheet setup like Figure 5-2. In this setup, there are maximum 4 denominations named Domain 1, 2, 3, and 4. There are a maximum of 20 outcomes. Be advised that we can treat the outcomes as denominations and vice versa, and we can easily revise the worksheet to include more denominations. Generally speaking, 4 denominations and 20 outcomes can meet most requirements. In the current example, we have only two domains and five outcomes.

---

[1] "E5."

	A	B	C	D	E	F	G	H	I	J	K	L	M	N	O
1		two-way table/original data									Chi-Square statistic				ERROR=
2		Domain 1	Domain 2	Domain 3	Domain 4		Expected counts			B- x^2	C-x^2	D-X^2	E-x^2	Total X^2	Rows=
3	outcome-1	85	441												columns=
4	outcome-2	81	398												P-Value=
5	outcome-3	69	579												
6	outcome-4	46	292												
7	outcome-5	21	70												
8	outcome-6														
9	outcome-7														
10	outcome-8														
11	outcome-9														
12	outcome-10														
13	outcome-11														
14	outcome-12														
15	outcome-13														
16	outcome-14														
17	outcome-15														
18	outcome-16														
19	outcome-17														
20	outcome-18														
21	outcome-19														
22	outcome-20														

Figure 5-2. *Setup of the project*

Pay attention to the sizes of the "Expected counts" table and the "Chi-Square statistic" table. Because every original count has an expected count and a statistic, these two tables must be as large as the original data table. In addition, cell N3 is allocated to store the "Total x^2," the sum of individual statistic.

Follow the given instructions to complete the project:

1. To compute the expected counts, we must know the total counts. It is a good idea to name this total. Click the Formulas tab ➤ click Name Manager ➤ create a new name S as shown in Figure 5-3.

   Pay close attention here that S represents the sum of B3:E22.

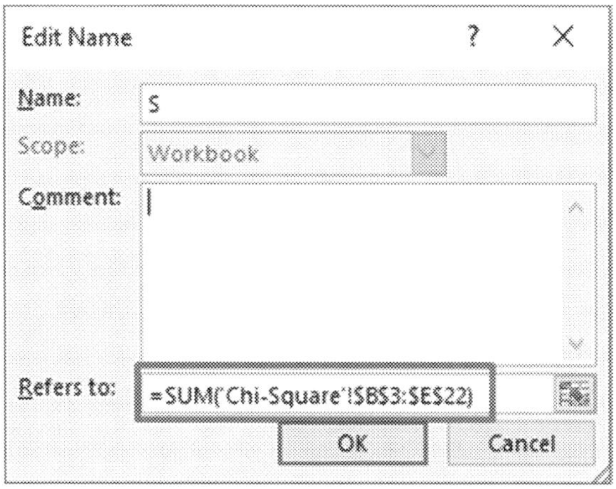

Figure 5-3. *Create the name S*

2.   In cell F3, enter the following formula:

```
=IF(OR(ISERROR(SUM(B$3:B$22) * SUM($B3:$E3) / S),
SUM($B3:$E3)=0, ISBLANK(B3)), "", SUM(B$3:B$22) *
SUM($B3:$E3) / S)
```

Cell F3 stores the expected count for cell B3, that is, the expected count for outcome-1 of domain 1. The expected count for outcome X of domain A is calculated as

Expect count = sum_of_domain_A * sum_of_outcome_X / total_counts

In this specific case, the expected count of B3 is =SUM(B3:B22) * SUM(B3:E3) / S.

The OR function tests the following three conditions:

1.   When there is no data in the worksheet, S = 0, which will result in a divided-by-zero error. Thus, the expression ISERROR(SUM(B$3:B$22) * SUM($B3:$E3) / S) is used to assert if any possible error(s) can happen.

2.   When SUM($B3:$E3)=0, we know that there is no data for outcome-1.

3.   When ISBLANK(B3) = TRUE, we know there is nothing in cell B3.

As long as the OR function returns true, nothing is displayed in cell F3 as defined by the IF function. Otherwise, the result of SUM(B$3:B$22) * SUM($B3:$E3) / S is presented in F3.

133

3. Autofill from F3 to I3, and then autofill together to F22:I22. Part of our worksheet should look like Figure 5-4.

	A	B	C	D	E	F	G	H	I
1	two-way table/original data								
2		Domain 1	Domain 2	Domain 3	Domain 4	Expected counts			
3	outcome-1	85	441			76.29779	449.7022		
4	outcome-2	81	398			69.48031	409.5197		
5	outcome-3	69	579			93.99424	554.0058		
6	outcome-4	46	292			49.02786	288.9721		
7	outcome-5	21	70			13.19981	77.80019		
8	outcome-6								
9	outcome-7								
10	outcome-8								
11	outcome-9								
12	outcome-10								

Figure 5-4. *Expected counts calculated*

4. Enter the formula =IFERROR((B3 - F3)^2 / F3, "") in cell J3.

   The chi-square statistic measures how far away the actual count (the observed count) is from the expected count. The larger the chi-square statistic, the farther the observed count is away from the expected count.

   For a given observed count, its chi-square statistic is

   (observed count – expected count)^2 / expected count

   Thus, (B3 - F3)^2 / F3 calculates the chi-square statistic for B3. Here, we use the IFERROR function to safeguard possible divided-by-zero error.

5. Autofill from J3 to M3, and then autofill together to J22:M22.

6. In cell N3, enter the formula =SUM(J3:M22). This is the total chi-square statistic. At this point, part of our worksheet should look like Figure 5-5.

	F	G	H	I	J	K	L	M	N
1					Chi-Square statistic				
2	Expected counts				B- x^2	C-x^2	D-X^2	E-x^2	Total X^2
3	76.29779	449.7022			0.992538	0.168397			16.77897
4	69.48031	409.5197			1.909941	0.324046			
5	93.99424	554.0058			6.646278	1.127627			
6	49.02786	288.9721			0.186994	0.031726			
7	13.19981	77.80019			4.609385	0.782042			

Figure 5-5. *Chi-square statistic calculated*

7. As we may know, the counts should all be positive. Thus, if some negative numbers are entered inside table B3:E22, we should issue a warning. In cell P1, enter the formula

```
=IF(COUNTIF(B3:E22, "<0") > 0, "Negative number(s) are not allowed", "")
```

It is a good idea for the error message to show up in red. So, select the cell P1 ➤ click the Home tab ➤ inside the Font group, select the red color to apply to cell P1.

After we have entered this formula, we can test its behavior by entering -1 in cell E10.

8. The CHITEST function of Excel has the syntax CHITEST(actual-range, expected-range). As we can imagine, our actual range can change, and, therefore, the expected range will change accordingly. We need a mechanism to detect the actual range and expected range. The principal is that the actual range always starts from cell B3 and the expected range always starts from cell F3 in this worksheet. If we know the number of rows and the number of columns of the actual range, we can then determine both the actual range and the expected range.

In cell P2, enter the formula =COUNT(B3:B22). This counts how many rows of cells contain numerical data. Remember that chi-square analysis only works with numerical data. Therefore, we are expecting numerical data, too.

9. In cell P3, enter the formula =COUNT(B3:E3). This counts how many columns of cells contain numerical data.

10. Given P2 and P3, how do we determine the actual and expected ranges?

    Recall that the actual range starts from cell B3 which is at row 3 and column 2. In this specific example, P2 = 5, which tells us that there are 5 rows including the third row for the actual range. Certainly, the last row is 3 + P2 - 1 = P2 + 2 = 7.

    As the starting column is 2 (column B), the last column = 2 + P3 - 1 = P3 + 1 = P3 + 1 = 3 translated to column C.

    In our worksheet setup, the expected range is immediately right to the actual range. Given that the actual range has a maximum of 4 columns, the starting column of the expected range = 2 + 4, and the last column = 2 + 4 + P3 - 1 = P3 + 5.

    The expected range has the same row range as the actual range, which is from row 3 to row (P2 + 2).

    Therefore, the formula in cell P4 can be

    =IFERROR(CHITEST(B3:INDIRECT(ADDRESS(P2+2, P3+1)), F3:INDIRECT(ADDRESS(P2+2, P3+5))), "")

    In this specific example, because P2 = 5 and P3 = 2, ADDRESS(P2+2, P3+1) = ADDRESS(7, 3), which creates a text "C7".

    INDIRECT(ADDRESS(P2+2, P3+1)) translates "C7" into the cell reference C7. Thus, we get the proper actual range B3:C7.

    Similarly, F3:INDIRECT(ADDRESS(P2+2, P3+5)) gives us the proper expected range F3:G7.

    IFERROR function is used to make sure when the actual range does not contain proper data; nothing is displayed in cell P4.

    CHITEST computes the famous probability P-value and stores it inside cell P4. Since in this specific example, it is less than 0.05, we can conclude that there is statistically significant difference between the outcomes of domain 1 and domain 2.

By now, our worksheet should look like Figure 5-6.

	A	B	C	D	E	F	G	H	I	J	K	L	M	N	O	P
1		two-way table/original data									Chi-Square statistic				ERROR=	
2		Domain 1	Domain 2	Domain 3	Domain 4		Expected counts			B- x²	C-x²	D-x²	E-x²	Total X²	Rows=	5
3	outcome-1	85	441			76.29779	449.7022			0.992538	0.168397			16.77897	columns=	2
4	outcome-2	81	398			69.48031	409.5197			1.909941	0.324046				P-Value=	0.002134
5	outcome-3	69	579			93.99424	554.0058			6.646278	1.127627					
6	outcome-4	46	292			49.02786	288.9721			0.186994	0.031726					
7	outcome-5	21	70			13.19981	77.80019			4.609385	0.782042					
8	outcome-6															
9	outcome-7															
10	outcome-8															
11	outcome-9															
12	outcome-10															
13	outcome-11															
14	outcome-12															
15	outcome-13															
16	outcome-14															
17	outcome-15															
18	outcome-16															
19	outcome-17															
20	outcome-18															
21	outcome-19															
22	outcome-20															

Figure 5-6. *Chi-square test completed*

We can certainly change the data in the B3:E22 range. For example, if the actual data is revised to be the same as shown in Figure 5-7, we shall notice that everything in the worksheet is automatically updated accordingly.

	B	C	D	E	F	G	H	I	J	K	L	M	N	O	P
1	two-way table/original data									Chi-Square statistic				ERROR=	
2	Domain 1	Domain 2	Domain 3	Domain 4		Expected counts			B- x²	C-x²	D-x²	E-x²	Total X²	Rows=	4
3	38	875	17	11	25.05215	893.5267	16.35825	6.06285	6.691911	0.384141	0.025176	4.020462	31.78056	columns=	4
4	122	3917	72	21	110.0058	3923.541	71.83029	26.62242	1.307749	0.010906	0.000401	1.187404		P-Value=	0.000217288
5	51	2496	43	12	69.27279	2470.73	45.23292	16.76465	4.820002	0.258463	0.110228	1.354152			
6	8	523	11	9	14.66922	523.2022	9.578531	3.550085	3.032097	7.81E-05	0.210948	8.36644			
7															
8															
9															
10															
11															
12															

Figure 5-7. *After revising the actual data, everything is automatically updated*

The file chapter-5-1b.xlsx presents the final product. Again, if we want this product to be used by other people, it would be a good idea to protect cells except those in the actual range. The file chapter-5-1c.xlsx is password protected, and the password is "Excel" (without the quotation marks).

Challenge: At step 10, the formula to compute the P-value makes use of the ADDRESS and INDIRECT functions to obtain proper ranges. The formula is a little bit complicated. If we make use of the OFFSET function, we can simplify the formula significantly. Please study the OFFSET function to try it. Refer to the file chapter-5-1d. xlsx which employs the OFFSET function.

Chapter Tip

So far, we have been creating names through Name Manager. This is the traditional fashion. We can also create names for data tables in a different way. Follow the given instructions to experience this interesting tip:

1. Open a blank worksheet, and enter some data as shown in Figure 5-8. Remember to leave the data inside columns H and I. If you leave them in A1:B6, remember to make the proper transition from my instructions.

H	I	J
Name	Wage	
A	957	
B	527	
C	946	
D	162	
E	173	

Figure 5-8. *A sample table*

2. Select table H1:I6 ➤ click the Home tab ➤ in the Styles group, click "Format as Table" as shown in Figure 5-9.

3. A screen shows up with many different table styles. Select one as you like. For example, I selected the one as the arrow pointed in Figure 5-9.

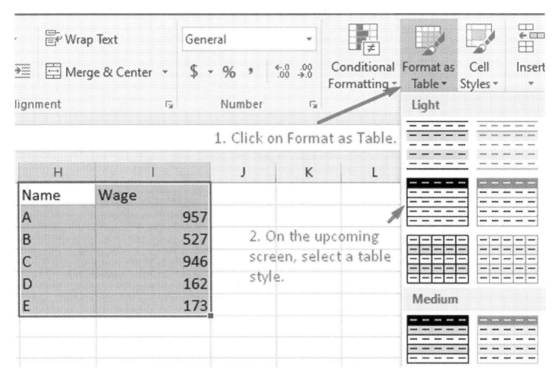

Figure 5-9. Format as Table

4. A small window named Format As Table jumps out as shown in Figure 5-10. Make sure that the formula is =$H$1:$I$6, and leave the option "My table has headers" checked. Click OK.

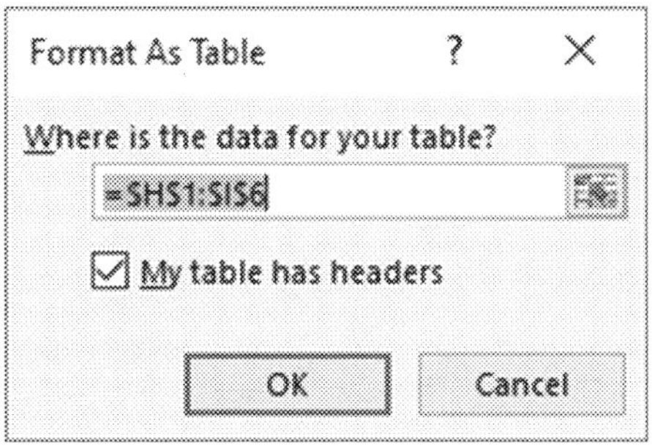

Figure 5-10. My table has headers

5. Now, the array H1:I6 has been formatted as a table. Click anywhere inside the table ➤ the Design tab shows up, and click it ➤ the Table Name box appears ➤ rename the table "wage." This process is illustrated in Figure 5-11.

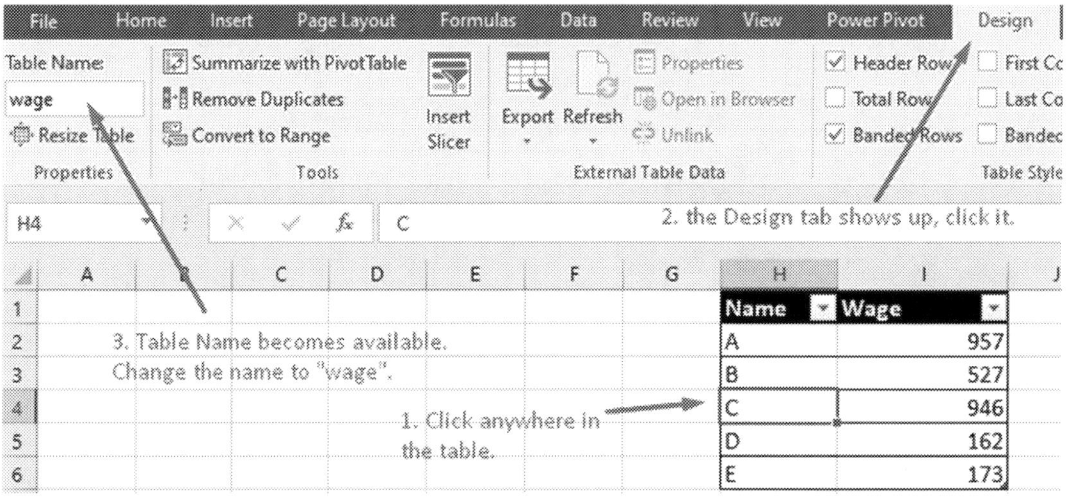

Figure 5-11. *Rename the table wage*

6. Now, if we click the Formulas tab ➤ Name Manager, we will see the name "wage" there.

Since our table has headers, we can access each column based on its header.

Assume we want to sum the wages (in column I) and leave the result in cell D2. In D2, enter a formula but do not complete it. Instead, leave it as "=SUM(wage[".

At this moment, a small menu comes up as shown in Figure 5-12. Use the down arrow key on our keyboard to select Wage, and then hit the tab key.

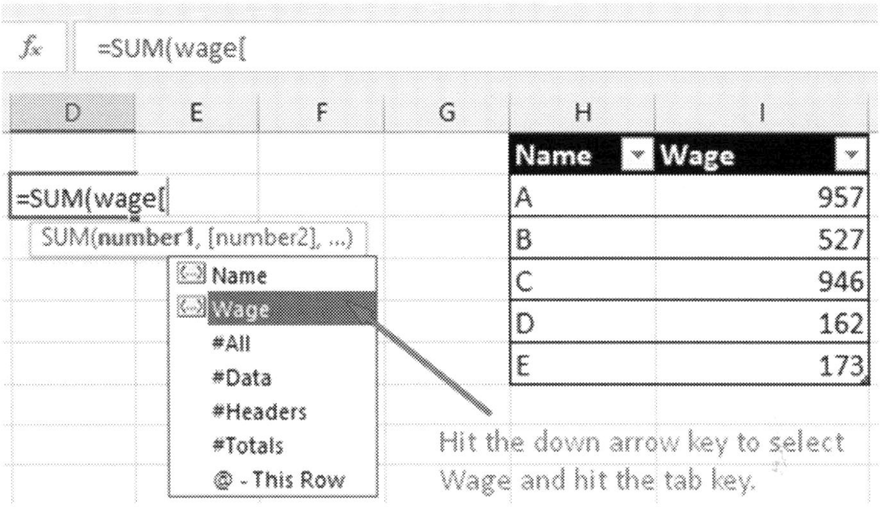

Figure 5-12. *Sum the wage*

7. Complete the formula as shown in Figure 5-13.

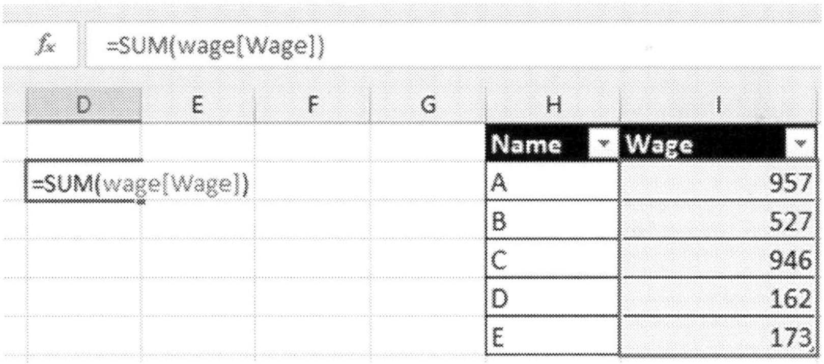

Figure 5-13. *Complete the SUM function*

8. We can also conduct other operations on the data. For example, we can average the wages by entering the formula =AVERAGE(wage[Wage]) in cell D3. This time, we do not wait for the small menu; we can directly type this formula in cell D3.

9. Enter the formula =INDEX(wage[Wage], 2) in cell D4.

Our worksheet should look like Figure 5-14.

D	E	F	G	H	I
				Name ▾	Wage ▾
2765				A	957
553				B	527
527				C	946
				D	162
				E	173

Figure 5-14. *Other operations on the table data*

Accessing table columns by name is a classical feature in programming languages Python and R. Certainly, Excel is becoming more and more programmable.

Review Points

1. Functions ISERROR, ADDRESS, and CHITEST (and probably the OFFSET function).

2. Using the function COUNT to determine the numerical data range.

3. Knowledge of two-way table and chi-square statistic.

4. The skill to construct an automatic two-way table for chi-square P-value calculation.

5. Another way of naming tables and accessing table columns by name.

CHAPTER 6

Kaplan–Meier Analysis

Please download the sample Excel files from `https://github.com/hhohho/master-Excel-through-projects` for this chapter's exercises.

The Kaplan-Meier method, also known as Kaplan-Meier estimator, is widely used in clinical research to estimate the likely survival times of patients after a certain treatment. As a nonparametric statistical method, it can also be used in other applications. For example, it can be used to estimate how long people are likely to remain unemployed after a job loss. In recent years, it is also used to help find genetic factors that can provide better prognosis for cancer patients.

Poor prognosis of cancer patients has been a challenge for many years, and therefore, medical researchers turn their eyes to modern technologies, thanks to the success of the Human Genome Project. Researchers have found that certain groups of genes, especially their expression levels, can provide better prognosis for certain cancer patients. The project in this chapter is to dive into a simple example in which we download colon adenocarcinoma (COAD) clinical data from the National Center for Biotechnology Information (NCBI) and use the data to study if the expression levels of the IL11 gene can be a potential prognosis indicator for COAD patients by applying Kaplan-Meier survival analysis on the obtained data. To apply Kaplan-Meier survival analysis, we need to divide the patients into two cohorts based on their gene expression levels (high or low). If there are significantly more patients in one cohort who survived longer, for example, the cohort with low IL11 expression levels, then we can assume that a patient with lower IL11 expression level has a higher chance to survive longer.

© Hong Zhou 2022
H. Zhou, *Mastering Excel Through Projects*, https://doi.org/10.1007/978-1-4842-7842-0_6

Kaplan-Meier analysis is often visually presented as a chart. A typical chart would look like Figure 6-1. In Figure 6-1, the x-axis marks the survival periods, and each period is of 30 days. As we can notice, the difference in survival probability between the two cohorts becomes larger when the survival time period goes up. This is usually a positive sign that the gene in study is a potential prognosis indicator. Please observe that the two lines are composed of either vertical or horizontal segments, which is the challenging part in conducting Kaplan-Meier analysis in Excel. Today, many statistical tools such as R and SPSS can allow us to perform Kaplan-Meier analysis easily, especially R. With a little bit of programming, R can automate Kaplan-Meier analysis (including drawing the charts) on many samples at one time. Nevertheless, this chapter will demonstrate that we can accomplish Kaplan-Meier survival analysis by using only the built-in features of Excel.

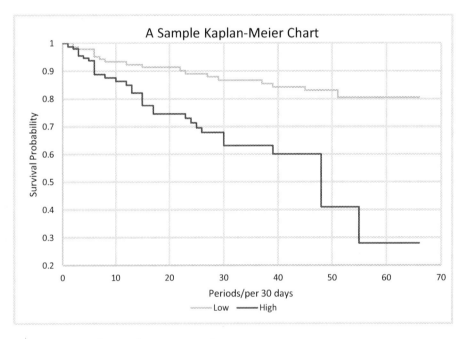

Figure 6-1. *A sample Kaplan-Meier chart*

Functions to Learn

The project of this chapter makes use of these functions: SUM, IF, INT, LOOKUP, MAX, COUNTIFS, MEDIAN, and CHITEST (or CHISQ.TEST). Thus, there are only two new functions with which we must become familiar before we step on our project. Again, learning functions is just the first step; how to make creative uses of them is the key skill that this book is trying to exhibit.

MEDIAN

Given a sequence of data points, for example, 1, 3, 3, 4, 6, 8, 9, 100, 100, since there are nine (odd) numbers, the median of this sequence is the middle one: the fifth number which is 6. If the sequence is 1, 3, 3, 4, 6, 8, 9, 100 instead (eight numbers), the median is then the average of the two middle numbers, that is, $(4 + 6)/2 = 5$.

Median is different from mean (average). For example, given the sequence 1, 3, 3, 4, 6, 8, 9, 100, its mean is 16.75. If we divide these eight numbers into two groups by average, we will get seven numbers below the average and only one number above the average.

However, if we divide these eight numbers by median, then we will get four numbers below the median and four numbers above the median. Clearly, median is resistant to outliers (the number 100 is the outlier in this case) in a dataset, but mean is not.

In Excel, we can apply the MEDIAN function as `=MEDIAN(1, 3, 3, 4, 6, 8, 9, 100)`, or if these numbers are stored in cells A1:A8, a simpler formula is `=MEDIAN(A1:A8)`.

COUNTIFS

COUNTIFS is a very popular and must-learn Excel function. It is available in version 2010 and higher. It has an elder brother named COUNTIF. However, COUNTIFS is much more powerful than COUNTIF. Whatever COUNTIF can accomplish, COUNTIFS can, too. But COUNTIFS can accomplish other tasks that COUNTIF is not capable of at all. For example, in this chapter's project, we must use COUNTIFS instead of COUNTIF. Once we have learned COUNTIFS, we should always use COUNTIFS even when COUNTIF is applicable.

COUNTIFS counts the number of cells that meet a given set of conditions. If there are more than one condition, it then counts the number of times when all the conditions are met. Its syntax is COUNTIFS(criteria_range1, criteria1, [criteria_range2, criteria2], ...).

Open the file chapter-6-1a.xlsx, and stay on the COUNTIFS-1 worksheet (there are five worksheets). As we can see in this worksheet and shown in Figure 6-2, there are 200 students, and we are counting how many of them have both their computer science and finance scores greater than or equal to 90.

	A	B	C	D	E	F	G	H
1	Student	CS Score	Finance Score					
2	12858	83	79		Your answer=			
3	27963	49	81		Here is the scenario: A Wall Street company			
4	51530	68	53		is looking for young students who are skilled			
5	16421	60	92		in both computer science and finance			
6	71460	77	73		(usually called Quantitative Finance). So, we			
7	92881	71	49		are going to count how many students there			
8	57721	54	92		are who meet the minimum requirement:			
9	13274	51	75		their computer science score and finance			
10	52516	96	43		score must both be >= 90.			
11	17652	98	64					
12	96643	93	91					
13	10729	70	40					

Figure 6-2. *The example of COUNTIFS*

The formula should be =COUNTIFS(B2:B201, ">=90", C2:C201, ">=90"). The first range is B2:B201, and the first criteria is ">=90". Note that if the criteria are in text, they must be enclosed in a pair of quotation marks. The second range is C2:C201, and the second criteria is ">=90", too.

Switch to the worksheet COUNTIFS-2. As shown in Figure 6-3, the criteria are specified in cells E1 and F1. In this case, our formula should be =COUNTIFS(B2:B201, E1, C2:C201, F1).

	A	B	C	D	E	F	G	H
1	Student	CS Score	Finance Score		>90	>90		
2	12858	83	79		Your answer=			
3	27963	49	81		We are counting how many students who			
4	51530	68	53		meet the minimum requirement: the criteria			
5	16421	60	92		for their computer science score and finance			
6	71460	77	73		score are stored in cells E1 and F1			
7	92881	71	49					
8	57721	54	92					

Figure 6-3. *When the criteria are specified in cells*

Sometimes, the criteria do not come with the ">" symbol as shown in Figure 6-4. In this case, our formula should be =COUNTIFS(B2:B201, ">"&E1, C2:C201, ">"&F1). Be aware that the & operator is frequently used to concatenate two strings into one. For example, the expression ">"&E1 concatenates ">" and "95" together as ">95".

	A	B	C	D	E	F	G	H
1	Student	CS Score	Finance Score		95	93		
2	12858	83	79		Your answer=			
3	27963	49	81		We are counting how many students who			
4	51530	68	53		meet the minimum requirement: their			
5	16421	60	92		computer science score must be greater than			
6	71460	77	73		the value in cell E1, and their finance score			
7	92881	71	49		must be greater than the value in cell F1.			
8	57721	54	92					

Figure 6-4. *Another type of criteria for COUNTIFS*

The fourth worksheet presents a different question regarding the use of COUNTIFS. It asks how many students scored no less than 80 but less than 90 in computer science. This time, the same column of data must be used twice. The correct formula is then

=COUNTIFS(B2:B201, ">=80", B2:B201, "<90")

The fifth worksheet is for practice only. I recommend you to try it out. The file chapter-6-1b.xlsx has all the answers to the practices.

Work on the Project

Open chapter-6-2a.xlsx. We will see a dataset looking like Figure 6-5. The data here was downloaded from NCBI and has been preprocessed such that it is ready for Kaplan-Meier analysis.

	A	B	C	D
1	Sample code	Gene expression	Days	Outcome
2	TCGA-AY-4071	92.228	29	dead
3	TCGA-AA-3818	52.7287	30	dead
4	TCGA-AZ-4323	136.9966	43	dead
5	TCGA-5M-AAT4	14.6299	49	dead
6	TCGA-AZ-6608	19.5918	59	dead
374	TCGA-QG-A5YX	4.91	526	censored
375	TCGA-QG-A5Z1	5.7205	202	censored
376	TCGA-QG-A5Z2	20.2263	449	censored
377	TCGA-QL-A97D	140.7652	295	censored
378	TCGA-RU-A8FL	26.7938	921	censored
379	TCGA-SS-A7HO	16.5364	1829	censored
380	TCGA-WS-AB45	785.6705	2038	censored

Figure 6-5. *A slice of the COAD dataset*

Below is a brief explanation of the dataset:

- *Sample code*: The codes of the patient COAD samples. They are irrelevant to our practice.

- *Gene expression*: The IL11 gene expression levels measured from patient tumor tissue samples.

- *Days*: The number of days between when a patient was diagnosed with COAD and when the patient's outcome was identified. In another word, how many days a patient has stayed alive to the knowledge of the study.

- *Outcome*: The outcomes of all patients in the study. There are two types of outcomes. One is "dead," indicating the patient passed away. Another is "censored," indicating the study lost track of the patient for various reason(s) and, therefore, has no further information about the patient except knowing that the patient was still alive at the time of "censored."

A close look at the data discloses that the outcomes of the majority of patients are censored. Censored data introduces uncertainty into the study. A large portion of censored data can make the study result unreliable. Nevertheless, we will continue our project and see what we can discover.

Follow the given instructions to complete our project:

1. Enter "Period" in cell E1 (without the quotation marks). Every medical study has a timeline, that is, a starting date and a completion date. It is very common to divide the timeline into a number of periods. For example, a medical study of 5 years may have 60 periods (each period is 1 month) or 20 periods (each period is about 90 days).

2. Enter the formula =INT((C2 - 1) / 30) + 1 in cell E2. Our period has 30 days. Period 1 is the first study period, and period 0 is the initial point right before the study starts. This formula can guarantee that patients passed away or left on the thirtieth day are included in period 1.

    Be advised that there are some patients whose "Days" are recorded as 0. They are placed in period 0.

    Autofill from E2 to E380.

3. Type "Median" in cell F1 and the formula =MEDIAN(B2:B380) in cell F2.

    We are going to divide the samples into two clusters. One cluster has gene expression levels higher than the median, while another cluster has gene expression levels below the median. We can use either mean or median to make the division. Because median can divide the samples into two clusters of equal size, median is selected in this project.

Our goal is to examine if the two clusters exhibit statistically significant difference in survival rates by following the Kaplan-Meier method.

4. Type "Max" in cell F3, and enter the formula =MAX(E2:E55) in cell F4. F4 should have the number 102.

We should have noticed that the dataset is sorted based on outcomes. All samples with outcome "dead" are listed first, and their range is E2:E55. We need to find the largest period of these samples marked "dead." There might be a larger period number for censored samples, but for Kaplan Meier analysis, it does not matter.

If the dataset is not sorted based on outcomes, the use of MAX function here is not going to work correctly. In such a case, we may hope to have a MAXIFS function similar to COUNTIFS. Yes, Office 365 and Excel 2019 do have such a MAXIFS function. Try to use it if it is available in your Excel. By using MAXIFS, the dataset does not need to be sorted. Such a formula using MAXIFS should be =MAXIFS(E2:E380, D2:D380, "dead").

5. Type "period" in cell G2. Enter 0 in cell G3 and 1 in cell G4. Select both G3 and G4 so as to autofill to cell G105. This action creates a series from 1 to 102 which is the max period for the "dead" outcome.

6. Select cells H1:L1 ➤ click the Home tab ➤ click Merge & Center as shown in Figure 6-6.

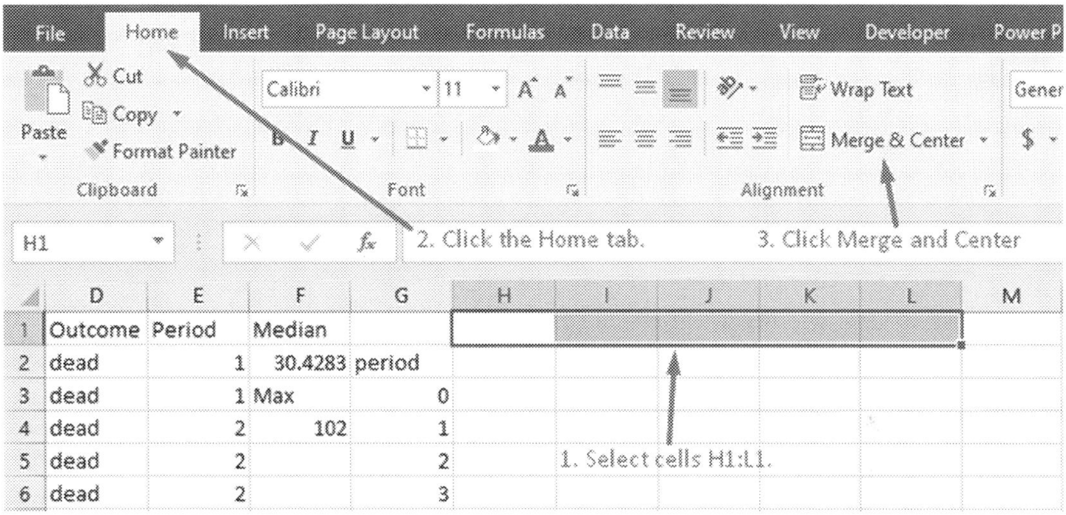

Figure 6-6. *Merge & Center*

After that, type "< Median" inside the merged cell. Since H1 is the first cell in H1:L1, the merged cell is referenced as H1. Columns H to L are to store data for the cluster whose gene expression levels are below the calculated median in cell F2.

At this moment, part of our worksheet should look like Figure 6-6.

7. Enter "at risk," "censored," "dead," "survived," and "probability" in cells H2, I2, J2, K2, and L2, respectively (without quotation marks).

    Be advised that "at risk" represents the number of alive patients in a given period. It is the starting number of alive patients in a given period subtracted by the number of patients censored in the same period.

8. Merge cells M1:Q1, and type "> Median" inside the merged cell. This merged cell is referenced by M1 because M1 is the first cell in M1:Q1.

9. Enter "at risk," "censored," "dead," "survived," and "probability" in cells M2, N2, O2, P2, and Q2, respectively. Part of our worksheet should look like Figure 6-7.

	D	E	F	G	H	I	J	K	L	M	N	O	P	Q
1	Outcome	Period	Median				< Median					> Median		
2	dead	1	30.4283	period	at risk	censored	dead	survived	probability	at risk	censored	dead	survived	probability
3	dead	1	Max	0										
4	dead	2	102	1										
5	dead	2		2										
6	dead	2		3										
7	dead	3		4										
8	dead	3		5										
9	dead	3		6										
10	dead	3		7										
11	dead	4		8										
12	dead	5		9										

Figure 6-7. *Set up the worksheet before calculation*

10. Enter in cell H3 the following formula:

    =COUNTIFS(B$2:B$380, "<"&$F$2, E$2:E$380, ">="&G3) - I3

    This formula counts how many patients are in period 0 and have their gene expression levels below the median. Note that those patients censored in this period (I3) must be excluded.

    Observe that in the recent formula, for the range B$2:B$380, the criteria are "<"&$F$2 (less than the median). However, for the range E$2:E$380, its criteria is ">="&G3. One important understanding here is that any patients who appear in a later period must have lived through all the periods before. For example, patients appearing in period 5 must have been in periods 0, 1, 2, 3, and 4. This is why the relational operator is ">=" instead of "=" in the criteria ">="&G3.

    Autofill from H3 to H105.

11. Enter =COUNTIFS(B$2:B$380, "<"&F$2, D$2:D$380, "censored", E$2:E$380, G3) in cell I3. This formula counts how many patients are censored in period 0 and have their gene expression levels below the median.

    Autofill from I3 to I105.

    We can notice that some numbers in H3:H105 are changing while we are completing the formulas in column I.

12. Enter `=COUNTIFS(B$2:B$380, "<"&F$2, D$2:D$380, "dead",` `E$2:E$380, G3)` in cell J3. This formula counts how many patients whose gene expression levels are below the median become dead during period 0. Autofill from J3 to J105.

13. Enter formula `=H3 - J3` in cell K3. This is the number of patients who survived period 0.

    Autofill from K3 to K105.

14. Enter formula `=K3/H3` in cell L3. This is the probability to survive period 0 for the patients whose gene expression levels are below the median.

    Do not autofill.

15. Enter `=L3 * K4 / H4` in cell L4. Note that this is how the probability is calculated in the Kaplan-Meier method. Except for the period 0, the probability of every period (also known as survival rate) is calculated as

    (the probability of the previous period) * (survived in this period) / (at risk in this period).

    This is because to live through period N, a patient must have lived through all the periods before the period N.

    Autofill from L4 to L105. At this point, part of our worksheet should look like Figure 6-8.

F	G	H	I	J	K	L	M	N
Median				< Median				
30.4283	period	at risk	censored	dead	survived	probability	at risk	censored
Max	0	184	5	0	184	1		
102	1	157	27	0	157	1		
	2	138	19	2	136	0.9855072		
	3	131	5	1	130	0.9779843		
	4	125	5	0	125	0.9779843		
	5	116	9	0	116	0.9779843		
	6	106	10	3	103	0.9503055		
	7	99	4	1	98	0.9407064		
	8	93	5	1	92	0.9305913		
	9	82	10	0	82	0.9305913		
	10	80	2	0	80	0.9305913		

Figure 6-8. *Calculate probabilities for one cluster*

16. Similarly, enter in cell M3 the formula

    =COUNTIFS(B$2:B$380, ">"&$F$2, E$2:E$380, ">="&G3) - N3

    Autofill from M3 to M105.

17. Enter =COUNTIFS(B$2:B$380, ">"&F$2, D$2:D$380, "censored", E$2:E$380, G3) in cell N3.

    Autofill from N3 to N105.

18. Enter =COUNTIFS(B$2:B$380, ">"&F$2, D$2:D$380, "dead", E$2:E$380, G3) in cell O3.

    Autofill from O3 to O105.

19. Enter =M3 - O3 in cell P3.

    Autofill from P3 to P105.

20. Enter =P3 / M3 in cell Q3. Do not autofill.

21. Enter =Q3 * P4 / M4 in cell Q4.

    Autofill from Q4 to Q105. At this moment, part of our worksheet should look like Figure 6-9.

	G	H	I	J	K	L	M	N	O	P	Q
1					< Median				> Median		
2	period	at risk	censored	dead	survived	probability	at risk	censored	dead	survived	probability
3	0	184	5	0	184	1	188	1	0	188	1
4	1	157	27	0	157	1	160	28	2	158	0.9875
5	2	138	19	2	136	0.9855072	122	36	1	121	0.9794057
6	3	131	5	1	130	0.9779843	117	4	3	114	0.9542928
7	4	125	5	0	125	0.9779843	110	4	1	109	0.9456174
8	5	116	9	0	116	0.9779843	103	6	1	102	0.9364366
9	6	106	10	3	103	0.9503055	94	8	5	89	0.8866262
10	7	99	4	1	98	0.9407064	78	11	0	78	0.8866262
11	8	93	5	1	92	0.9305913	72	6	1	71	0.8743119
12	9	82	10	0	82	0.9305913	68	3	0	68	0.8743119
13	10	80	2	0	80	0.9305913	63	5	1	62	0.860434

Figure 6-9. Count the patients in various categories

22.   Enter "risk-for-death," "<M-expected-death," and ">M-expected-death" in cells R2, S2, and T2, respectively (without quotation marks).

risk-for-death = the total deaths in a period divided by the total patients at risk in the period. It measures the risk of death in a given period.

expected-death = (the number of patients at risk in a cluster) * risk-for-death.

<M-expected-death records the expected death count of the cluster with gene expression levels less than the median.

>M-expected-death records the expected death count of the cluster with gene expression levels greater than the median.

23.   Enter =SUM(J3, O3)/SUM(H3, M3) in cell R3. Autofill from R3 to R105.

24.   Enter =H3 * R3 in cell S3 and =M3 * R3 in cell T3. Select both S3 and T3, and autofill them together to S105:T105.

25.   Type "Observed Death" and "Expected Death" in cells U2 and U3, respectively.

26. Type "< Median" and "> Median" in cells V1 and W1, respectively.

   At this point, part of our worksheet should look like Figure 6-10.

R	S	T	U	V	W
				< Median	> Median
risk-for-death	<M-expected-death	>M-expected-death	Observed Death		
0	0	0	Expected Death		
0.006309148	0.990536278	1.009463722			
0.011538462	1.592307692	1.407692308			
0.016129032	2.112903226	1.887096774			
0.004255319	0.531914894	0.468085106			
0.00456621	0.529680365	0.470319635			
0.04	4.24	3.76			
0.005649718	0.559322034	0.440677966			
0.012121212	1.127272727	0.872727273			

Figure 6-10. *Risk and expected values calculated*

27. Now, it is time to complete table V2:W3.

   Enter =SUM(J3:J105) in cell V2. This formula adds all the observed dead outcomes for the cluster whose gene expression levels are below the median.

28. Enter =SUM(O3:O105) in cell W2. This formula adds all the observed dead outcomes for the cluster whose gene expression levels are above the median.

29. Enter =SUM(S3:S105) in cell V3 and =SUM(T3:T105) in cell W3.

   These are the expected death outcomes.

30. Enter "P-value=" in cell U5.

31. Enter =CHITEST(V2:W2, V3:W3) in cell V5. The CHITEST function computes the P-value of our Kaplan-Meier survival analysis. Since the P-value is about 0.0155 which is less than 0.05, it indicates that the difference in the numbers of deaths between the two clusters is statistically significant. Because survival probability is directly related to death rate, this further shows that the two clusters have significantly different survival probabilities.

Part of our worksheet should look like Figure 6-11.

U	V	W
	< Median	> Median
Observed Death	23	31
Expected Death	31.75430471	22.24569529
P-value=	0.015501756	

Figure 6-11. *Calculate the P-value*

32. We need to draw the Kaplan-Meier chart as shown in Figure 6-1. This is a scatter chart in which the X-axis is the survival period, and the Y-axis is the survival probability (survival rate). As the line segments in the chart are either horizontal or vertical, we need to reorganize data in the three columns: periods (column G), probability for <Median cluster (column L), and probability for >Median cluster (column Q).

    Enter "Period," "IL11-Low," and "IL11-High" in cells U8, V8, and W8, respectively.

    IL11-Low represents the survival probability for the cluster <Median (from column L).

    IL11-High represents the survival probability for the cluster >Median (from column Q).

33. Take a close look at Figure 6-1. When the line segment is horizontal, what does that mean? When it is vertical, what does it tell us?

    Well, a vertical line segment tells us that the probability drops while the period does not change. This gives us two hints. The first one is that each period number (except for the first period) must be repeated. But when a period is repeated, how can the probability drop? Take period 2 as an example. After it is repeated as 2_1 and 2_2, they can have different probability values such that the probability drops to display a vertical segment.

Thus, we need to repeat every period number except for the very first period (0) and the last period. For example, our periods should be 0, 1, 1, 2, 2, 3, 3, 4, 4, ...

A horizontal line segment discloses that the probability does not change even when the period increments. This indicates that when the period increments, the probability carries over. For example, given the periods 0, 1, 1, 2, 2, 3, 3, 4, 4, the survival probability of the first period 2 should be the same as that of the second period 1. Only the probability of the second period 2 has the true probability of period 2 which is carried over to the first period 3. From the first period 2 to the second period 2, the probability drops vertically if there is a drop.

So, enter 0 and 1 in cells U9 and U10, respectively.

34. We want to obtain a series like 0, 1, 1, 2, 2, 3, 3, 4, 4, ..., 101, 101, 102. How?

Enter the formula =IF(U10>U9, U10, U10+1) in cell U11.

Notice that this formula resides in cell U11. This formula accomplishes the two cases.

   a. If the cell right before U11 (which is U10) is larger than the two cells before U11 (which is U9), an increment was just made; therefore, U11, the current cell, should repeat the last period number (U10).

   b. Else, this cell should increment the period number of the last cell by 1 (U10 + 1).

Autofill from U11 to U212 such that U212 = 102. Recall that the last period is 102.

35. Enter the formula =LOOKUP($U9, $G$3:$G$105, $L$3:$L$105) in cell V9. This formula finds the survival probability of period 0 for the cluster whose gene expression levels are lower than the median.

Do not autofill.

36. Enter the formula =LOOKUP($U9, $G$3:$G$105, $Q$3:$Q$105) in cell W9. This formula finds the survival probability of period 0 for the cluster whose gene expression levels are above the median.

    Do not autofill.

37. Enter the formula =IF(U10>U9, V9, LOOKUP(U10, $G$3:$G$105, $L$3:$L$105)) in cell V10.

    If U10 > U9, the probability should carry over from the cell right before V10, which is V9.

    Else, use the corresponding period number in U10 to find a matched survival probability.

    Autofill from V10 to V212.

38. Enter =IF(U10>U9, W9, LOOKUP(U10, $G$3:$G$105, $Q$3:$Q$105)) in cell W10.

    Autofill from W10 to W212.

    Part of our worksheet should look like Figure 6-12.

U	V	W
Period	IL11-Low	IL11-High
0	1	1
1	1	1
1	1	0.9875
2	1	0.9875
2	0.985507246	0.979405738
3	0.985507246	0.979405738
3	0.97798429	0.95429277
4	0.97798429	0.95429277
4	0.97798429	0.945617381
5	0.97798429	0.945617381
5	0.97798429	0.93643663
6	0.97798429	0.93643663
6	0.95030549	0.886626171

Figure 6-12. *Some numbers are repeated*

39. Select cells U8:W212. Click the Insert tab ➤ select Scatter Charts. This procedure is depicted in Figure 6-13.

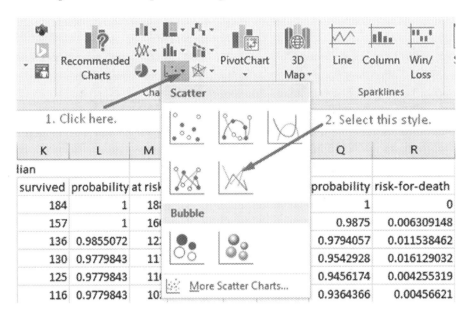

Figure 6-13. *Draw a scatter chart*

40. The default chart needs to be modified. The first modification is on the Y-axis because the maximum should not be more than 1.0. Follow the instructions in Figure 6-14 to adjust the Y-axis options.

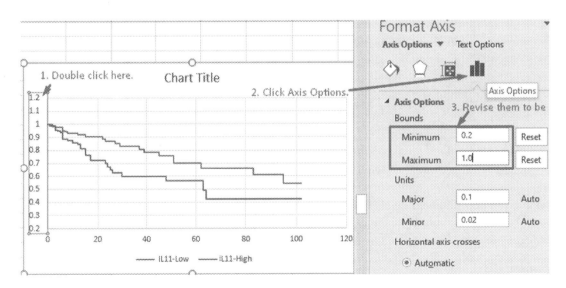

Figure 6-14. *Readjust the Y-axis options*

41. We need to add a title to the chart and set the X-axis title and
     Y-axis title. See Figure 6-15.

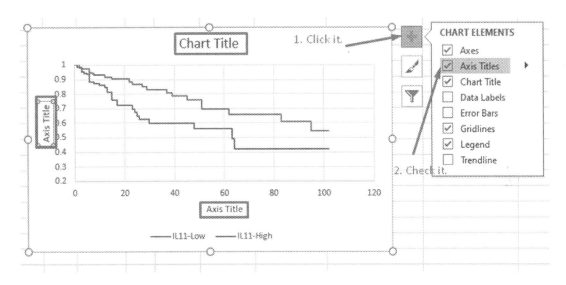

Figure 6-15. *Add chart titles*

42. We can also change the colors of the two lines to be green and red,
     respectively. Follow the instructions in Figure 6-16 to change the
     colors of the two lines one by one.

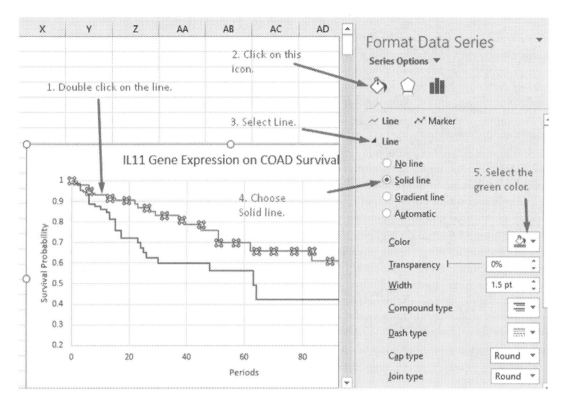

Figure 6-16. *Change the color of one line*

The final chart may look like Figure 6-17. Though the P-value = 0.0155, the chart does not support the notion that IL11 gene expression level can be a good predictor for COAD patient survival probability. The first reason was mentioned before: there are too many censored data points. The second reason is that in a typical Kaplan-Meier analysis, not only we need to have a very small P-value, but also we need to observe that the distance between the two lines goes wider and wider when the number of periods increases.

The final result can be found in the file chapter-6-2b.xlsx.

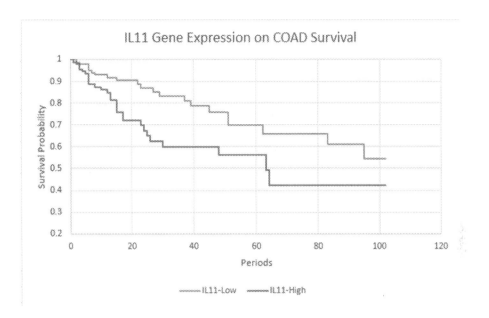

Figure 6-17. *The final chart*

Chapter Tip

This chapter's tip will be on Excel form controls.

By default, the Developer tab does not show up on the Excel menu. Let's click File ➤ Options ➤ on the Excel Options window, click Customize Ribbon ➤ check the option Developer as shown in Figure 6-18.

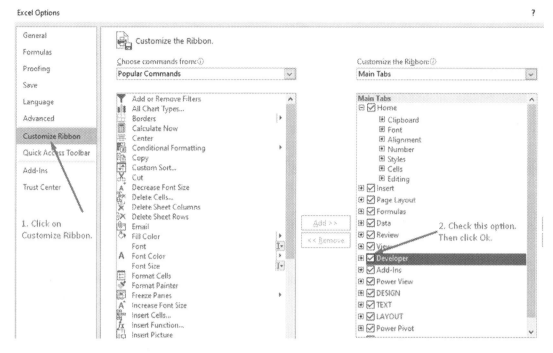

Figure 6-18. *Enable Developer tab*

Now, the Developer tab shows up on top of our Excel worksheet. Let's follow the given instructions to experience a little bit of Excel form controls:

1. Click the Developer tab ➤ click Insert ➤ click the Scroll Bar (Form Control) to select it as shown in Figure 6-19. After the Scroll Bar form control is clicked once, it is selected, and then we are ready to draw a scroll bar in our worksheet.

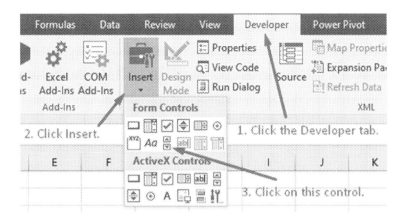

Figure 6-19. *Access Excel Form Controls*

2. Let's draw a scroll bar in our Excel worksheet by pressing down the left mouse button and dragging from left to right. We shall see a scroll bar, similar to the one in Figure 6-20.

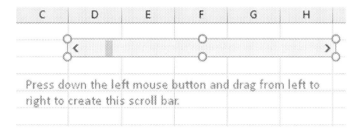

Figure 6-20. *Draw a scroll bar*

3. We are going to link this scroll bar with a cell which holds an integer. In cells A1 and B1, type "Left" and "Right," respectively.

4. In cell A2, enter 50.

5. In cell B2, enter the formula =100 - A2.

6. Right click the scroll bar ➤ click Properties as shown in Figure 6-21.

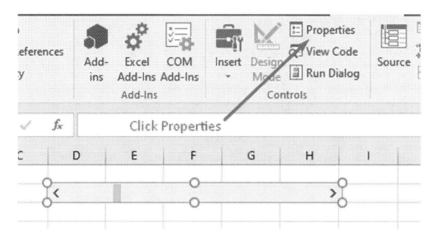

Figure 6-21. *Access Properties of a control*

7. The Format Control window shows up. On this window, select the Control tab ➤ Enter =A2 in the box for "Cell link" ➤ then click OK.

This process is demonstrated in Figure 6-22.

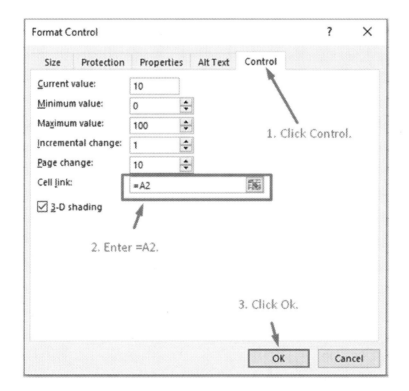

Figure 6-22. *Link the scroll bar to cell A2*

8. The formula =A2 (shown in Figure 6-22) links the scroll bar to the cell A2. This means that we can move the slider to change the number in A2 as shown in Figure 6-23.

Please try to move the slider to experience it.

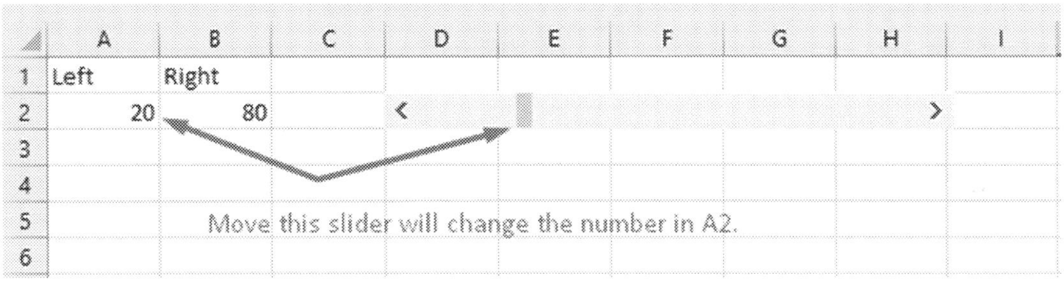

	A	B	C	D	E	F	G	H	I
1	Left	Right							
2	20	80	‹		▮			›	
3									
4									
5		Move this slider will change the number in A2.							
6									

Figure 6-23. *Move the slider to change the number in A2*

9. We can also draw a column chart or a pie chart based on table A1:B2. The chart can be controlled by the scroll bar, too. Figure 6-24 shows a pie chart that can be controlled by the scroll bar.

Move the slider to observe how the pie chart is changing.

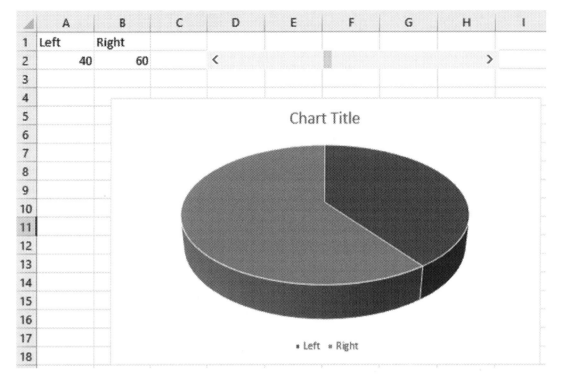

Figure 6-24. *A pie chart controlled by the scroll bar*

The completed work can be found in the file chapter-6-3b.xlsx.

Review Points

1. Knowledge of Kaplan-Meier method.

2. Functions MEDIAN and COUNTIFS.

3. How to conduct a Kaplan-Meier survival analysis in Excel.

4. How to customize a scatter chart into a typical Kaplan-Meier chart.

5. Merge & Center.

6. The Developer tab.

7. The Form Control Scrollbar and its link to a cell.

CHAPTER 7

PivotTable Data Analysis

Please download the sample Excel files from https://github.com/hhohho/master-Excel-through-projects for this chapter's exercises.

Excel is a great tool for data analysis including data visualization. As part of the Microsoft Office tool set designed for office tasks, Excel is naturally suitable for information management and presentation. Generating various reports from raw data is so critical in office jobs that Excel has a dedicated feature for it: PivotTable and PivotChart. In recent versions of Excel, more data analysis features have emerged, including Subtotal, Group, What-If Analysis, Forecast Sheet, and PowerPivot.

In this chapter, we are going to learn PivotTable, Group, Subtotal, and What-If Analysis. The project of this chapter focuses on PivotTable and PivotChart only, however.

One advantage of these data analysis features is that in most occasions, they can be easily applied without writing any formulas. Excel is a very smart tool; it makes easy many routine data analysis jobs for us.

Group and Subtotal

Open an Excel worksheet and click the Data tab. We shall notice that there are quite a few built-in features available as shown in Figure 7-1.

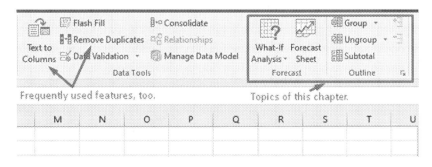

Figure 7-1. *Some built-in features under the Data tab*

© Hong Zhou 2022
H. Zhou, *Mastering Excel Through Projects*, https://doi.org/10.1007/978-1-4842-7842-0_7

The two built-in features shown in Figure 7-1, Text to Columns and Remove Duplicates, are very important and handy but won't be covered in this book. I personally apply Text to Columns in many of my Excel-related works. This feature is also related to importing external data into Excel. Be aware that different Excel versions may present a somewhat different procedure in applying Text to Columns and importing external data.

Open the Excel file chapter-7-1a.xlsx. There is only one worksheet that records sales amounts for four sales agents as shown in Figure 7-2. The sales records are further detailed with product numbers and seasonal quarters. As a manager, we may want to know who performs the best and which product is sold the most. We can achieve this quickly by using the Subtotal data analysis feature.

	A	B	C	D
1	Agent	Quarter	Product	Sales
2	Rose	3	p824	7062
3	Rachel	2	p824	7182
4	Rose	2	p456	10127
5	Nancy	4	p456	3589
6	Nancy	4	p456	4477
7	Rose	2	p824	10055
8	Rose	1	p987	11702
9	Jack	2	p987	1081
10	Nancy	2	p987	1912
11	Nancy	4	p123	8607
12	Rose	4	p123	5049

Figure 7-2. *A glance at the sample data*

Of the 64 records, Figure 7-2 only displays 11 of them. We can make use of the Freeze Panes feature of Excel to show the top rows and the bottom rows, omitting the middle ones. For example, if we want to freeze the displaying of the first five rows of records (in addition to the heading), we need to click row number 7 such that row 7 is selected ➤ click the View tab ➤ select Freeze Panes as demonstrated in Figure 7-3. After this, we can scroll down, and only the top five records plus the heading are always displayed.

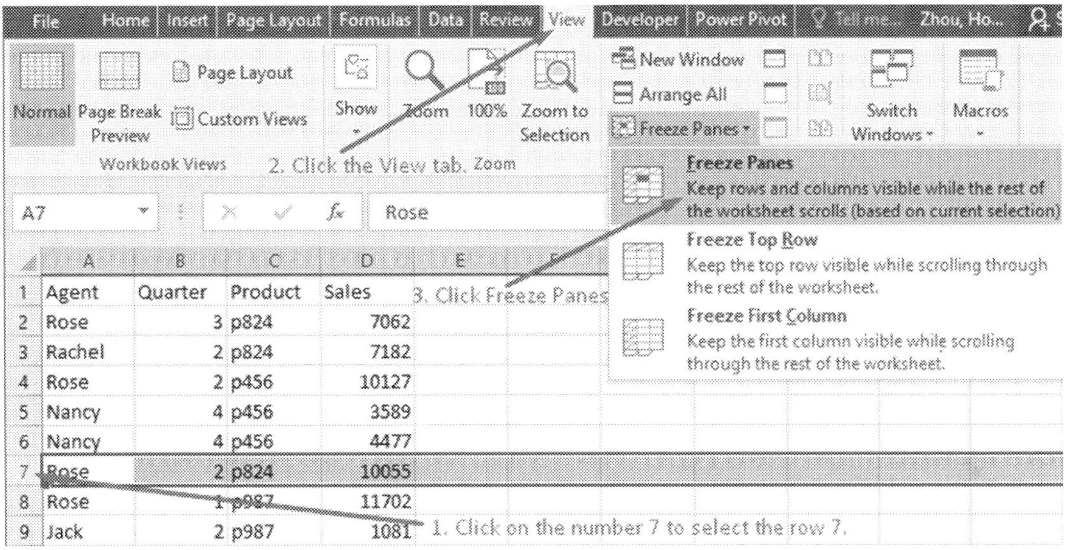

Figure 7-3. *Freeze Panes*

To unfreeze, click the View tab ➤ then select Unfreeze Panes. By now, the worksheet is unfrozen and back to its original view.

The Group feature is similar to and also different from Freeze Panes. For easy demonstration, let's select rows 5 to 10. Click on the Data tab ➤ click Group. Our worksheet shall look like Figure 7-4. As shown in Figure 7-4, if we click the dash, rows 5–10 will be hidden.

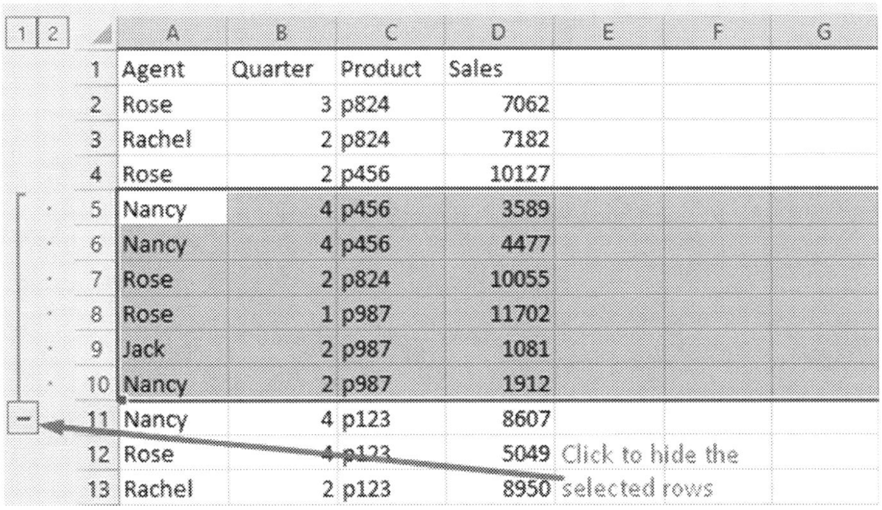

Figure 7-4. *Group rows 5-10 to hide them*

One advantage of the Group feature is that it can be applied at multiple locations inside a single worksheet.

To remove the Group format in our worksheet, click the Data tab ➤ Ungroup ➤ select Clear Outline. This is explained in Figure 7-5.

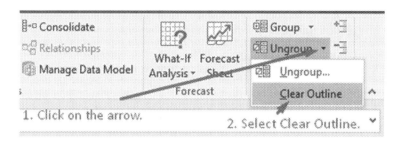

Figure 7-5. *Clear Outline to ungroup*

After removing the Group format, let's experience the Subtotal feature:

1. Click any data item in the table, for example, click cell A1 ➤ click the Data tab ➤ click Subtotal; a small window comes up as shown in Figure 7-6. Click OK.

    Excel is intuition-oriented. The default setting of the Subtotal window is accomplishing exactly what we want: sum the sales amounts for the four agents. Note that in addition to the SUM function, there are other popular functions available, such as AVERAGE, MAX, MIN, COUNT, etc.

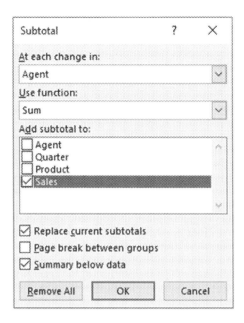

Figure 7-6. *Subtotal setup*

2. Unfortunately, what jumps into our eyes is not pleasant as illustrated in Figure 7-7. The reason is that the column Agent is not sorted.

   Since we want to compare the sales amounts among the four agents, we need to sort their names alphabetically first. Otherwise, Subtotal cannot render the result we want.

   We need to cancel the Subtotal. To do so, click the Data tab ➤ select Subtotal ➤ on the upcoming Subtotal window, click Remove All (the button to the left of the OK button in Figure 7-6).

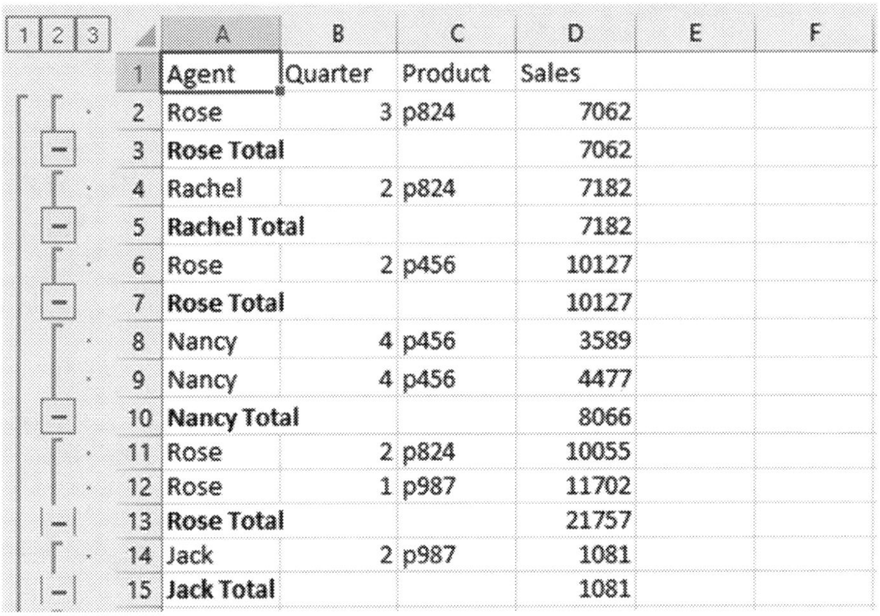

	A	B	C	D	E	F
1	Agent	Quarter	Product	Sales		
2	Rose	3	p824	7062		
3	**Rose Total**			7062		
4	Rachel	2	p824	7182		
5	**Rachel Total**			7182		
6	Rose	2	p456	10127		
7	**Rose Total**			10127		
8	Nancy	4	p456	3589		
9	Nancy	4	p456	4477		
10	**Nancy Total**			8066		
11	Rose	2	p824	10055		
12	Rose	1	p987	11702		
13	**Rose Total**			21757		
14	Jack	2	p987	1081		
15	**Jack Total**			1081		

Figure 7-7. *Subtotal does not work if the data is not sorted*

3. To sort the data based on Agent, click inside the data range (e.g., click cell A1) ➤ click the Data tab ➤ click Sort ➤ on the upcoming Sort window, make sure that the option "My data has headers" is checked ➤ select Agent for Sort by, as shown in Figure 7-8.

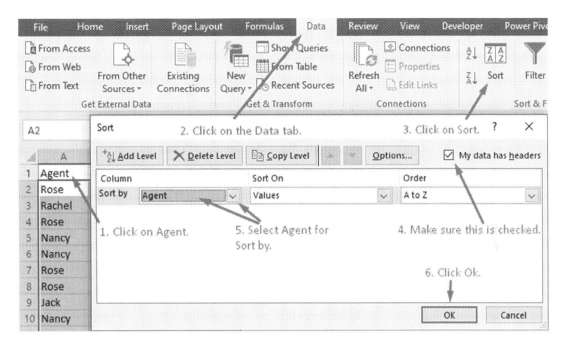

Figure 7-8. *Sort the data by Agent*

4.   Once the data is sorted, let's repeat step 1: click the Data tab
     ➤ click Subtotal ➤ Once the Subtotal window comes up (see
     Figure 7-6) ➤ click OK. Part of our worksheet should look like
     Figure 7-9.

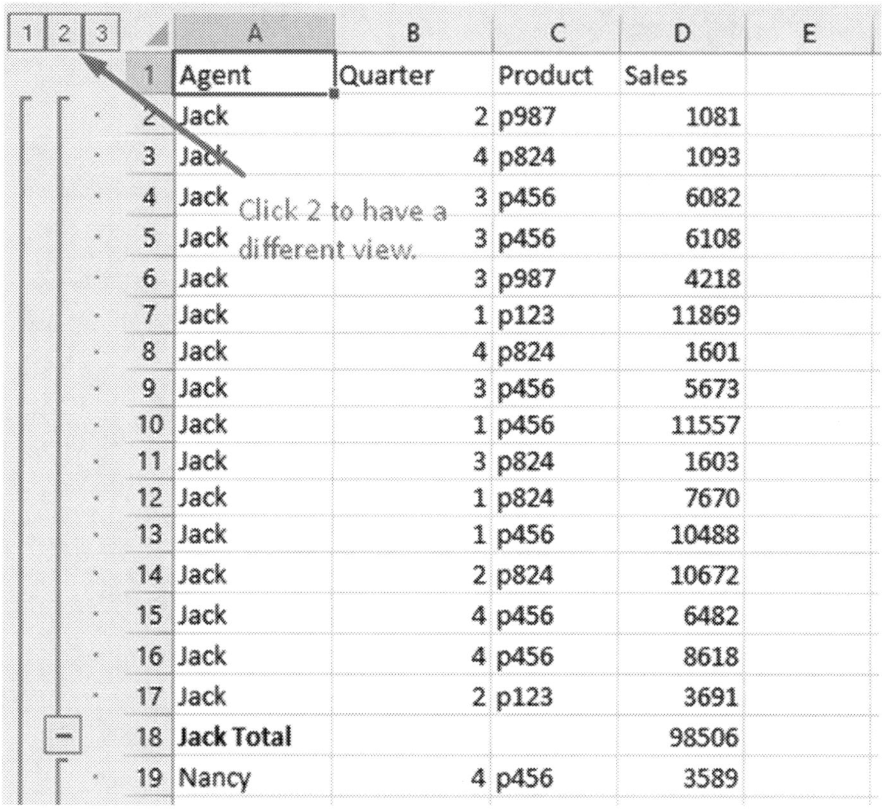

	A	B	C	D	E
1	Agent	Quarter	Product	Sales	
2	Jack	2	p987	1081	
3	Jack	4	p824	1093	
4	Jack	3	p456	6082	
5	Jack	3	p456	6108	
6	Jack	3	p987	4218	
7	Jack	1	p123	11869	
8	Jack	4	p824	1601	
9	Jack	3	p456	5673	
10	Jack	1	p456	11557	
11	Jack	3	p824	1603	
12	Jack	1	p824	7670	
13	Jack	1	p456	10488	
14	Jack	2	p824	10672	
15	Jack	4	p456	6482	
16	Jack	4	p456	8618	
17	Jack	2	p123	3691	
18	**Jack Total**			98506	
19	Nancy	4	p456	3589	

Figure 7-9. *Subtotal by Agent with a detailed view*

5. If we click the number 2 as instructed in Figure 7-9, we will get a summarized view similar to Figure 7-10.

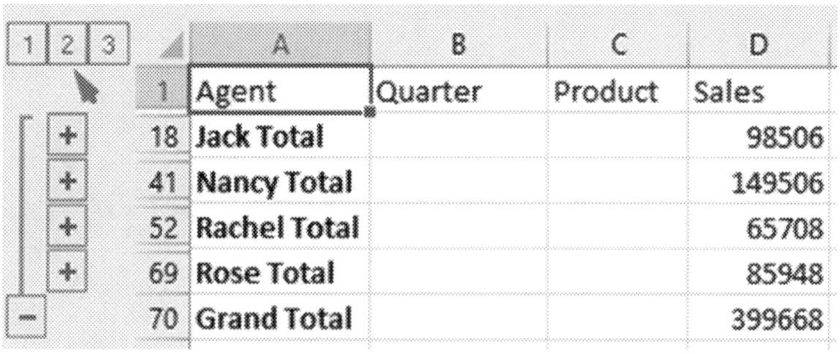

	A	B	C	D
1	Agent	Quarter	Product	Sales
18	**Jack Total**			98506
41	**Nancy Total**			149506
52	**Rachel Total**			65708
69	**Rose Total**			85948
70	**Grand Total**			399668

Figure 7-10. *The level 2 view of Subtotal*

6. If we want to view the subtotals based on product numbers, we need to sort the data based on Product, then apply Subtotal to the dataset. Figure 7-11 shows the setup of Subtotal by Product and the level 2 view of the result.

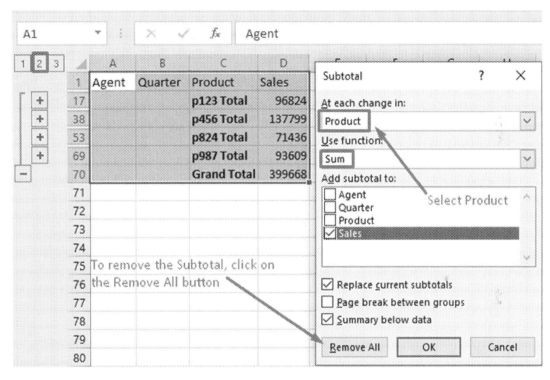

Figure 7-11. *Subtotal by Product*

What-If Analysis

What-If Analysis has three options: Scenario Manager, Goal Seek, and Data Table. Let's experience both Goal Seek and Data Table.

Assume that we are financing (borrowing money from a bank) to buy a house. Also, assume that we cannot afford more than $1400 per month to pay back the bank. Thus, we need to examine several options including the cost of the house, the amount of down payment and interest rate, and the number of payments for the loan.

Open a blank worksheet, and enter the following data in the worksheet as illustrated in Figure 7-12.

	A	B	C
1	Total Cost	$300,000	
2	Down Payment	$60,000	
3	Npers	180	
4	Interest Rate	2.75%	
5	Monthly Payment		

Figure 7-12. *Make a loan*

In Figure 7-12, we assume that the total cost of the house is $300,000, the down payment is $60,000, the number of payments (Npers) is 180 monthly payments, and the interest rate is 2.75%. Excel has a function called PMT that can calculate the monthly payment based on these values. In cell B5, enter the formula

`= -PMT(B4/12, B3, B1-B2)`

The default syntax of the PMT function is `PMT(rate, nper, pv)`, where rate is the monthly interest rate, nper is the number of payments, and pv (present value) represents the size of the loan, that is, how much we borrow from the bank.

Since the interest rate in cell B4 is yearly interest rate, we need to divide B4 by 12 inside the formula. In addition, the amount we need to borrow is B1 – B2.

The expression `PMT(B4/12, B3, B1-B2)` generates a negative number. That is why we place a negative sign in the front of PMT to get a positive number.

At this moment, our worksheet looks like Figure 7-13.

	A	B	C
1	Total Cost	$300,000	
2	Down Payment	$60,000	
3	Npers	180	
4	Interest Rate	2.75%	
5	Monthly Payment	$1,628.69	

Figure 7-13. *Calculate monthly pay by PMT*

Clearly, the monthly payment is over our budget. We need to either cut down the Total Cost or Interest Rate or increase the Down Payment or Npers. We can use the Goal Seek option of What-If Analysis to test each option.

Click cell A1 ➤ click Data tab ➤ click What-If Analysis ➤ select Goal Seek ➤ on the upcoming small window, specify the parameters exactly as Figure 7-14. Here, the Set cell is the target cell containing the PMT formula, and we want its value to be no greater than 1400 by changing the value in cell B1.

⊿	A	B	Goal Seek	?	✕
1	Total Cost	$300,000			
2	Down Payment	$60,000	Set cell:	$B$5	▦
3	Npers	180	To value:	1400	
4	Interest Rate	2.75%	By changing cell:	$B$1	▦
5	Monthly Payment	$1,628.69	OK		Cancel
6					

Figure 7-14. *Goal Seek parameters*

After clicking OK on the menu, we shall see something like Figure 7-15.

⊿	A	B	Goal Seek Status	?	✕
1	Total Cost	$266,301	Goal Seeking with Cell B5		
2	Down Payment	$60,000	found a solution.	Step	
3	Npers	180			
4	Interest Rate	2.75%	Target value: 1400	Pause	
5	Monthly Payment	$1,400.00	Current value: $1,400.00		
6			OK		Cancel

Figure 7-15. *Total Cost is down to meet the goal*

Figure 7-15 tells us if we keep everything else unchanged, we must seek for a cheaper house. We can try the same procedure on Interest Rate and Npers.

Goal Seek can work on only one parameter a time. If we want to adjust both Interest Rate and Total Cost at the same time, we need to make use of Data Table.

Starting from what we have as shown in Figure 7-13, enter data exactly (using autofill) as what is shown in Figure 7-16. The row E1:O1 lists different Total Cost values; the column D2:D14 lists different Interest Rate values.

▲	D	E	F	G	H	I	J	K	L	M	N	O
1		250000	255000	260000	265000	270000	275000	280000	285000	290000	295000	300000
2	2.2%											
3	2.3%											
4	2.4%											
5	2.5%											
6	2.6%											
7	2.7%											
8	2.8%											
9	2.9%											
10	3.0%											
11	3.1%											
12	3.2%											
13	3.3%											
14	3.4%											

Figure 7-16. *Set up the data table*

In cell D1, enter the formula =B5. Note that the table is D1:O14 and the cell D1 represents the monthly payment which is what we want to know depending on different Total Cost and Interest Rates.

Select cells D1:O14, and then click the Data tab ➤ What-If Analysis ➤ Data Table. We shall see a small menu coming up as shown in Figure 7-17. Make sure that the Row input cell is B1 and the Column input cell is B4, then click OK.

D	E	F	G	H	I	J	K	L	M	N	O
$1,628.69	250000	255000	260000	265000	270000	275000	280000	285000	290000	295000	300000
2.2%											
2.3%			Data Table		?	✕					
2.4%											
2.5%			Row input cell:		$B$1						
2.6%			Column input cell:		$B$4						
2.7%											
2.8%			OK		Cancel						
2.9%											
3.0%											
3.1%											
3.2%											
3.3%											
3.4%											

Figure 7-17. *Enter parameters for the data table*

Part of our worksheet should look like Figure 7-18.

D	E	F	G	H	I	J	K	L	M	N	O
$1,628.69	250000	255000	260000	265000	270000	275000	280000	285000	290000	295000	300000
2.2%	1240.2	1272.9	1305.5	1338.2	1370.8	1403.4	1436.1	1468.7	1501.3	1534	1566.6
2.3%	1249.1	1282	1314.8	1347.7	1380.6	1413.4	1446.3	1479.2	1512.1	1544.9	1577.8
2.4%	1258	1291.1	1324.2	1357.3	1390.4	1423.5	1456.6	1489.7	1522.8	1555.9	1589
2.5%	1266.9	1300.2	1333.6	1366.9	1400.3	1433.6	1466.9	1500.3	1533.6	1567	1600.3
2.6%	1275.9	1309.4	1343	1376.6	1410.2	1443.7	1477.3	1510.9	1544.5	1578	1611.6
2.7%	1284.9	1318.7	1352.5	1386.3	1420.1	1453.9	1487.7	1521.6	1555.4	1589.2	1623
2.8%	1293.9	1328	1362	1396.1	1430.1	1464.2	1498.2	1532.3	1566.3	1600.4	1634.4
2.9%	1303	1337.3	1371.6	1405.9	1440.1	1474.4	1508.7	1543	1577.3	1611.6	1645.9
3.0%	1312.1	1346.6	1381.2	1415.7	1450.2	1484.8	1519.3	1553.8	1588.3	1622.9	1657.4
3.1%	1321.3	1356	1390.8	1425.6	1460.3	1495.1	1529.9	1564.7	1599.4	1634.2	1669
3.2%	1330.5	1365.5	1400.5	1435.5	1470.5	1505.5	1540.5	1575.5	1610.6	1645.6	1680.6
3.3%	1339.7	1374.9	1410.2	1445.5	1480.7	1516	1551.2	1586.5	1621.7	1657	1692.2
3.4%	1349	1384.5	1420	1455.5	1491	1526.5	1562	1597.5	1633	1668.5	1704

Figure 7-18. *The data table result*

Now, we can evaluate the combinations of Total Cost and Interest Rate that can give us a monthly payment no larger than $1400. Be aware that the table is generated by Excel array formula. So, try not to click any cells inside the table because array formulas cannot be changed. Personally, I try to avoid using array formulas. In fact, such a data table can be generated easily by using regular formulas, too. This would be a good exercise. Take a look at the file chapter-7-1b.xlsx for such regular formulas.

PivotTable and PivotChart

PivotTable is a critical skill that all Excel users must have. We have just learned Subtotal, but PivotTable is much more powerful and popular than Subtotal. Soon, we will experience how PivotTable simplifies the data management and presentation tasks.

Let's open the original chapter-7-1a.xlsx again. Click cell A1 ➤ Click the Insert tab on the top of the worksheet ➤ Select PivotTable ➤ A window shows up with default data range ➤ Click OK as shown in Figure 7-19. Note that Excel automatically detects the data range.

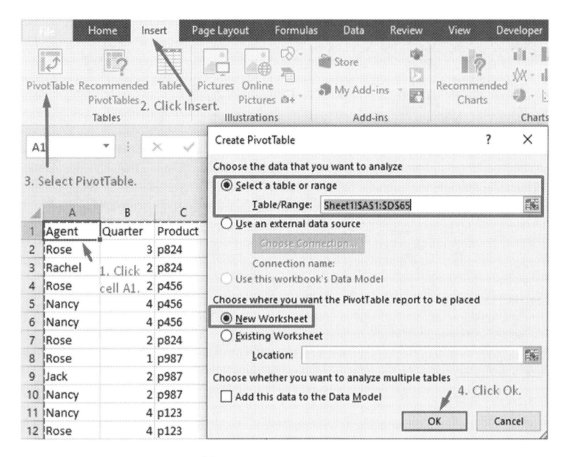

Figure 7-19. *Create PivotTable*

After clicking OK, a new worksheet is created. At the left side of the new worksheet, there is a formatted area which is where the future PivotTable resides. At the right side of the new worksheet is the PivotTable Fields. There are four fields (Agent, Quarter, Product, Sales), though Figure 7-20 only displays three of them. If the PivotTable Fields does not show up, click the formatted area on the left.

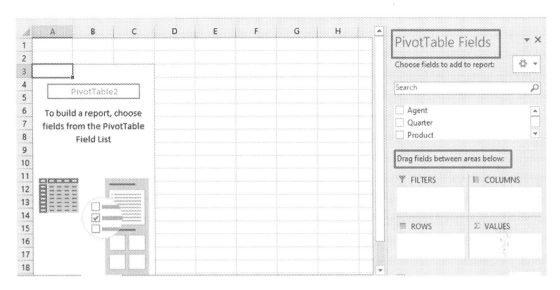

Figure 7-20. *PivotTable Fields*

Figure 7-20 shows that a PivotTable has four areas: FILTERS, COLUMNS, ROWS, and VALUES. At this point, we may not be clear what they are for. Let's create one PivotTable first so that we can have some live experience.

Drag Agent and Quarter into ROWS one after another. Drag Product into COLUMNS and Sales into Values. We should notice that the formatted area is changing while we are dragging those fields. Our worksheet should look like Figure 7-21.

	A	B	C	D	E	F
1						
2						
3	Sum of Sales	Column Labels				
4	Row Labels	p123	p456	p824	p987	Grand Total
5	⊟Jack	15560	55008	22639	5299	98506
6	1	11869	22045	7670		41584
7	2	3691		10672	1081	15444
8	3		17863	1603	4218	23684
9	4		15100	2694		17794
10	⊟Nancy	36142	49869	8907	54588	149506
11	1	11805	11373		20383	43561
12	2	2858			1912	4770
13	3	7750	18669	8907	22151	57477
14	4	13729	19827		10142	43698
15	⊟Rachel	22894	12388	18757	11669	65708
16	1				11669	11669
17	2	15964		12398		28362
18	3		4070			4070
19	4	6930	8318	6359		21607
20	⊟Rose	22228	20534	21133	22053	85948
21	1	9742			19931	29673
22	2		10127	10055		20182
23	3	4487		9174	2122	15783
24	4	7999	10407	1904		20310
25	Grand Total	96824	137799	71436	93609	399668

PivotTable Fields ▾ ✕

Choose fields to add to report:

Search

☑ Agent
☑ Quarter
☑ Product
☑ Sales

MORE TABLES...

Drag fields between areas below:

▼ FILTERS   ⯿ COLUMNS
                   Product ▼

≡ ROWS   Σ VALUES
Agent ▼   Sum of Sales ▼
Quarter ▼

Figure 7-21. *Drag fields into areas*

As both Agent and Quarter are in ROWS, the rows of the PivotTable are arranged by agents first and further divided by quarters. If we collapse each agent as indicated in Figure 7-21, we will then see a higher-level summary as illustrated in Figure 7-22.

	A	B	C	D	E	F
1						
2						
3	Sum of Sales	Column Labels				
4	Row Labels	p123	p456	p824	p987	Grand Total
5	⊞Jack	15560	55008	22639	5299	98506
6	⊞Nancy	36142	49869	8907	54588	149506
7	⊞Rachel	22894	12388	18757	11669	65708
8	⊞Rose	22228	20534	21133	22053	85948
9	Grand Total	96824	137799	71436	93609	399668

Figure 7-22. *A collapsed PivotTable*

Both Figure 7-21 and Figure 7-22 present us an understanding of the overall performance of all four agents. In addition, Figure 7-21 allows us to analyze their sales in each quarter and on each product item. This is the power of a PivotTable. Moreover, we can drag fields into and/or out from the four areas, and then conduct different analysis immediately, and we do not need to sort the data at all. For example, we can drag Product into ROWS, drag Agent out from ROWS, and drag Quarter into COLUMNS. Doing so, we can then compare the sales of the four products in each quarter.

Whenever our cursor is inside the PivotTable, there are two additional tabs on the top menu: Analyze and Design (note that in some Excel versions, it is PivotTable Analyze instead of Analyze). Click the Analyze tab ➤ click PivotChart as instructed in Figure 7-23.

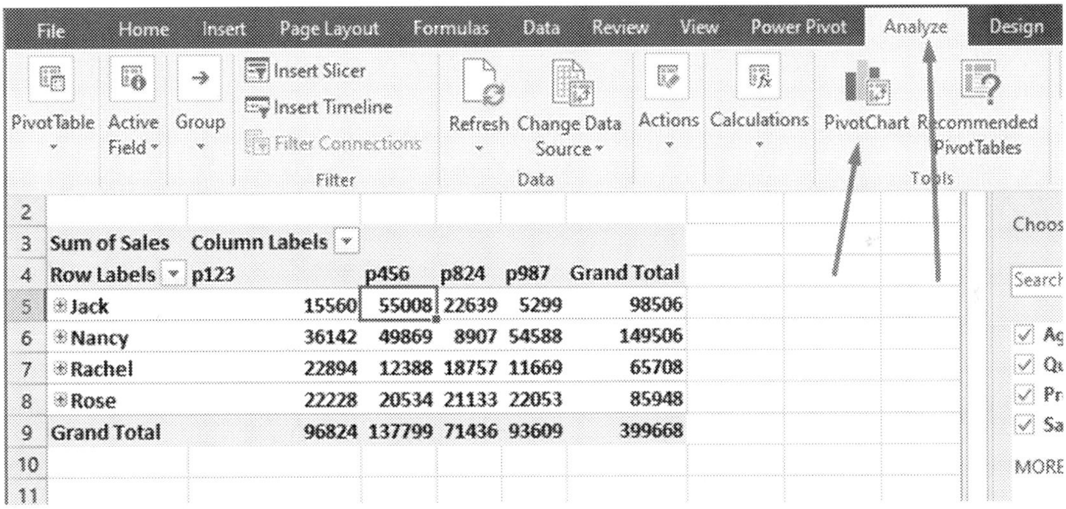

Figure 7-23. *Insert a PivotChart*

The window Insert Chart shows up with a Clustered Column chart preselected. In most cases, Excel makes the right choice for us, and it does so this time too. Let's take it, and click OK as shown in Figure 7-24. We shall see a PivotChart in our worksheet which is illustrated in Figure 7-25. Figure 7-25 instructs us to expand the PivotChart. If we do so, both the chart and the table are expanded to display more information regarding Quarters.

The completed work can be found in chapter-7-1c.xlsx.

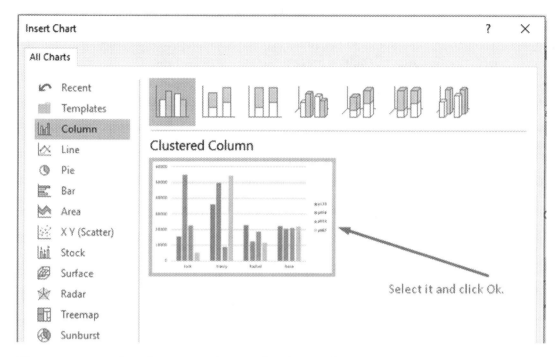

Figure 7-24. *Select the given Clustered Column chart*

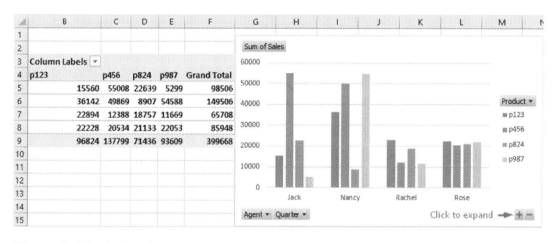

Figure 7-25. *A PivotChart*

Work on the Project

Open the Excel file chapter-7-2a.xlsx. What jumps into our eyes is a worksheet showing the numbers of students of different races in school districts. Depending on what we want to know, we can set up different PivotTables. Figure 7-26 presents a slice of the data.

	A	B	C	D	E	F	G	H	I	J	K	L	M
1	District	School	Grade	% of Non-Wh	American Inc	Asian Americ	Black	White	Hispanic	Pacific Islander	Two or More race	Non White	Total
2	1	1	0		0	0	0	26		0		0	26
3	1	1	0		0	0	0	26		0		0	26
4	1	1	1		0	0		37	0	0		0	37
5	1	1	2		0		0	40		0	0		40
6	1	1	3	7	0	0		40		0		7	40
7	1	1	4		0		0	42		0	0	0	42
8	1	1	5		0	0		46	0	0		0	46
9	1	1	6		0	0	0	33		0	0	0	33
10	2	3	0	54		0	18	17	32			54	67
11	2	3	1	54			18	34	33	0	0	54	85
12	2	3	2	46	0		0	16	42	29	0	46	87
13	2	3	3	55	0		0	21	38	30		55	89
14	2	3	4	36			0	13	59	19	0	36	91
15	2	3	5	52	0		16	41	32		0	52	89
16	2	3	6	50	0		17	41	29		0	50	87
17	2	8	0	64			15	41	43	0		64	99
18	2	8	1	68	0		27	43	36		0	68	106

Figure 7-26. *Numbers of students of different races*

We may have noticed that there are discrepancies among some data items. For example, at row 6, while there are 40 White and 7 Non White, the total is 40. This can happen frequently when data are manually recorded or entered. We can do some data cleansing, but let's just work on the given data and employ the Calculated Field feature of PivotTable to make corrections.

Let's get an idea of the numbers of White, Non White, and Total among all the districts first. To achieve that, follow these instructions:

1. Click anywhere inside the data range ➤ click the Insert tab ➤ select PivotTable.

2. Keep the default setting on the upcoming window named Create PivotTable, then click OK.

3. PivotTable Fields appear on the right side of the new worksheet. Drag the District field into ROWS, and drag the other three fields White, Non White, and Total into VALUES as shown in Figure 7-27.

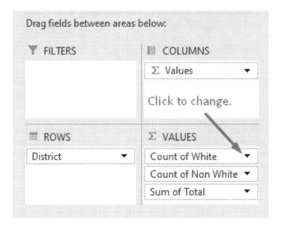

Figure 7-27. *Set up the PivotTable for school districts*

Note that because the values of all the three fields (White, Non White, and Total) are numerical, we should not drag anyone of them into COLUMNS.

4. We shall find out that Excel applies function COUNT on White and Non White. By default, Excel applies SUM if the column contains numbers only and COUNT if the column contains text. But if there is at least one empty cell in a column with numbers, the column is treated as a text column, and therefore, COUNT is applied. If we take a close look at the two columns White and Non White, we shall find some empty cells in them. We need to change COUNT to SUM. Click the arrow to the right of Count of White as instructed in Figure 7-27.

5. On the upcoming menu, select Value Field Settings... as shown in Figure 7-28.

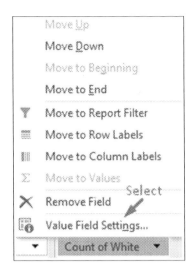

Figure 7-28. *Value Field Settings*

6. The window Value Field Settings shows up. On this window, select
    function Sum as instructed in Figure 7-29. Click OK.

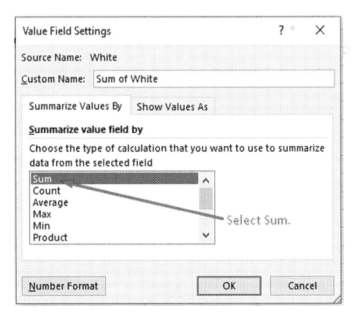

Figure 7-29. *Switch to function Sum*

7. We can certainly repeat steps 4–6 for Non White. However, let's try a different approach for Non White here. Inside the PivotTable, right-click the column name "Count of Non White" or any number under it. Then, on the upcoming menu, select Summarize Value By ➤ choose Sum. This procedure is demonstrated in Figure 7-30.

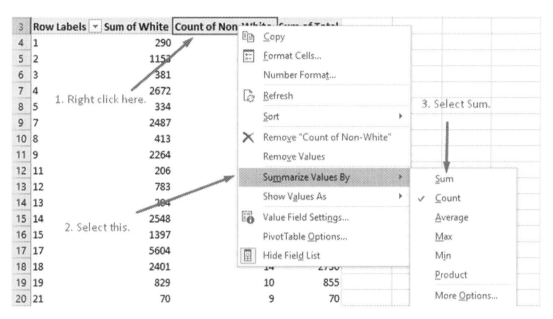

Figure 7-30. *Another way to change function type*

Once completed, part of our worksheet should look like Figure 7-31.

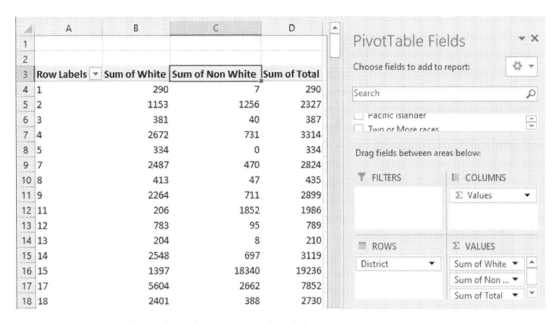

Figure 7-31. *Student distribution in school districts*

8. Be aware that there are discrepancies among the data so that
    (Sum of White) + (Sum of Non White) > (Sum of Total) for every
    district. We need to display a correct Sum of Total for White and
    Non White. To do so, we need to remove Sum of Total first. To
    remove it, simply go to the PivotTable Fields to drag Sum of Total
    out of the field VALUES.

    To place a correct Sum of Total for White and Non White, we need
    to insert a Calculated Field into our PivotTable. Click the Analyze
    tab ➤ click the drop-down arrow of Fields, Items, & Sets ➤ select
    Calculated Field. This is shown in Figure 7-32.

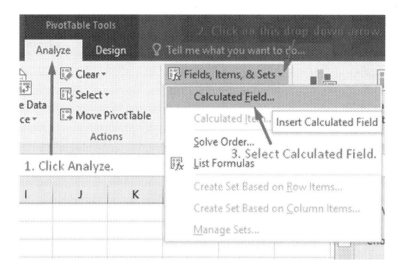

Figure 7-32. *Select Calculated Field*

9. On the upcoming window, add a field named "White+Non White" (without quotation marks) as shown in Figure 7-33. Note that the formula is =White + Non White.

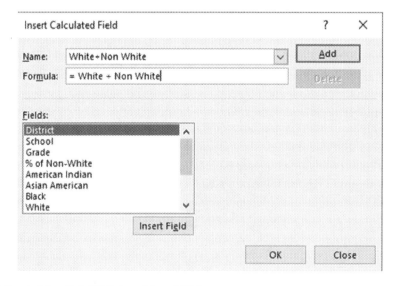

Figure 7-33. *Add a field White+Non White*

After clicking OK as shown in Figure 7-33, part of our worksheet should look like Figure 7-34.

	A	B	C	D
1				
2				
3	Row Labels	Sum of White	Sum of Non White	Sum of White+Non White
4	1	290	7	297
5	2	1153	1256	2409
6	3	381	40	421
7	4	2672	731	3403
8	5	334	0	334
9	7	2487	470	2957
10	8	413	47	460
11	9	2264	711	2975

Figure 7-34. *The PivotTable with Sum of White+Non White*

10. Assume we now want to know the race distribution by grades in individual districts. Drag the District field to FILTERS, and drag the Grade field into ROWS.

    By default, we get an overview of race distribution by grade in all school districts. This is shown in Figure 7-35.

	A	B	C	D
1	District	(All) ▼		
2				
3	Row Labels ▼	Sum of White	Sum of Non White	Sum of White+Non White
4	0	13466	15465	28931
5	1	23020	18143	41163
6	2	28709	18866	47575
7	3	30726	24129	54855
8	4	24177	16365	40542
9	5	23687	16157	39844
10	6	24696	16024	40720
11	7	25065	16214	41279
12	8	25761	15976	41737
13	9	26521	18443	44964
14	10	26088	15842	41930
15	11	26811	15174	41985
16	12	26815	13651	40466
17	Grand Total	325542	220449	545991

Figure 7-35. *Race distribution by grade*

11. If we only want to know the race distribution by grade in District 7, for example, we need to filter for District 7. Follow the instructions in Figure 7-36.

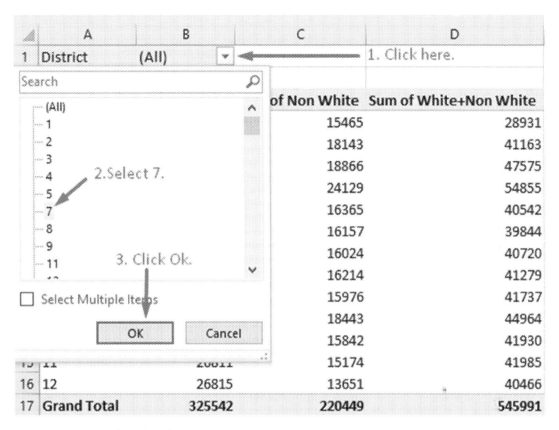

Figure 7-36. *Filter for district 7*

12. Assume we want to combine the data of Districts 7, 8, and 9. We then need to check the box Select Multiple Items as shown in Figure 7-37. Our PivotTable should look like Figure 7-38.

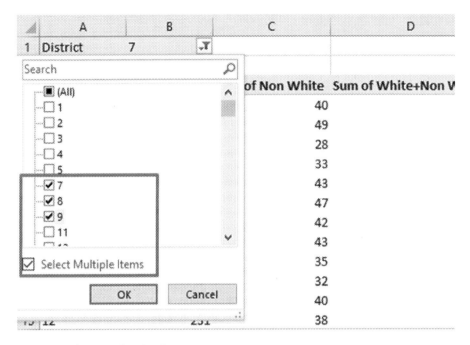

Figure 7-37. *Select multiple districts*

	A	B	C	D
1	District	(Multiple Items) 🔽		
2				
3	Row Labels 🔽	Sum of White	Sum of Non White	Sum of White+Non White
4	0	231	60	291
5	1	332	81	413
6	2	540	98	638
7	3	506	91	597
8	4	436	104	540
9	5	392	117	509
10	6	443	114	557
11	7	375	91	466
12	8	364	96	460
13	9	393	102	495
14	10	359	85	444
15	11	382	99	481
16	12	411	90	501
17	**Grand Total**	**5164**	**1228**	**6392**

Figure 7-38. *The PivotTable for districts 7, 8, and 9*

13. We may find it unnecessary to display the Sum of White+Non White. To remove it, simply go to the PivotTable Fields ➤ drag Sum of White+Non White out of the field VALUES.

14. We can also draw a PivotChart. Click anywhere inside our PivotTable ➤ click the Analyze tab ➤ select PivotChart ➤ on the Insert Chart window, select Bar ➤ select the default Clustered Bar. We shall get a chart looking like Figure 7-39.

As indicated in Figure 7-39, the Grade is ordered from 12 to 0 (top down), the reverse order of our PivotTable.

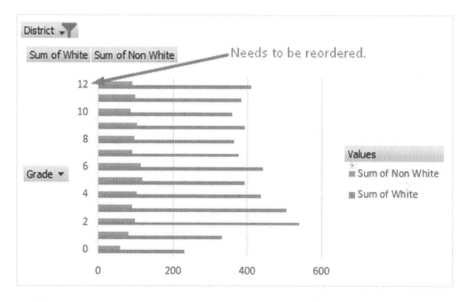

Figure 7-39. *A pivot bar chart whose Grade needs to be reordered*

15. To reverse the order of the Grades, click inside the chart first ➤ double-click the numbers of Grade to let the Format Axis menu to show up ➤ Choose Axis Options, and check the box "Categories of reverse order." This is illustrated in Figure 7-40.

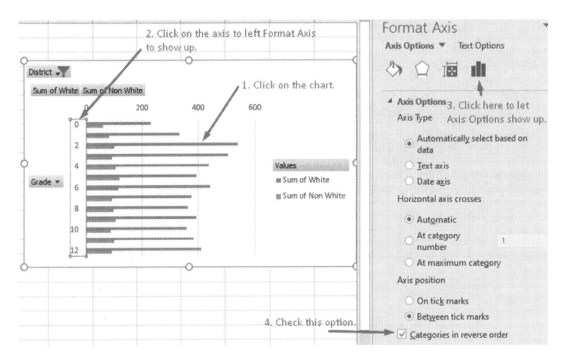

Figure 7-40. *Check the option "Categories in reverse order"*

Our final worksheet should look like Figure 7-41. The final result is available in chapter-7-2b.xlsx.

▲	A	B	C	D	E	F	G	H	I
1	District	(Multiple Iter ▼							
2									
3	Row Lal ▼	Sum of White	Sum of Non White						
4	0	231	60						
5	1	332	81						
6	2	540	98						
7	3	506	91						
8	4	436	104						
9	5	392	117						
10	6	443	114						
11	7	375	91						
12	8	364	96						
13	9	393	102						
14	10	359	85						
15	11	382	99						
16	12	411	90						
17	Grand Tot	5164	1228						

Figure 7-41. *The PivotTable with its pivot bar chart*

Chapter Tip

This chapter's tip is about adding rows or columns. Assume we want to add a column before the current column D, and later add a row before the current row 3. Follow the instructions here to experience it:

1. Open a blank worksheet, and type "D" in D1, 3 in A3, and 100 in D3.

2. In cell B2, enter the formula =INDIRECT(D1&A3). This formula gives us cell reference D3.

3. In cell B3, enter the formula =D3. Our worksheet should look like Figure 7-42.

◢	A	B	C	D
1				D
2		=INDIRECT(D1&A3)		
3	3	=D3		100

Figure 7-42. *Set up the worksheet to experience adding a column and a row*

4. To insert a column before the current column D, right-click the column letter D. A small menu appears. Click Insert to insert a column before the current column D. This is shown in Figure 7-43.

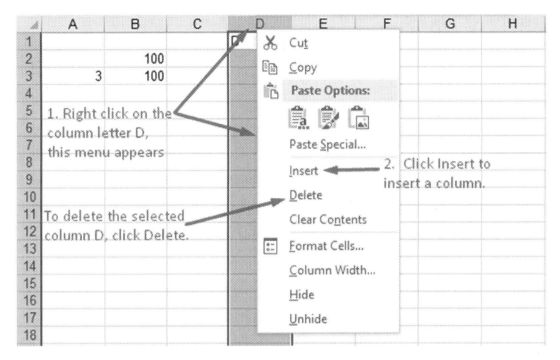

Figure 7-43. *The menu to insert or delete a column*

5. To insert a row before the current row 3, we follow the same procedure. Right-click the row number 3 ➤ on the upcoming menu, click Insert. Our worksheet should look like Figure 7-44. The beauty is that the cell references inside the formulas are automatically updated.

	A	B	C	D	E
1					D
2		=INDIRECT(E1&A4)			
3					
4	3	=E4			100
5					

Figure 7-44. *The cell references are updated automatically*

For example, in the formula of cell B2, the original "D1" becomes "E1" because the old column D is now column E, and the original "A3" becomes "A4" because the old row 3 becomes row 4.

The formula originally inside cell B3 is now in cell B4 and is updated to be =E4, too.

Be aware that while even the two formulas (originally in cell B2 and B3) are automatically updated, their calculation results are now different, however. Why?

Excel always updates cell references in all formulas when row(s)/column(s) are inserted or deleted. The updated formulas generate the same result. For example, before inserting a column and a row, the original formula in B2 creates a formula =D3 by the function INDIRECT. After insertion, it still creates the same formula =D3. In this sense, the update formula keeps the same result. However, cell D3 is now empty.

Note that we can insert a row/column only *before* the selected row/column.

Review Points

1. Freeze Panes.

2. Group rows or columns.

3. Subtotal.

4. Data sorting.

5. What-If analysis.

6. PivotTable and PivotChart.

7. Inserting or deleting row(s)/column(s).

8. Function PMT.

CHAPTER 8

K-Means Clustering and Iterative Calculation

This is our last chapter. Hopefully we have become more and more familiar with Excel. We should have realized that under every main tab, there are quite a few icon groups, each presenting some quick-access tools or features. For example, under the Home tab, there are groups Font, Alignment, Number, Styles, Editing, etc. We can find that under the Formulas tab, the Function Library group organizes functions into different categories including Financial, Logical, Text, Date & Time, Lookup & Reference, and Math & Trig. This Function Library group also lists those Recently Used functions and some other More Functions. Remember that Excel is adding more and more functions, and for general purpose, it is very likely that Excel has all the functions we need for our projects. The same understanding applies to Excel's built-in features, that is, Excel is likely to have all the built-in features we need.

Therefore, whenever we run into a new task or project, think about what functions and/or features we must have, navigate through available Excel functions and features, then think again how to apply available functions and/or features to accomplish the task. By the end of this book, this is the most important skill we want to develop.

In this last chapter, let's see how we can learn some machine learning knowledge through an Excel project.

Excel can also be a powerful tool for certain data science tasks. For instance, Excel can easily perform linear regression analysis on a numerical dataset. Nevertheless, this last chapter is dedicated to the demonstration that Excel can nicely accomplish a popular data mining method: k-means clustering.

Clustering is a widely used classification method in data mining or machine learning. It categorizes subjects, also known as data points, into different clusters each with a number of characteristic measurements. For example, an insurance company may want to categorize clients into different risk groups when determining insurance premiums. Such a categorizing process relies on the selected characteristics and the adopted algorithm.

© Hong Zhou 2022
H. Zhou, *Mastering Excel Through Projects*, https://doi.org/10.1007/978-1-4842-7842-0_8

In machine learning (we are not differentiating the two terminologies in this book – machine learning and data mining), data is organized into tables, while Excel is truly a huge table. Thus, Excel is naturally suitable for some machine learning operations. In a data table, a row is called a record. Since a record can be composed of multiple numerical values, it can also be called a data point. In addition, a record can contain characteristics that are used to describe somebody, so in some cases, a record is also called a subject. In machine learning, data point, record, and subject, all have the same meaning.

The two most popular types of clustering methods are partitioning clustering and hierarchical clustering. K-means clustering, where k represents the desired number of clusters, is a type of partitioning clustering. In k-means clustering, each cluster is defined by the centroid (also known as mean) of the data points in the cluster. For instance, suppose a cluster has three data points expressed as three vectors: (1, 2, 3, 4, 3), (0, 2, 4, 6, 8), and (5, 5, 2, 2, 1). The centroid of this cluster is then ((1+0+5)/3, (2+2+5)/3, (3+4+2)/3, (4+6+2)/3, (3+8+1)/3), that is, (2, 3, 3, 4, 4). Note that the k-means clustering method requires all data to be numerical.

To start the k-means clustering process, the first task is to decide how many clusters are needed, that is, the value of k. The second task is to select k data points as the initial centroids. We can randomly select the k centroids, or we can pick them based on the data distribution. The distances from each data point to every centroid are computed, and a data point is pushed into a cluster that is the closest to it. Once every data point has been pushed into a cluster, the centroid of the points in a cluster is recomputed. The distances of each data point to every new centroid are recomputed again, followed by categorizing points into clusters based on the shortest-distance rule. Such a process is repeated until all data points are assigned into the same clusters in two consecutive iterations, at which point the cluster centroids have stabilized and will remain the same thereafter. This process can also be stopped when a predefined maximum number of iterations have been reached.

There are different methods to compute the distances between any two data points, though Euclidean distance is commonly used. Given two data points (x1, x2, x3, x4) and (y1, y2, y3, y4), their Euclidean distance is computed as

$$\sqrt{\left(x1 - y1\right)^2 + \left(x2 - y2\right)^2 + \left(x3 - y3\right)^2 + \left(x4 - y4\right)^2} \qquad (8\text{-}1)$$

In this chapter, Euclidean distance is applied to practice k-means clustering through Excel. As usual, we try to minimize manual work but automate the process as much as possible. For this purpose, we are going to learn two ways of conducting k-means clustering in Excel, that is, we are going to work on two projects, both on the same dataset.

Functions to Learn

There are several new functions to learn for this chapter's projects. They are SQRT, SUMXMY2, AVERAGEIFS, and SHEET.

SQRT

This function calculates the square root of a number. For example, if we want to calculate the square root of 100, our formula should be =SQRT(100). Similarly, if the number is stored in cell A1, then our formula should be =SQRT(A1).

SUMXMY2

This function has the syntax as SUMXMY2(array_x, array_y). It sums the squares of the differences in two corresponding ranges or arrays specified by the two arguments array_x and array_y.

For example, given A1:A4 as the array_x and C1:F1 as the array_y as shown in Figure 8-1, if we want to sum the squares of the differences between A1:A4 and C1:F1, our formula can be

=SUM((A1-C1)^2, (A2-D1)^2, (A3-E1)^2, (A4-F1)^2)

This formula works fine when the two arrays are small. What if we have two arrays A1:A1000 and B1:B1000?

◢	A	B	C	D	E	F
1	1		3	4	5	6
2	2					
3	3					
4	4					

Figure 8-1. *Learn function SUMXMY2*

Certainly, for A1:A4 and C1:F1, a better formula would be =SUMXMY2(A1:A4, C1:F1). When the two arrays are A1:A1000 and B1:B1000, =SUMXMY2(A1:A1000, B1:B1000) is the only solution.

If we want to apply equation (8-1) to the two arrays A1:A4 and C1:F1, our formula should then be =SQRT(SUMXMY2(A1:A4, C1:F1)).

AVERAGEIFS

This is another popular function in the IF family. Its syntax is AVERAGEIFS(average-range, criteria-range1, criteria1, ...). It calculates the average for the cells specified by a given set of criteria. Let's start a blank worksheet and enter data as shown in Figure 8-2 (the dataset is available in chapter-8-example.xlsx).

	A	B	C
1	Gender	Level	Sales amount
2	F	1	$ 58,262.00
3	F	2	$ 41,736.00
4	F	1	$ 97,941.00
5	M	1	$ 78,292.00
6	M	1	$ 18,751.00
7	M	2	$ 48,555.00
8	F	2	$ 99,517.00
9	F	1	$ 28,305.00
10	M	2	$ 75,816.00
11	M	1	$ 75,111.00
12	M	2	$ 64,055.00
13	M	1	$ 98,462.00
14	F	1	$ 96,547.00
15	F	2	$ 79,542.00
16	M	1	$ 4,373.00

Figure 8-2. *Learn function AVERAGEIFS*

Assume that in a company, there are two levels of employees: level 1 and level 2. We want to average the sales amount for the female employees who are in level 1. Observe that what we want to average is in C2:C16, and there are two criteria: female (F) and level 1. Such a task can be easily accomplished by using the formula

=AVERAGEIFS(C2:C16, A2:A16, "F", B2:B16, 1). In this formula, only certain cells in C2:C16 are averaged, for example, cell C2, because C2 is aligned with A2 and B2, while A2 = "F" and B2 = 1. The same applies to cells C4, C9, and C14.

Test Yourself: write a formula to average the sales amount for male employees who are in level 2.[1]

Challenge: write a formula to average the single sales amounts over $50000 for female employees who are in level 2.[2]

SHEET

SHEET is a very interesting function which returns the sheet number of the referenced sheet. Its syntax is SHEET(reference), where the argument is usually a cell reference. We need to practice an example, or we will be lost. Follow these instructions:

1. Open chapter-8-1a.xlsx. This Excel file has only one default worksheet named Sheet1 which is almost empty except for cells C2, D2, and C3 as shown in Figure 8-3.

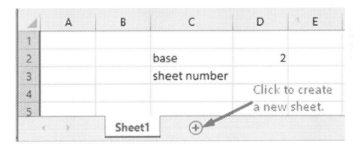

Figure 8-3. *Sheet1 is the only sheet*

2. Inside an Excel workbook, all worksheets are numbered from left to right based on their positions. As we currently have only one worksheet, this worksheet's number must be 1. Enter the formula =SHEET(A1) inside cell D3. D3 now displays 1.

---

[1] =AVERAGEIFS(C2:C16, A2:A16, "M", B2:B16, 2).
[2] =AVERAGEIFS(C2:C16, A2:A16, "F", B2:B16, 2, C2:C16, ">50000").

3. Click the circled + as shown in Figure 8-3 to create a new worksheet. We now have another worksheet named Sheet2. Inside Sheet2, enter "previous sheet" in C1, "2 times" in C2, and "sheet number" in C3. Then, in cell D3, enter the formula =SHEET(A1). Now, our Sheet2 should look like Figure 8-4.

Like previously mentioned, the sheet number is determined by the position of the specific worksheet. Currently, Sheet2 is right after Sheet1; thus, its sheet number is 2.

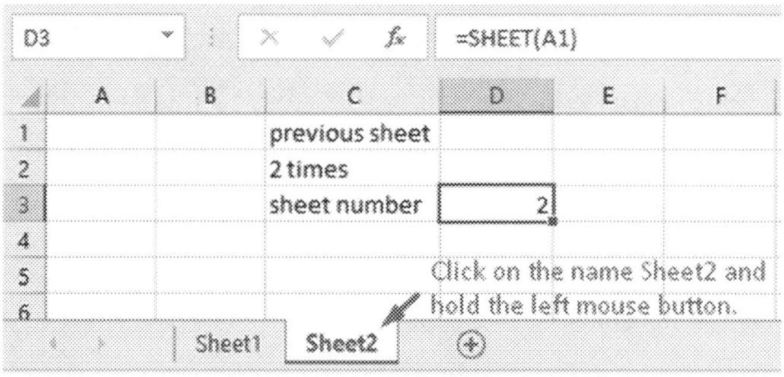

Figure 8-4. *The sheet number of Sheet2 is 2*

4. Click the name "Sheet2" as shown in Figure 8-4, and then hold the left mouse button, and drag/move Sheet2 to the left of Sheet1. Now, Sheet2 is placed before Sheet1, and therefore, its sheet number becomes 1. This is illustrated in Figure 8-5.

At this point, the sheet number of Sheet1 must be 2.

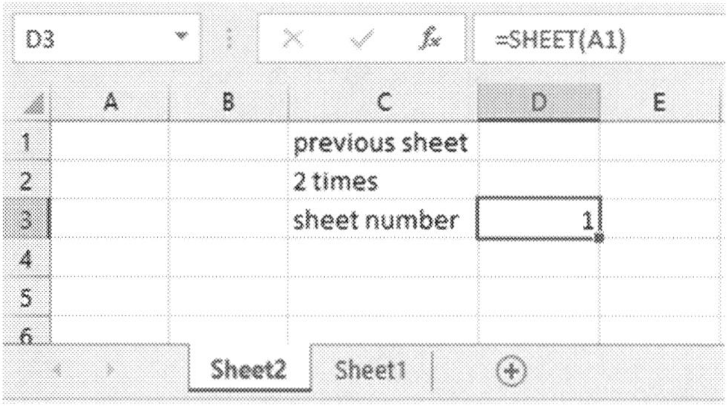

Figure 8-5. *The sheet number of Sheet2 is 1*

5. Drag Sheet2 back to the right of Sheet1. Its sheet number becomes 2 again.

6. Right-click on the name Sheet1, and select Rename as show in Figure 8-6. Rename Sheet1 to be 1 (yes, the number 1). Repeat the procedure to rename Sheet2 to be 2.

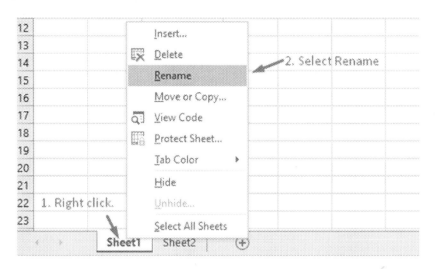

Figure 8-6. *Right-click to rename a worksheet*

7. Inside worksheet 2, enter the formula =SHEET(A1) - 1 in cell D1. Because the sheet number of worksheet 2 = 2, cell D1 stores number 1 which happens to be the name of worksheet 1.

8. Enter the formula =2 * INDIRECT(D1 & "!D2") in cell D2. This formula accesses the previous worksheet's cell D2 and doubles its value. Now, our worksheet 2 should look like Figure 8-7.

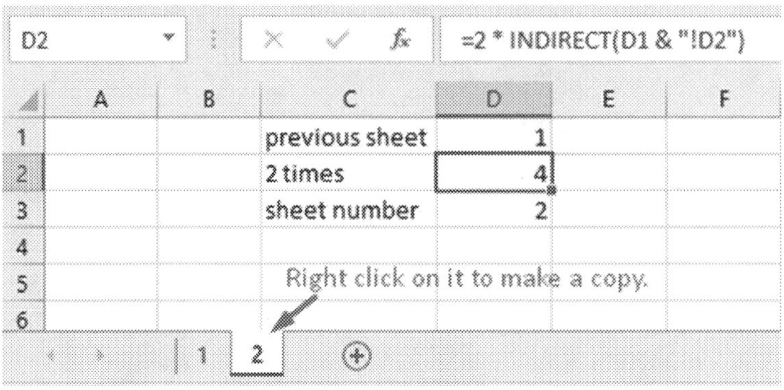

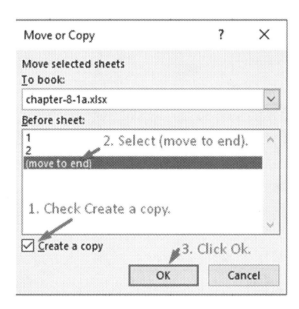

Figure 8-7. *Worksheet 2 accesses its previous worksheet*

9.   Right-click on the name 2 as shown in Figure 8-7. On the upcoming menu, select Move or Copy. The Move or Copy window shows up.

10.   Follow the instructions in Figure 8-8 to create a copy of worksheet 2, and move it to end. The new worksheet is automatically named "2 (2)" and should look like Figure 8-9.

Figure 8-8. *Create a copy and move to end*

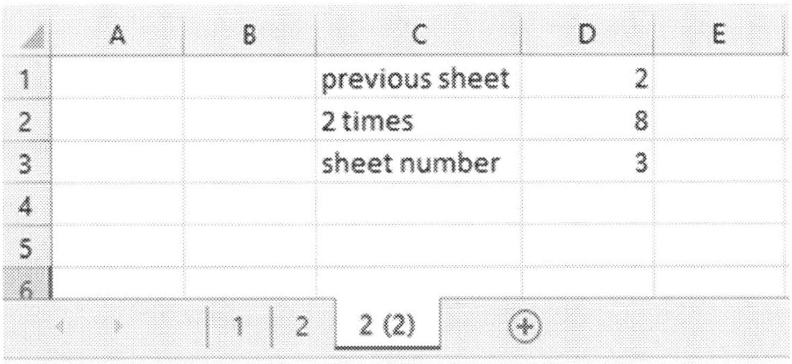

▲	A	B	C	D	E
1			previous sheet	2	
2			2 times	8	
3			sheet number	3	
4					
5					
6					

Sheet tabs: 1 | 2 | **2 (2)** | ⊕

Figure 8-9. *Worksheet 2 (2)*

11. Notice that the previous sheet in cell D1 becomes 2 now. Let's rename this worksheet "2 (2)" to be 3, then repeat the previous procedure to make a copy of worksheet 3, and rename the new worksheet 4.

12. Continue the process to copy worksheet 4, and rename the new worksheet 5. Our worksheet 5 should now look like Figure 8-10.

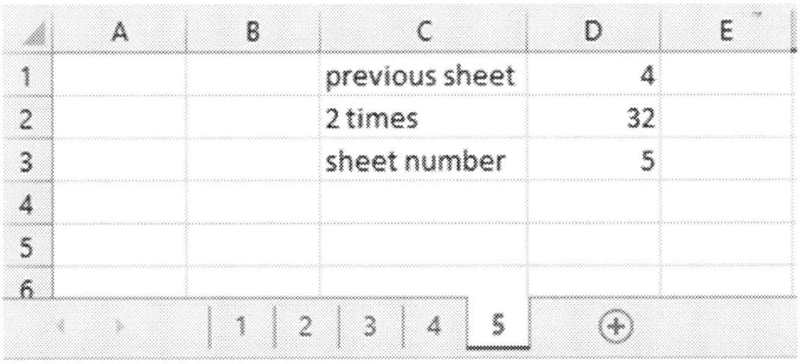

▲	A	B	C	D	E
1			previous sheet	4	
2			2 times	32	
3			sheet number	5	
4					
5					
6					

Sheet tabs: 1 | 2 | 3 | 4 | **5** | ⊕

Figure 8-10. *Worksheet 5 is created*

Please make sure that the worksheets are properly named and ordered as shown in Figure 8-10. Because every worksheet's name matches to its sheet number, every worksheet can reference its "previous sheet" correctly. If the names or order is incorrect, our worksheet 5 may have errors inside. The final result can also be found in the file chapter-8-1b.xlsx.

The reason why so many words and figures are spent on the function SHEET is because we are going to use it to help maximize the automation of our project 1.

Work on Project 1

Please open the file chapter-8-2a.xlsx. We will notice there is only one worksheet named "1" which looks like Figure 8-11.

	A	B	C	D	E	F	G	H	I	J	K	L	M	N	O
1	Patient/Feature	F1	F2	F3	F4	F5	F6	F7				C1	C2	C3	C4
2	P1	-0.8408	1.3330	1.4755	-1.3908	0.0278	-2.5495	-1.2420		F1		-5.00	1.00	2.00	2.00
3	P2	0.0180	0.7625	0.3245	-1.4873	-0.2065	-2.7658	-0.3030		F2		3.00	-3.00	-3.00	1.00
4	P3	0.3549	0.1348	0.6340	-0.8305	0.0667	-2.7638	-0.0132		F3		1.00	3.00	3.00	-1.00
5	P4	-0.2038	2.4988	0.4831	-0.4633	2.1560	-2.4823	-0.0635		F4		-2.00	-2.00	2.00	-4.00
6	P5	0.6890	1.1573	0.9526	-2.2230	0.1502	-2.1108	-0.6090		F5		0.00	-3.00	-4.00	-1.00
7	P6	-0.6789	-0.0878	1.5736	-1.6678	-0.7148	-2.4963	-1.0927		F6		-4.00	1.00	-1.00	-5.00
8	P7	0.0776	2.2815	0.4514	-0.1113	0.2840	-2.5458	-1.0632		F7		3.00	2.00	-3.00	2.00
9	P8	0.5876	0.5685	0.8083	-1.6613	1.0735	-2.0618	-0.8283							
10	P9	-0.7700	0.7413	1.5640	-2.9843	-1.5688	-1.2460	-0.6345							
11	P10	-0.8243	2.2150	0.8194	-1.8460	-0.8620	-1.7265	-0.9145							
12	P11	-0.7328	0.5258	0.8918	-1.5978	-1.6905	-2.1125	-0.8562							
13	P12	0.8811	2.0940	0.8181	-1.0492	-1.4525	-2.1693	-0.8022							

Figure 8-11. *Worksheet 1*

Let's first get some understanding of this scenario. In worksheet 1, there are 155 patients whose conditions can be clustered based on the values of the seven features. Please do not worry about what the features are. We can imagine they are gene expression levels, blood sugar concentrations, etc. They are irrelevant. We are going to cluster these patients into four clusters.

Since the cell range A2:H156 will be used frequently, it has been named AA through Name Manager as shown in Figure 8-12. In addition, the worksheet has an initial setup such that the four centroids are already initialized. We can certainly initialize them with different values later. For now, please keep them.

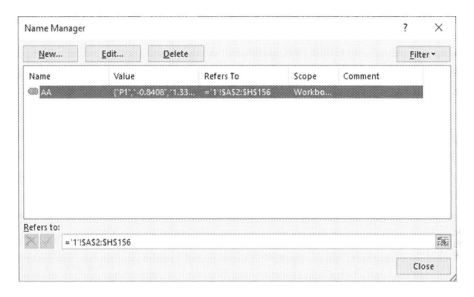

Figure 8-12. *The data range A2:H156 is named AA*

Our first task is to compute the distances of each data point to every centroid marked as C1, C2, C3, and C4. Based on the distances, we then need to assign each data point into a cluster closest to it.

Follow these instructions to complete this project:

1. Enter formula =SQRT(SUMXMY2($B2:$H2, L$2:L$8)) in cell R2. This formula calculates the distance between the patient P1 and centroid C1. Pay close attention to the use of absolute references. We will autofill this formula both horizontally and vertically.

2. Autofill from R2 to U2, and then autofill together from R2:U2 to R156:U156. Now, the distances between each data point to every centroid are computed.

3. Enter formula =INDEX($R$1:$U$1, MATCH(MIN(R2:U2), R2:U2, 0)) in cell V2.

    MIN(R2:U2) finds the smallest among the four distances between the patient P1 and the four centroids.

    MATCH(MIN(R2:U2), R2:U2, 0) finds the position of the smallest distance in the array R2:U2. For example, if R2 is the smallest, this expression returns 1. If U2 is the smallest, it returns 4. Based on the position, we need to fetch the cluster name from R1:U1. That is why we have the formula =INDEX($R$1:$U$1, MATCH(MIN(R2:U2), R2:U2, 0)).

Autofill from V2 to V156. Part of our worksheet should look like Figure 8-13.

K	L	M	N	O	P	Q	R	S	T	U	V
	C1	C2	C3	C4		Distance:	C1	C2	C3	C4	Cluster
F1	-5.00	1.00	2.00	2.00			6.38546	7.5588	7.8982	6.2201	C4
F2	3.00	-3.00	-3.00	1.00			6.58648	7.0591	7.8858	4.7936	C4
F3	1.00	3.00	3.00	-1.00			6.99989	6.6956	7.3968	5.1344	C4
F4	-2.00	-2.00	2.00	-4.00			6.49777	9.1296	9.8087	6.5091	C1
F5	0.00	-3.00	-4.00	-1.00			7.2408	6.9302	8.0747	5.0191	C4
F6	-4.00	1.00	-1.00	-5.00			6.94029	6.3604	6.9147	6.0281	C4
F7	3.00	2.00	-3.00	2.00			6.9908	8.4586	8.1876	6.2946	C4
							7.5399	7.1965	8.0325	5.6438	C4
							6.89471	5.8476	7.7551	6.0582	C2
							6.27247	7.4701	8.3333	6.0524	C4
							6.76722	6.2929	6.961	5.8322	C4
							6.15141	7.472	7.8466	6.1793	C1
							6.62129	6.3396	7.6491	5.3922	C4

Figure 8-13. *First round of clustering*

4. Now, we have finished our first round of clustering. We need to recalculate the centroids, and then reassign the data points into clusters based on the shortest-distance rule. To do so, we need to make a copy of worksheet 1 and rename the new worksheet 2.

Right-click the name "1," and a small menu shows up ➤ select Move or Copy ... ➤ on the upcoming window, check the box Create a copy ➤ select the option (move to end) ➤ click OK. This process is shown in Figure 8-8 and Figure 8-14. After that, we will notice that the name of the new worksheet is "1 (2)." Right-click on the name and rename it "2" (the number 2).

A shortcut for copying a worksheet is to press SHIFT + CTRL ➤ press the left mouse button ➤ drag the sheet tab to the right side.

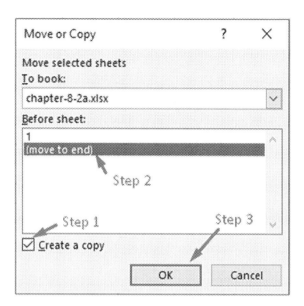

Figure 8-14. *Copy a worksheet*

5. In worksheet 2, enter =SHEET(A1) - 1 in cell J1. The cell J1 should have number 1 displayed. If not, make sure that worksheet 2 is to the right of worksheet 1. The order is important as we have experienced before with the SHEET function.

    The number 1 inside cell J1 will be used to reference worksheet 1.

6. Enter 2 and 3 in cells J2 and J3. Select both cells, and then autofill to J8.

    Since many cells around cells J2 and J3 are having floating-point numbers (numbers with digits after the decimal point), by default, J2 and J3 may be displayed as 2.0000 and 3.0000. This is because their format is Number. If this happens, we need to apply the General format to reformat them.

    Select cells J2:J8 ➤ click the Home tab ➤ inside the Number group ➤ select General. This process is shown in Figure 8-15.

    By now, J2:J8 should display integers 2–8. Integers 2–8 can be used to reference columns B-H by the function INDIRECT.

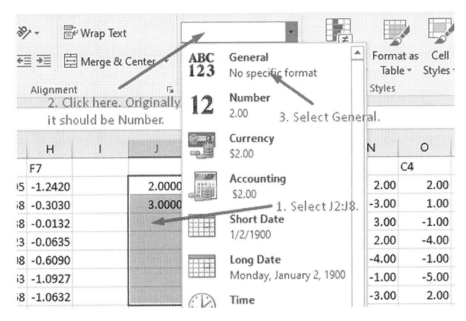

Figure 8-15. *Apply format General to cells*

7. Enter "change=" in cell J10. By now, part of our worksheet 2 looks like Figure 8-16.

	I	J	K	L	M	N	O	P
1		1		C1	C2	C3	C4	
2		2	F1	-5.00	1.00	2.00	2.00	
3		3	F2	3.00	-3.00	-3.00	1.00	
4		4	F3	1.00	3.00	3.00	-1.00	
5		5	F4	-2.00	-2.00	2.00	-4.00	
6		6	F5	0.00	-3.00	-4.00	-1.00	
7		7	F6	-4.00	1.00	-1.00	-5.00	
8		8	F7	3.00	2.00	-3.00	2.00	
9								
10		change=						

Figure 8-16. *Setup of worksheet 2*

8. Let's recalculate the centroids. In cell L2, enter the following formula:

```
=IFERROR(AVERAGEIFS(INDEX(AA, 0, $J2), INDIRECT($J$1 &
"!$V$2") : INDIRECT($J$1 & "!$V$156"), L$1), 0)
```

The AVERAGEIFS function has a division operation. If no cell meets its criteria set, the denominator will be zero, and the division operation will have an error. In this case, we need to return 0 instead of having an error. That is why we need to use the function IFERROR here.

Cell L2 stores the average of feature 1 (column B) of those data points which are assigned into cluster 1 (C1) in worksheet 1. How do we calculate such a value?

`INDEX(AA, 0, $J2)` finds column B. This is for feature 1. We will average feature 1 based on one criterion: the assigned clusters are C1 in the column V of worksheet 1.

The intended expression of the criteria range and criteria would be

`1!$V$2 : 1!$V$156, "C1"`

The expression `INDIRECT($J$1 & "!$V$2")` generates the reference `1!$V$2`, and the expression `INDIRECT($J$1 & "!$V$156")` generates the reference `1!$V$156`.

Certainly, L$1 gives "C1." Thus, the previous formula can be correctly translated to

`=IFERROR(AVERAGEIFS(INDEX(AA, 0, 2), 1!$V$2 : 1!$V$156, "C1"), 0)`

9. Autofill from L2 to O2, and then autofill together to L8:O8. We should notice that values inside R2:V156 are changed automatically.

Part of our worksheet should look like Figure 8-17.

◢	J	K	L	M	N	O	P	Q	R	S	T	U	V
1	1		C1	C2	C3	C4		Distance:	C1	C2	C3	C4	Cluster
2	2	F1	-0.87	-0.41	-0.60	-0.31			1.18556	2.4258	2.5826	1.2125	C1
3	3	F2	1.88	0.03	1.71	1.23			1.98018	2.1539	3.0839	1.0066	C4
4	4	F3	1.04	1.26	1.29	0.88			2.45524	2.4382	3.1348	1.7236	C4
5	5	F4	-0.75	-2.05	0.80	-1.52			2.77551	4.6726	4.0115	3.1433	C1
6	6	F5	-0.23	-1.23	-1.25	-0.43			2.30676	2.231	3.7144	1.3689	C4
7	7	F6	-2.02	-1.47	-2.54	-2.25			2.35822	1.4754	3.1173	1.6816	C2
8	8	F7	-0.83	-0.36	-1.27	-0.53			1.55159	3.6964	2.1723	2.0792	C1
9									2.53381	2.739	3.8492	1.9157	C4
10	change=								2.99982	1.3588	4.1896	2.3133	C2

Figure 8-17. *The centroids are recalculated*

10. Enter 2 and 3 inside cells W2 and W3, respectively, and then autofill them to cell W156. Make sure that the numbers are 2, 3, 4, 5, ..., 156 in column W.

11. Enter text "Old Cluster" in cell X1 and "Difference" in cell Y1. We will copy worksheet 1's clusters (inside column V) into this column X.

12. Enter formula =INDIRECT($J$1 & "!V" & W2) in cell X2.

    This formula references cell V2 of worksheet 1. As the text in cell X1 suggests, column X stores the assigned clusters of worksheet 1.

    Autofill from X2 to X156.

13. Enter formula =IF(V2=X2, 0, 1) in cell Y2. This formula examines if a data point has been reassigned to a cluster different from the previous round. If yes, returns 1; else, returns 0.

14. Enter formula =SUM(Y2:Y156) in cell K10. The number in K10 tells how many data points have been reassigned into a different cluster in this iteration.

    Part of our worksheet 2 should look like Figure 8-18. Notice that in Figure 8-18, columns N-R are not shown.

	J	K	L	M	S	T	U	V	W	X	Y
1	1		C1	C2	C2	C3	C4	Cluster		Old Cluster	Difference
2	2	F1	-0.87	-0.41	2.4258	2.5826	1.2125	C1	2	C4	1
3	3	F2	1.88	0.03	2.1539	3.0839	1.0066	C4	3	C4	0
4	4	F3	1.04	1.26	2.4382	3.1348	1.7236	C4	4	C4	0
5	5	F4	-0.75	-2.05	4.6726	4.0115	3.1433	C1	5	C1	0
6	6	F5	-0.23	-1.23	2.231	3.7144	1.3689	C4	6	C4	0
7	7	F6	-2.02	-1.47	1.4754	3.1173	1.6816	C2	7	C4	1
8	8	F7	-0.83	-0.36	3.6964	2.1723	2.0792	C1	8	C4	1
9					2.739	3.8492	1.9157	C4	9	C4	0
10	change=	46			1.3588	4.1896	2.3133	C2	10	C2	0
11					2.3871	2.913	1.3934	C1	11	C4	1

Figure 8-18. *Count how many data points are reassigned to a different cluster*

15. As shown in Figure 8-18, there are 46 data points that are reassigned into a different cluster. This means that our clustering process is not converged. We need no data points to be reassigned into a different cluster, that is, cell K10 must be 0. Thus, we need to repeat our clustering process.

Make a copy of worksheet 2, rename the new worksheet 3, and make sure it is at the rightmost position. By placing it at the rightmost, its sheet number is 3; therefore, its previous worksheet must automatically be worksheet 2 (cell J1 must display number 2).

We should notice that everything in worksheet 3 has been updated automatically, and the value in cell K10 becomes 18, as shown in Figure 8-19.

	J	K	L	M	N	O	P	Q	R	S	T	U	V	W	X	Y
1	2		C1	C2	C3	C4		Distance:	C1	C2	C3	C4	Cluster		Old Cluster	Difference
2	2	F1	-0.62	-0.40	-0.53	-0.29			1.25305	2.1923	2.1142	1.266	C1	2	C1	0
3	3	F2	1.95	0.32	1.59	1.19			1.80067	1.8009	2.5256	1.0136	C4	3	C4	0
4	4	F3	0.84	1.09	0.88	0.92			2.29597	2.2752	2.5783	1.7397	C4	4	C4	0
5	5	F4	-0.71	-2.18	0.53	-1.66			2.54039	4.4764	3.2113	3.1801	C1	5	C1	0
6	6	F5	-0.11	-1.24	-0.47	-0.40			2.18619	1.9909	3.1846	1.2631	C4	6	C4	0
7	7	F6	-2.25	-1.91	-2.45	-2.21			2.4688	1.3822	2.8676	1.6677	C2	7	C2	0
8	8	F7	-0.83	-0.34	-1.22	-0.47			1.18786	3.4645	1.4336	2.2097	C1	8	C1	0
9									2.3885	2.6463	3.1285	1.8643	C4	9	C4	0
10	change=	18							3.21455	1.3495	4.0751	2.2199	C2	10	C2	0
11									1.49668	2.1115	2.6298	1.4264	C4	11	C1	1

Figure 8-19. *Worksheet k3*

16. *Continue the process*: Make a copy of worksheet 3, rename the new worksheet 4, and make sure worksheet 4 is at the rightmost position. In worksheet 4, cell J1 should display number 3.

The number in cell K10 becomes 12.

17. We need to make a copy of worksheet 4, and rename it 5, and make sure worksheet 5 is placed to the right of worksheet 4. The number in cell J1 inside worksheet 5 should be 4 automatically.

18. Repeat the process until we have worksheet 15. The number in cell K10 of worksheet 15 becomes 0. Note that we may find the number in cell K10 go up in the process of copying worksheets. This is normal. We just need to continue the process until the number in K10 becomes 0. Part of our worksheet 15 should look like Figure 8-20.

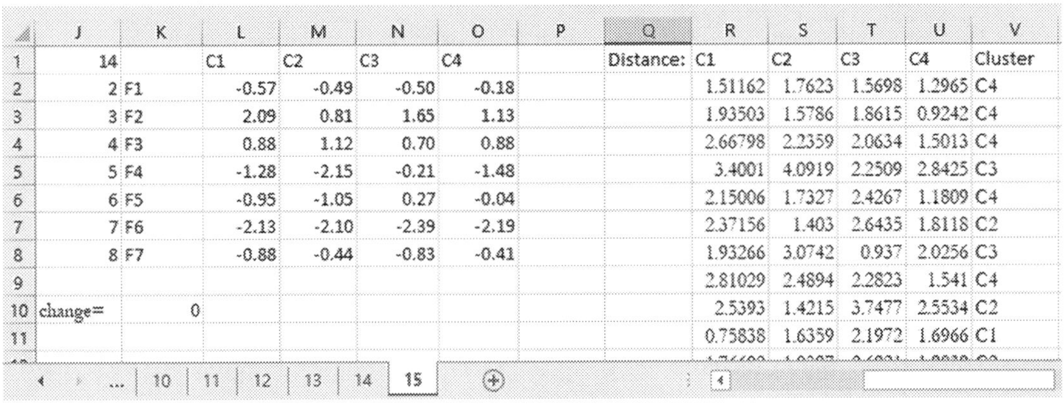

	J	K	L	M	N	O	P	Q	R	S	T	U	V
1	14		C1	C2	C3	C4		Distance: C1		C2	C3	C4	Cluster
2	2	F1	-0.57	-0.49	-0.50	-0.18			1.51162	1.7623	1.5698	1.2965	C4
3	3	F2	2.09	0.81	1.65	1.13			1.93503	1.5786	1.8615	0.9242	C4
4	4	F3	0.88	1.12	0.70	0.88			2.66798	2.2359	2.0634	1.5013	C4
5	5	F4	-1.28	-2.15	-0.21	-1.48			3.4001	4.0919	2.2509	2.8425	C3
6	6	F5	-0.95	-1.05	0.27	-0.04			2.15006	1.7327	2.4267	1.1809	C4
7	7	F6	-2.13	-2.10	-2.39	-2.19			2.37156	1.403	2.6435	1.8118	C2
8	8	F7	-0.88	-0.44	-0.83	-0.41			1.93266	3.0742	0.937	2.0256	C3
9									2.81029	2.4894	2.2823	1.541	C4
10	change=	0							2.5393	1.4215	3.7477	2.5534	C2
11									0.75838	1.6359	2.1972	1.6966	C1

... 10 | 11 | 12 | 13 | 14 | **15** | ⊕

Figure 8-20. *The clustering process converges*

19. We can try one more round to have worksheet 16. The number in cell K10 of worksheet 16 is still 0. This confirms that our clustering process has reached convergence, that is, each data point is stably clustered.

In many cases, we do not need to go up to worksheet 15. If we are lucky, we can reach convergence in five worksheets. However, it is also possible that we must go up to a much larger worksheet number. That is why we need to study Iterative Calculation and make use of it in project 2. The final result of project 1 can be found in chapter-8-2b.xlsx.

Iterative Calculation

Before we step on project 2, it is a good idea to develop a solid understanding of circular reference and iterative calculation in Excel. The name "circular reference" indicates that the formula inside a cell is referencing the cell itself, either directly or indirectly. By default, Excel does not allow circular reference.

To obtain live experience with circular reference and iterative calculation, let's try the following two experiments.

Experiment 1

Open a blank worksheet, and enter the numbers 1, 2, 3, and 4 inside cells A1, B1, C1, and D1, respectively. In cell E1, enter the formula =SUM(A1:E1). This is shown in Figure 8-21.

Figure 8-21. *Cell E1 references itself*

Because the formula =SUM(A1:E1) is inside the cell E1, it is adding its own value to itself. Certainly, there is a circular reference, and we will get a warning as shown in Figure 8-22. After clicking OK, cell E1 will display 0.

A	B	C	D	E	F	G	H	I	J	K	L	M
1	2	3	4	=SUM(A1:E1)								

Microsoft Excel   ✕

⚠ There are one or more circular references where a formula refers to its own cell either directly or indirectly. This might cause them to calculate incorrectly.

Try removing or changing these references, or moving the formulas to different cells.

OK   Help

Figure 8-22. *Circular reference is not allowed by default*

We can, however, allow circular reference by enabling iterative calculation in Excel. Click File ➤ Options ➤ on the upcoming Excel Options window, click Formulas ➤ check the option Enable iterative calculation, and set the Maximum Iterations to be 1. This is illustrated in Figure 8-23.

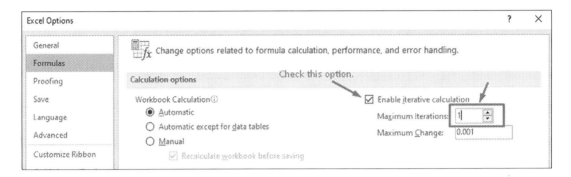

Figure 8-23. *Enable iterative calculation*

When the Maximum Iterations = 1, the formula =SUM(A1:E1) can reference itself for one round. Therefore, because cell E1 is initially 0, cell E1 will now display 10 because 1+2+3+4+0=10. If we set Maximum Iterations = 2 and re-enter the values and the formula in cells A1:E1, then E1 should display 20 because 1+2+3+4+10=20.

Test yourself: If we set Maximum Iterations = 3 and re-enter the values and the formula in cells A1:E1, what will E1 display?[3]

Experiment 2

Open a new Excel file, and make sure that the option Enable iterative calculation is unchecked. Enter the formula =SUM(C2+1) in cell D1 and then the formula =SUM(D1+1) in cell C2. We should get the warning message as shown in Figure 8-22. After clicking OK on the warning message window, we shall see something as shown in Figure 8-24. The blue line traces the circular references.

---

[3] 30.

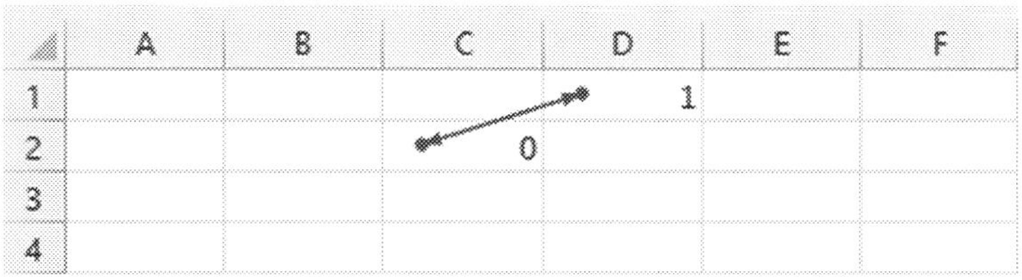

Figure 8-24. *Circular reference is marked*

Now, let's open another new Excel file and enable iterative calculation and set Maximum Iterations = 1. Because the iterative calculation is top-down and initially C2=0 and D1=1, the iterative calculation will set D1=0+1=1 again but set C2=1+1=2. Thus, the final answer is D1=1 and C2=2.

If we repeat the recent procedure from the beginning but set Maximum Iterations = 2, the second iterative calculation will set D1=C2+1=2+1=3 and C2=D1+1=3+1=4.

Note again that the iterative calculation is top-down, that is, the previous cells are calculated first. In the same row, the iterative calculation is also evaluated from left to right.

Test yourself: If we repeat the recent procedure from the beginning but set Maximum Iterations = 3, what are inside cell D1 and C2?[4]

Work on Project 2

Open the Excel file chapter-8-3a.xlsx. There is only one worksheet named k1. The setup of worksheet k1 is similar to that of chapter-8-1a.xlsx but slightly different as shown in Figure 8-25. The difference is that in chapter-8-3a.xlsx, cells J2:J8 already have numbers stored.

---

[4] 5 and 6.

J	K	L	M	N	O	P	Q	R	S	T	U	V
		C1	C2	C3	C4		Distance: C1	C2	C3	C4		Cluster
2	F1	-5.00	1.00	2.00	2.00							
3	F2	3.00	-3.00	-3.00	1.00							
4	F3	1.00	3.00	3.00	-1.00							
5	F4	-2.00	-2.00	2.00	-4.00							
6	F5	0.00	-3.00	-4.00	-1.00							
7	F6	-4.00	1.00	-1.00	-5.00							
8	F7	3.00	2.00	-3.00	2.00							

Figure 8-25. *A new setup of worksheet k1*

Note that the worksheet is named "k1" instead of 1. This indicates that in this project, we do not need to number the worksheets; therefore, the function SHEET is not required. Instead, we are going to make use of the Iterative Calculation feature of Excel. Note that the Enable iterative calculation option is unchecked for chapter-8-3a.xlsx.

Follow the instructions to complete this project:

1. Enter formula =SQRT(SUMXMY2($B2:$H2,L$2:L$8)) in cell R2.

2. Autofill from R2 to U2, and then autofill together to R156:U156.

3. Enter formula =INDEX($R$1:$U$1, 1, MATCH(MIN(R2:U2), R2:U2,0)) in cell V2.

4. Autofill from V2 to V156. So far, we are repeating steps in project 1.

5. Click the File tab ➤ click Options (near the bottom), the Excel Options window shows up. On this window, click Formulas, then check Enable Iterative Calculation, leave Maximum Iterations to be 100, and set the Maximum Change to be 0, as shown in Figure 8-26. We are making use of Excel's Iterative Calculation feature to complete our clustering process automatically.

6. Click OK to close Excel Options.

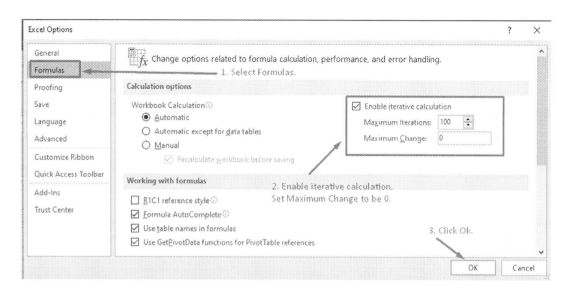

Figure 8-26. *Enable iterative calculation*

7. Enter formula =IFERROR(AVERAGEIFS(INDEX(AA, 0, $J2),
    $V$2:$V$156, L$1), 0) in cell L2. After hitting the ENTER key,
    we shall see that the number inside cell L2 has changed, as shown
    in Figure 8-27. Note that our number in cell L2 may not be
    exactly -0.40.

J	K	L	M	N	O
		C1	C2	C3	C4
2	F1	-0.40	1.00	2.00	2.00
3	F2	3.00	-3.00	-3.00	1.00
4	F3	1.00	3.00	3.00	-1.00
5	F4	-2.00	-2.00	2.00	-4.00
6	F5	0.00	-3.00	-4.00	-1.00
7	F6	-4.00	1.00	-1.00	-5.00
8	F7	3.00	2.00	-3.00	2.00

Figure 8-27. *Start iterative calculation*

8. Autofill from L2 to O2, then autofill together to L8:O8. We shall see that all the centroids are recalculated. At the same time, the clusters in column V are updated, too. The formulas inside L2:O8 reference cells in V2:V156 which reference cells L2:O8. There are circular references among them.

   Important: only autofill once here. Repeating the autofill action here can cause unexpected results.

   Part of our worksheet may look like Figure 8-28. Be advised that we may get different numbers in cells L2:O8.

J	K	L	M	N	O	P	Q	R	S	T	U	V
		C1	C2	C3	C4		Distance: C1	C2	C3	C4	Cluster
2	F1	-0.52	-0.20	0.66	-0.55		1.42852	1.304	3.5456	1.6517	C2
3	F2	1.95	1.16	-0.76	1.02		1.92294	0.8899	2.6726	1.6148	C2
4	F3	0.81	0.80	1.24	1.11		2.29343	1.5111	1.9905	2.311	C2
5	F4	-0.40	-1.45	-1.01	-2.02		2.433	2.8418	4.3003	4.011	C1
6	F5	0.00	-0.08	0.11	-1.10		2.37324	1.2256	2.8052	1.7835	C2
7	F6	-2.39	-2.19	-1.37	-2.08		2.63174	1.8346	2.9104	1.4985	C4
8	F7	-0.93	-0.43	0.84	-0.52		0.89328	1.976	4.0064	2.9121	C1
							2.44873	1.5846	2.562	2.5559	C2
							3.55344	2.5699	3.6469	1.479	C4
							1.85405	1.6537	4.0092	1.3937	C4
							2.54135	1.8721	3.2739	0.9855	C4
							1.68173	1.9183	4.0979	1.6052	C4
							2.02341	0.7053	2.0782	1.2956	C2
							1.5076	1.3002	3.4875	1.1016	C4

Figure 8-28. *Iterative calculation updates clusters*

9. Our job is done! How can we verify if this clustering process has reached convergence?

   Well, if this clustering process has reached convergence, then after we copy/paste the values inside L2:O8 into the original file chapter-8-2a.xlsx to serve as the starting centroids and repeat the project 1 process, the worksheet 2 must confirm the convergence.

   The following procedure repeats some steps in project 1 but is slightly different as our worksheet is named k1 in project 2.

   Make a copy of worksheet k1, and rename the new worksheet k2 (the order of the two worksheets does not matter since we are not using the function SHEET).

10. Inside worksheet k2, enter text "k1" (without quotation marks) in cell J1. Recall that the first worksheet is named k1. Be aware that we can make use of the SHEET function to skip this step as we did in project 1. Since the verification is an extra step, I didn't plan to apply the SHEET function to maximize the automation.

11. Enter text "changes=" in cell J10.

12. In cell L2, enter the following formula:

    ```
    =IFERROR(AVERAGEIFS(INDEX(AA, 0, $J2), INDIRECT($J$1 &
    "!$V$2") : INDIRECT($J$1 & "!$V$156"), L$1), 0)
    ```

13. Autofill from L2 to O2, and then autofill together to L8:O8.

    Though this step recalculates the centroids, we should notice that the values inside L2:O8 are not changed.

14. Enter 2 and 3 in cells W2 and W3, respectively, autofill to W156. Make sure that the numbers are 2, 3, 4, 5, ..., 156 in column W.

15. Enter text "Old Cluster" in cell X1 and "Difference" in cell Y1. We will copy worksheet k1's clusters (in column V) into column X.

16. Enter formula =INDIRECT($J$1 & "!V" & W2) in cell X2. Autofill from X2 to X156.

17. Enter formula =IF(V2=X2, 0, 1) in cell Y2. Autofill from Y2 to Y156.

18. Enter formula =SUM(Y2:Y156) in cell K10. We should realize that the number in cell K10 is 0, indeed. This is shown in Figure 8-29. This verification result can be found in the file chapter-8-3b.xlsx.

J	K	L	M	N	O	P	Q	R	S	T	U	V	W	X	Y
k1		C1	C2	C3	C4		Distance:	C1	C2	C3	C4	Cluster		Old Cluster	Difference
	2 F1	-0.52	-0.20	0.66	-0.55			1.42852	1.304	3.5456	1.6517	C2	2	C2	0
	3 F2	1.95	1.16	-0.76	1.02			1.92294	0.8899	2.6726	1.6148	C2	3	C2	0
	4 F3	0.81	0.80	1.24	1.11			2.29343	1.5111	1.9905	2.311	C2	4	C2	0
	5 F4	-0.40	-1.45	-1.01	-2.02			2.433	2.8418	4.3003	4.011	C1	5	C1	0
	6 F5	0.00	-0.08	0.11	-1.10			2.37324	1.2256	2.8052	1.7835	C2	6	C2	0
	7 F6	-2.39	-2.19	-1.37	-2.08			2.63174	1.8346	2.9104	1.4985	C4	7	C4	0
	8 F7	-0.93	-0.43	0.84	-0.52			0.89328	1.976	4.0064	2.9121	C1	8	C1	0
								2.44873	1.5846	2.562	2.5559	C2	9	C2	0
changes=	0							3.55344	2.5699	3.6469	1.479	C4	10	C4	0
								1.85405	1.6537	4.0092	1.3937	C4	11	C4	0
								2.54135	1.8721	3.2739	0.9855	C4	12	C4	0
								1.68173	1.9183	4.0979	1.6052	C4	13	C4	0
								2.02341	0.7053	2.0782	1.2956	C2	14	C2	0

Figure 8-29. *Confirmation of the convergence by iterative calculation*

An easier verification would be to copy/paste the values inside L2:O8 into the worksheet 1 of the file chapter-8-2b.xlsx to serve as the initial centroids. We should then immediately find out that starting from worksheet 2 inside the file chapter-8-2b.xlsx, the number inside the cell K10 becomes 0. This again confirms that the Iterative Calculation has successfully clustered the data points.

One important reminder is that by default, a copy/paste action will copy and paste the formulas and formats of the source cells. However, the preceding paste action needs to paste the values only. Pasting formulas will result in an error. Please follow the instructions to exercise how to paste value only:

1. Copy the cells L2:O8 from worksheet k1 (see the cells L2:O8 in Figure 8-28).

2. Open the file chapter-8-2b.xlsx, and click worksheet 1.

3. Click the cell L2 to select it.

4. Right-click on cell L2; on the upcoming menu, select the icon marked with number "123" under the "Paste Options:". This procedure is illustrated in Figure 8-30.

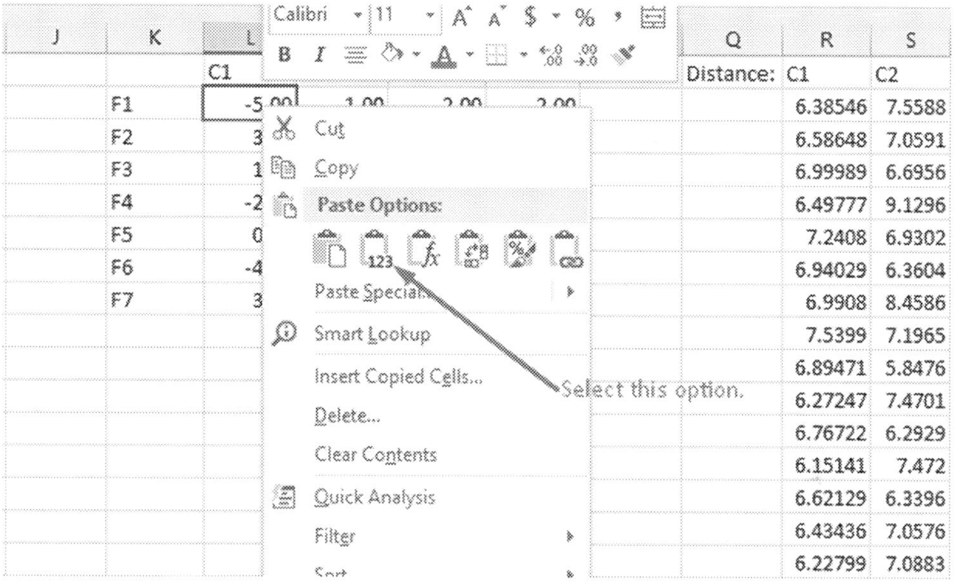

Figure 8-30. *Paste values to confirm the convergence by Iterative Calculation*

The recent verification result is recorded in file chapter-8-3c.xlsx.

If we compare the final result of project 2 with that of project 1, we will notice that the centroid values in cells L2:O8 are different between the two projects. Of course, the clusters in column V of the two projects are different, too. We should raise the question: why?

In project 1, the recalculation of the centroids is independent from each other. The recalculation of cell L3 does not impact the result in cell L2, and vice versa. In addition, every recalculation is just a one-time calculation. That means the recalculation is one time each round.

In project 2, however, once cell L2 starts iterative calculation, it repeats multiple times as specified by the parameter "Maximum Iterations" shown in Figure 8-26. When we autofill from L2 to O2, those cells M2, N2, and O2 all have repeated iterative calculation for up to 100 times before we can autofill further. Most importantly, the recalculations of the cells L2:O8 are not independent. Every cell's recalculation can change other cells' values.

Thus, the working processes of project 1 and project 2 are different indeed. However, both processes can result in convergence, indicating that there is more than one optimal clustering solution.

Strictly speaking, the approach in project 1 is much more reliable and always produces the same result. The approach in project 2 won't, however. If we try project 2 multiple times, we can realize that when we autofill from L2 to O2, and from L2:O2 to L8:O8, the speed and smoothness of our autofill action can have an impact on the values in L2:O8.

Chapter Tip

The tip of this chapter is about another two functions: CELL and SEARCH. In project 1, we make use of the function SHEET to automatically find the name of the previous worksheet. The disadvantage of SHEET function is that all the worksheets must be positioned in order, though the formula is fairly simple. We can make use of the CELL and SEARCH functions to achieve the same purpose, but the worksheets do not need to be positioned in order.

CELL function is not used often. It returns the formatting, location, and other information about a worksheet. Its syntax is CELL(information type, [reference]). The information type can be "address," "color," "filename," etc. For our purpose, the information type is "filename." The reference is optional. It is usually a cell reference such as A1. If the reference is omitted, the function CELL assumes the reference of the currently active cell. This may result in an unpredicted result. Thus, the reference is always encouraged.

In any of our Excel files, in an empty cell, type the formula =CELL("filename", A1), we should notice that a text string appears which denotes the absolute file path of our Excel file and ends with the name of the current worksheet. Take a look at Figure 8-31.

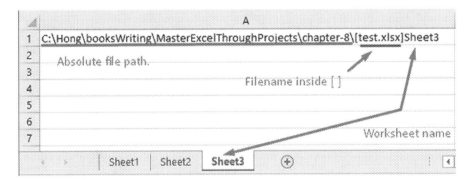

Figure 8-31. *The information regarding the filename by the function CELL*

My formula =CELL("filename", A1) is inside cell A1 of the worksheet named Sheet3. The name of the Excel file is test.xlsx. Every computer has many files which are stored at different locations called folders or directories. All these folders are organized as a hierarchical tree such that the operating system can follow the tree branches (think a folder as a branch) to locate any file (think a file as a tree leaf) by starting from the tree root (think the root as the top-level folder). An absolute file path denotes how to find a file by starting from the root folder. In Figure 8-31, the root is the hard disk C, and the last branch (folder) is chapter-8.

Observe that the filename is enclosed inside a pair of square brackets as revealed in Figure 8-31. After some analysis, we can soon realize that the name of the current worksheet is right after the filename, specifically, right after the closing square bracket "]." This understanding renders us the opportunity to make use of the SEARCH and MID functions to fetch the sheet name from the text string.

There are two functions in Excel that can perform a search operation inside a text string: SEARCH and FIND. They are very much the same except that SEARCH is not case-sensitive, while FIND is. The syntax of the SEARCH function is SEARCH(find-text, within-text, [start-number]). It finds the location of the find-text inside the within-text by starting the search from the position specified by start-number. If start-number is not given, it is assumed to be 1.

For example, assume we want to search for "He" inside the text string "Hello World" stored in cell B1. Our formula should be =SEARCH("He", B1), and this formula must return 1. Be aware that if the formula is =SEARCH("Hi", B1), an error is returned because "Hi" cannot be found.

Let's open file chapter-8-4a.xlsx. This file is the same as chapter-8-2b.xlsx except that it does not have worksheets 3-16.

Go to worksheet 2. Inside cell J1, replace the existing formula with the following one:

```
=MID(CELL("filename", A1), SEARCH("xlsx]", CELL("filename", A1)) + 5, 5) - 1
```

The expression CELL("filename", A1) gives the absolute file name plus the worksheet name 2.

The SEARCH function is searching for "xlsx]" instead of "]." This is to avoid the rare case when there is another "]" inside the file name.

The MID function picks characters from the full file name (plus the worksheet name 2). The picking starting position is SEARCH("xlsx]", CELL("filename", A1)) + 5. This is because "xlsx]" is of length 5. The picking must be after "xlsx]".

The MID function picks a maximum of 5 characters after "xlsx]", which should be large enough. Note that when there are less than five characters left to be picked, the MID function just picks whatever is available.

Because the MID function is applied inside worksheet 2, it returns 2. In the given formula, the result of the MID function is subtracted by 1; thus, it finds the name of the previous worksheet.

Test yourself: will the following formula work too?[5]

```
=MID(CELL("filename", A1), SEARCH("]", CELL("filename", A1)) + 1, 5) - 1
```

Now, make a copy of worksheet 2, and rename the new worksheet 3. Repeat this process until we have worksheets 15 and 16. After completion, we can reposition these worksheets, but the results inside each worksheet do not change. Take a look at Figure 8-32 in which worksheets 5 and 15 are repositioned.

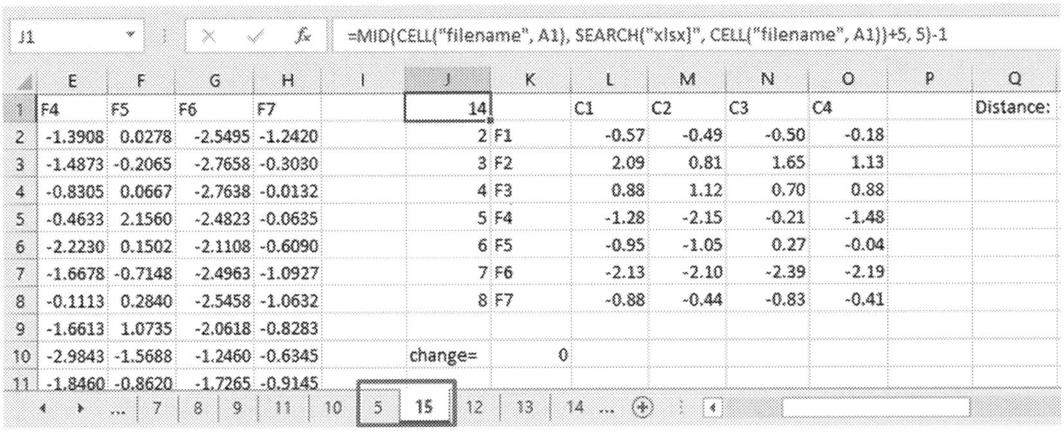

J1 =MID(CELL("filename", A1), SEARCH("xlsx]", CELL("filename", A1))+5, 5)-1

	E	F	G	H	I	J	K	L	M	N	O	P	Q
1	F4	F5	F6	F7		14		C1	C2	C3	C4		Distance:
2	-1.3908	0.0278	-2.5495	-1.2420		2	F1	-0.57	-0.49	-0.50	-0.18		
3	-1.4873	-0.2065	-2.7658	-0.3030		3	F2	2.09	0.81	1.65	1.13		
4	-0.8305	0.0667	-2.7638	-0.0132		4	F3	0.88	1.12	0.70	0.88		
5	-0.4633	2.1560	-2.4823	-0.0635		5	F4	-1.28	-2.15	-0.21	-1.48		
6	-2.2230	0.1502	-2.1108	-0.6090		6	F5	-0.95	-1.05	0.27	-0.04		
7	-1.6678	-0.7148	-2.4963	-1.0927		7	F6	-2.13	-2.10	-2.39	-2.19		
8	-0.1113	0.2840	-2.5458	-1.0632		8	F7	-0.88	-0.44	-0.83	-0.41		
9	-1.6613	1.0735	-2.0618	-0.8283									
10	-2.9843	-1.5688	-1.2460	-0.6345		change=	0						
11	-1.8460	-0.8620	-1.7265	-0.9145									

... 7 8 9 11 10 5 15 12 13 14 ...

Figure 8-32. *Worksheets 5 and 15 are repositioned*

The final result can also be found in chapter-8-4b.xlsx.

[5] Yes.

Review Points

1. New functions SQRT, SUMXMY2, AVERAGEIFS, SHEET, CELL, SEARCH, and FIND.

2. Copy and rename Excel worksheets.

3. The concept of k-means clustering and its working mechanism.

4. Simulate each re-clustering procedure via worksheet copy.

5. Excel circular reference and iterative calculation.

6. Apply iterative calculation in k-means clustering.

7. Paste value only.

Chapter Summary and Book Summary

So far, we have learned quite some functions. Like I mentioned before, the IF family functions are very important. In this chapter, we learned the AVERAGEIFS function. Please study another function SUMIFS which is a must-know function, too.

This chapter presents two different approaches to accomplish a k-means cluster example. The chapter tip further presents two revised formulas for project 1. These deliver us a strong message that there is more than one solution to an Excel task. Which solution to adopt depends on our considerations including efficiency, quality, and simplicity. My personal experience is whenever I find out a better solution, I study and adopt the better solution.

Chapter 1 once mentioned four data types commonly seen in cells: text, number, date, and formula. This is from my own experience which is different from how Excel categorizes value types. From the viewpoint of computer science, date is in fact an integer, that is, a number. So, clearly, my saying is for easy understanding only and is not precisely correct. Excel has a TYPE function which lists five value types: number, text, logical value, error value, and array. Expression including formula is not listed as a value type because only the result of an expression is typed. Please take time to access the help-page of the TYPE function to learn more about Excel's value types.

The fundamental goal is that we should never stop learning or exploring new knowledge. Excel has been here for several decades and has been excelling all the time; it must be a product of the accumulation of many people's intelligence and experience. As I mentioned at the beginning of this chapter, for general purpose, Excel is likely to have all the functions/features we need. What we need to do is to explore the available functions and built-in features to construct a creative solution.

Hope you have enjoyed reading this book and it does help.

Index

A, B, C

Chi-square analysis
    ADDRESS, 130
    CHITEST, 130
    definition, 130
    functions, 130
    ISERROR tests, 130
    project
        actual and expected ranges, 136
        CHITEST function, 135
        expected counts, 134
        formula, 133
        IFERROR function, 134
        instructions, 132
        name creation, 133
        setup, 131, 132
        statistic calculation, 135
        test completion, 137
        updation, 137
Colon adenocarcinoma (COAD), 143

D

Data analysis, *see* PivotTable/PivotChart
Data mining method, 1, 203
Data visualization, 169

E

Encryption techniques, 103
Euclidean distance, 204

F

Food nutrition ranks
    categories, 35
    chronic health problems, 37
    functional features, 36
    functions, 38
        AND/OR, 40, 41
        IF statement, 38, 39
        ISBLANK, 39, 40
        VLOOKUP, 41–47
    information, 37
    long date format, 63
    name manager/data validation
        access data validation, 52
        access name manger, 49
        array, 51
        drop-down list, 53
        formulas tab, 48–54
        set up, 53
        table creation, 49, 50
    overview, 35
    project instructions
        conditional format/equal to, 56, 62
        content table, 61
        food items, 56
        format cells window, 60, 61
        format selection, 57
        formula, 54, 55
        green color selection, 58, 59
        home tab, 59
        steps, 54

© Hong Zhou 2022
H. Zhou, *Mastering Excel Through Projects*, https://doi.org/10.1007/978-1-4842-7842-0

Printed in the United States
by Baker & Taylor Publisher Services